Enterprise Linux at Work
How to Build 10 Distributed Applications for Your Organization

Stephen Asbury

WILEY COMPUTER PUBLISHING

John Wiley & Sons, Inc.

NEW YORK · CHICHESTER · WEINHEIM · BRISBANE · SINGAPORE · TORONTO

Publisher: Robert Ipsen
Editor: Theresa Hudson
Associate Developmental Editor: Kathryn A. Malm
Managing Editor: Brian E. Snapp
Text Design & Composition: Publishers' Design and Production Services, Inc.

Designations used by companies to distinguish their products are often claimed as trademarks. In all instances where John Wiley & Sons, Inc., is aware of a claim, the product names appear in initial capital or ALL CAPITAL LETTERS. Readers, however, should contact the appropriate companies for more complete information regarding trademarks and registration.

This book is printed on acid-free paper. ∞

Published by John Wiley & Sons, Inc.

Published simultaneously in Canada.

This publication is designed to provide accurate and authoritative information in regard to the subject matter covered. It is sold with the understanding that the publisher is not engaged in professional services. If professional advice or other expert assistance is required, the services of a competent professional person should be sought.

Library of Congress Cataloging-in-Publication Data:

Asbury, Stephen.
      Enterprise Linux at work: how to build 10 distributed applications for your organization / Stephen Asbury.
          p.   cm.
      Includes index.
      ISBN 0-471-36349-9 (pbk./CD-ROM)
      1. Linux.   2. Application sofware—Development.   3. Electronic data processing—Distributed processing.   I. Title.
      QA76.76.063 A78 2000
      005.4'469—dc21

                                                                          99-059493

Printed in the United States of America.

10 9 8 7 6 5 4 3 2 1

for Cheryl
—Stephen Asbury

CONTENTS

Stephen Asbury is the Chief Technology Officer for Paradigm Research, Inc., a training company in the heart of Silicon Valley. Stephen has written numerous courses on Java, JavaScript, Active Server pages, CORBA, HTML and just about everything else that Web programmers need to know. This is Stephen's fifth book; the first four discussed Perl, CGI, the Java Foundation Classes, and enterprise Java applications. In addition, Stephen has designed and built several Web-based training environments and a number of other commercial applications and frameworks. Stephen lives in Sunnyvale, California, with his beloved wife, Cheryl.

Stephen can be reached at sasbury@crl.com.

First, I would like to thank the PRI gang: Karen, Mila, Nicole, Richard, Shrinand, Tyler, and especially Kerry. Sometimes writing takes away from work, and I appreciate their dedication in my stead.

Thanks to Alberto for listening to me complain, motivating me to keep writing, telling worse stories about how bad computers can be, and all the stuff it takes to be a good friend despite a 2000-mile separation. I take all of my cues on Linux from the man who wrote the book.

And where would I be without editors? Many thanks to Terri Hudson, Kathryn Malm, and Gerrie Cho for transforming my sometimes confused expositions into logical explanations.

Finally, I must thank my wife, Cheryl. I know that work and hobbies can burden a marriage by taking the most important resource, time. But no matter how many books I write or games I play, I will always be grateful to Cheryl for each second I get to spend with her. With Cheryl, I wear black, complain, mope, and am a general grouch. Without her . . . I shudder to think.

—Stephen Asbury

As you probably know, Linux is a public domain version of Unix that has been growing in popularity over the last couple of years. In particular, hobbyists are trying out Linux, and system administrators are switching server machines to Linux because it is inexpensive and runs on standard PC hardware. With the growing popularity and ongoing acknowledgment of Linux's stability as an operating system, it is becoming a platform for deploying applications. Numerous Web servers already are deployed on Linux servers. My hope with this book is to help push Linux both as a Web server host and as a generic application host, including acting as a messaging server, CORBA server, and even as part of a cluster of computers used for parallel programming.

Although a handful of books have been published recently on Linux programming, these have focused on writing Linux device drivers and using toolkits and languages that have not gained popularity in the mainstream enterprise. Rather than focus on Linux-specific technologies, the 10 projects in this book are real projects that can be deployed on Linux. Most could be deployed on other platforms, but as you try them out, you will see that Linux provides a robust, inexpensive, high-performance platform for deploying enterprise applications. The projects themselves touch on all of the major technologies people are using today:

- Java, Perl, and C++
- CGI, servlets, and server-side scripting for Web servers
- CORBA
- LDAP
- Messaging
- XML
- Parallel programming

Along the way I have included some discussions of Java technologies like JNDI and JDBC as well as topics on performance. At the time I am writing this book, I realize that Java has not yet made itself the most popular Linux development technology. But as Linux and Java both invade the enterprise, it is only logical that these two powerful technologies merge and leverage each other. At the same time, Perl and C++ are fundamental resources in the enterprise, so I have tried to give them time as well.

I hope that this will be a great, balanced resource for all developers who want to begin creating applications for their company on Linux.

How This Book Is Organized

This book consists of 10 projects. Each project is described using the same basic format. First, you'll find a list of the techniques used in the project, followed by a description of the project and how it could be used in your enterprise, and the skills and tools needed to complete the project. What follows is some background to the project and a discussion of the basic concepts and design issues for the project. Finally, a series of steps or parts is used to walk through the project itself. These steps discuss the code or techniques used to implement the project.

Because each project is basically independent of the others, you can jump around looking for specific discussions, technologies, or techniques. To help you navigate I have provided a number of resources. First there are the table of contents and the index. The Quick Reference table relates the techniques and topics to specific projects. Finally, to get started, scan the following list of short descriptions for each project to get an idea of what that project contains.

Project 1: An Online Catalog describes a basic Web application written in Perl. This online catalog uses a database to maintain a list of products. Web pages are used to view the items in the catalog and add new items.

Project 2: Java-based Web Page Scripting Engine introduces a server-side scripting engine that allows you to create dynamic Web pages by embedding Java in your HTML. This scripting engine is written as a servlet, so it also provides some information about how servlets can be used.

Project 3: Web-based Bug Tracker uses the scripting engine from Project 2 to create a Web-based bug-tracking system. Users can enter bugs into the system and search for existing bugs using several criteria. The information for each bug is stored in a relational database. This project includes both a Perl and Java version so that you can compare the two technologies.

Project 4: CORBA-based Course Registration Framework and Server uses CORBA to create a distributed course registration server. Data for courses is stored in a database. This database is publicized via a framework of objects that represent the various elements in the registration process. Both Java and C++ are used to create the server and test programs.

Project 5: A JNDI Service Provider introduces the Java Naming and Directory Interface as a way to access information services. This project uses the Java Remote Method Invocation technology to create a networked naming service.

Project 6: Accessing an LDAP Server builds on Project 5 and shows how Java programs can use JNDI to access information stored in an LDAP database. The test program is provided in C, Perl, and Java so that you can compare the various libraries for accessing LDAP servers.

Project 7: A Messaging Server implements a messaging service like MQ-Series in Java. This service relies on the Java Messaging Service (JMS) interface to support client-to-client messaging via queues and topics. This is a very large project and should indicate the power that Java can have on a Linux platform. This project uses JNDI and a relational database to support the messaging service.

Project 8: XML Data Backup Utility has two goals. First, it introduces XML and shows how you can write programs that use XML to define a data format. Second, this project creates a simple database utility that can be used to back up a relational database in a neutral format, allowing the data to be used to restore the original or replicate it.

Project 9: A Performance Toolkit discusses performance issues for Java programs and provides a number of tools for improving actual and perceived performance.

Project 10: A Parallel Program introduces a library called PVM that can be used to create parallel programs. The example program for this project is simple, but it should provide you with a basic understanding of how you can use parallel programs in your own projects.

Who Should Read This Book

This book is designed for two types of readers:

- Technical evaluators should be able to scan the introductory information in each chapter to learn about the various technologies at a high level.

- Experienced programmers can use code to see how the programs really work and get ideas for their own projects.

Both types of readers should be able to leverage the rules and guidelines throughout the book in future projects.

This book covers a lot of topics. You may want to read it straight through or jump around. If you are planning to read the code for the examples, be sure to check the prerequisites for each project. Some will require more programming experience than others.

Tools on the CD-ROM

One problem I encountered when writing this book is that enterprise programming needs a lot of software support. Each project can require one, two, or even more libraries, server programs, or packages. These packages include the following:

- The Java Developer Kit (JDK)
- The Servlet Development Kit (JSDK)
- Perl
- The Apache Web server
- JServ, a servlet engine for Apache
- MySQL, a relational database
- MySQL access drivers for Perl and Java
- JacORB and MICO, two CORBA ORBs
- The Java Naming and Directory interfaces (JNDI)
- The Java Messaging Service interfaces (JMS)
- OpenLDAP, an open source LDAP server
- XML4J, an XML library for Java written by IBM
- The Parallel Virtual Machine (PVM)

All of the code for each project is contained on the CD-ROM, and each project contains a list of the specific tools you will need for that project. The appendix provides a basic discussion about installing the supporting software for all of the projects. These two guides, plus the installation notes for each tool, will make it easy for you to try out these projects at home. I tried out the projects myself on SUSE 6.2 and RedHat 5.2 distributions of Linux. Both had their own idiosyncrasies, and I will admit that you may find yourself spending a measurable amount of time working on the installation of some tools. I hope that once you have the projects working, you will find the time well spent.

The CD-ROM also contains all the tools you need to complete the projects:

- JacORB 1.0 beta 14
- Apache JServ 1.0
- MICO 2.3.0

- MySQL JDBC driver (1.1i)
- MySQL Perl Modules
- MySQL 3.22.22 RPM
- MySQL benchmark package
- MySQL developer package
- Open LDAP 1.2.1
- PVM 3.4.2—Parallel Virtual Machine System
- IBM's alphaWorks XML Parser for Java 2.0.15
- IBM's VisualAge for Java, Entry Edition for Linux, Version 3.0
- Trial version of IBM WebSphere Application Server V2.03, Standard Edition for Linux

Also included are links to additional tools and resources on the Web:

- Java Developer Kit for Linux from Blackdown.org
- Java Developer Kit for Linux from Sun
- Java Servlet Development Kit (JSDK)
- Java Naming and Directory Interfaces (JNDI)
- MySQL Perl Modules
- Perl BER, WWW and LDAP modules (Search for ::BER, LWP::, and ::LDAP).

Wrap Up

My goal in writing this book is to provide a solid, example-rich introduction to enterprise programming on Linux. I couldn't hope to discuss every issue in enterprise development, despite how hard I tried. Please let me know how you do and what you would like to see in future books so that I can continue to provide a solid programming introduction to new technology. You can reach me at sasbury@crl.com.

To help navigate the projects and technologies in this book, use the following table to relate techniques and concepts that you are looking for with the project that discusses that technique.

TECHNIQUE	PROJECT
Access a database in Java	Project 3, 4, 7, 8, and 9
Access a database in Perl	Project 1 and 3
Access an LDAP server	Project 6 (Perl, Java, and C)
Access database metadata in Java	Project 8
Access information passed to a servlet by the server	Project 2 and 3
Access objects across the network using RMI	Project 5 and 7
Access objects across the network with CORBA	Project 4 (Java and C++)
Access services using JNDI	Project 5, 6, and 7
Associate a servlet with a URL type	Project 2
Bind, unbind, and look up objects with JNDI	Project 5, 6, and 7
Cache files in memory	Project 2
Combine Web pages and scripts into a Web application	Project 1 and 3 (Perl), Project 3 (Java)
Define a custom ClassLoader in Java	Project 2
Define a new language, file format in XML	Project 8
Define an interface for CORBA using IDL	Project 4
Define the interface between a client and a server	Project 4 (CORBA), Project 5 and 7 (RMI)
Dynamically generate links with query strings	Project 1 and 3
Encode special characters in strings	Project 8 (Java)
Generate HTML pages with CGI scripts	Project 1 and 3
Generate XML files programmatically	Project 8
Implement a CORBA server process	Project 4

TECHNIQUE	PROJECT
Implement a JMS service provider	Project 7
Implement a persistent messaging server	Project 7
Implement a simple transaction management system	Project 7
Implement an IDL interface in Java	Project 4
Implement producer-consumer relationships between threads	Project 7
Install a Java servlet	Project 2
Install the tools, servers used in this book	Appendix
Interoperate between Java and C++ using CORBA	Project 4
Manage child processes in Java	Project 9
Parse an HTML or other tag-based file in Java	Project 2
Parse XML files in Java	Project 8
Partition a program into server and client	Project 4, 5, and 7
Perform background tasks using threads	Project 9 (Java)
Pool database connections and threads	Project 9
Prepare the Apache Web server to run servlets	Project 2 and Appendix
Read and write files in Java	Project 8
Retrieve data from a relational database	Project 1 and 3 (Perl), Project 3, 4, 7, and 8 (Java)
Return error codes from a servlet	Project 2
Return references to objects in CORBA	Project 4
Search database contents using LIKE	Project 3
Send messages between programs as part of a parallel application	Project 10
Send messages between two ORBs using IIOP	Project 4
Separate a program into parallel processes	Project 10
Set up a class path for RMI applications	Project 7
Store data in a relational database	Project 1, 3, 4, 7, and 8
Store Java objects in a relational database	Project 7
Synchronize background tasks and drawing	Project 9
Use a resource bundle to store configuration information for a Java program	Project 3, 4, 5, and 7
Use command-line arguments	Project 6 (C, Perl, and Java) and 8 (Java)
Use synchronization to protect data from multithreaded access	Project 2, 7, and 9 (Java)

TECHNIQUE	PROJECT
Use the path info in a URL	Project 2
Using messaging to communicate between programs	Project 7
Validate data submitted to a CGI script	Project 1
Write a database backup utility	Project 8
Write a DTD for XML	Project 8
Write a JHTML file containing HTML and Java	Project 2 and 3
Write a JNDI service provider	Project 5
Write a servlet	Project 2
Write CGI scripts	Project 1 and 3 (Perl), Project 4 (C++)
Write multithreaded programs in Java	Project 7 and 9

An Online Catalog

 ## YOU WILL NEED

✔ Perl 5

✔ Apache Web Server 1.3 or higher

✔ MySQL database 3.22 or higher

✔ The Perl DBI modules for MySQL

✔ Experience programming in Perl

✔ Familiarity with SQL and HTML

Although this project is implemented using MySQL you could port it to other databases available on Linux, including Postgres and mSQL.

Memo

To: Stephen
From: The Manager

Stephen, we have decided to become the premier online store. I need you to put together a demo site to show the board how we can put our entire product catalog online. By the way, I need it tomorrow.

Thanks, The Manager

Memo

To: The Manager
From: Stephen

Manager, the online catalog is available at http://catalog/cgi-bin/display.pl. I used a database to store the data so we should be able to update this to the final Web site without too much work.

Stephen

About This Project

A few years ago, when client/server programming was popular and people were deploying powerful applications to each user's desktop, the idea was to create a "pretty" graphical interface that a customer or employee would use to access information from a database or some other data source. These interfaces had a lot of possibilities and resulted in the creation of sometimes large, often form-like applications that made it possible for a user to enter and retrieve data in a single program.

When the Web came along, people began to put information on their network by using Web pages. I remember the first time I saw Mosaic and started to "surf" the Web looking for information; I was, to say the least, intrigued. My buddies and I realized that there was a lot of potential in the Web, and we began to create some primitive Web training tools. We decided to try to put an application on the Web, and we created a room reservation system similar to the one we had used at NeXT Computer. The difference was that our reservation system used dynamic Web pages for the interface instead of a graphical user interface that was created with NEXTSTEP.

At the same time that we were thinking about the idea of Web applications, other programmers were, too. The Web provides an easy-to-access graphical user interface (GUI), which makes it a great solution to a problem that I am all too familiar with. Having trained a lot of NeXT programmers to create GUIs with what is arguably the best tool for the job, I knew how hard it was for programmers to architect a large database-driven client application. The Web changed that. HTML 1.0 was easy to learn and limited enough so that even a programmer could make an okay-looking Web page. And so the idea of *Web applications* was born—a collection of Web pages both fixed and dynamically generated that work together to provide a unified interface to the user.

At first, the Web was used for internal applications. In the course of a year and a half, numerous companies replaced expensive client/server solutions with Web applications that took a fraction of the time to develop, were more often completed successfully, were easier to use, and worked almost as well, and sometimes better. With that the Web exploded and, as more and more households got wired, companies sprang up to take advantage of the new communication medium that the Web provides, using applications to provide services not available previously.

One of the more popular commercial uses that people have found for the Web is the online store. Companies such as Amazon.com have sprung up in the last few years that sell their products directly over the Web. Other companies that sell their products through other channels, like Ford, have also begun to put their catalogs online while they move into the online commercial market. Companies are also putting catalogs and inventories online to make them more accessible to suppliers and partners. All of these electronic storefronts rely on a Web application that manages a database of products.

In this project, you create a simple online catalog system. The catalog data is stored in a database, and it is displayed as Web pages using Perl CGI scripts. Because this type of application is both popular and familiar, I have included it in the hope that you will find direct applications of the ideas discussed here in your own projects.

Design and Concepts

The inventors of the Web originally created a mechanism that provided access to resources on a network. The address of a resource was provided in the form of a Uniform Resource Locator, or URL. As shown in Figure 1.1, this URL uniquely identifies the computer, communication scheme, and document that the client wants to receive. When a client, usually a Web browser, wants a resource, the user of that client enters a URL or clicks on a link containing a URL. The browser uses the information in that URL to request the resource from the server. This request includes the URL itself as well as information about the client. If the request was made because the user filled in an HTML form and submitted it, the information in the form is sent to the server as well.

But I am getting ahead of myself. You see, originally, there were no forms, just links and documents. When you wanted something you clicked a link or typed in a URL. If you wanted to publish a document, you just created an HTML page or some other resource and put it on the Web server.

Unfortunately, that approach doesn't fulfill all of your needs. And it didn't fulfill the Web's inventors' needs either. So they added the idea of *dynamically created resources*. These resources were to be created by programs that worked with the Web server to generate the response to a particular URL. With a dynamic

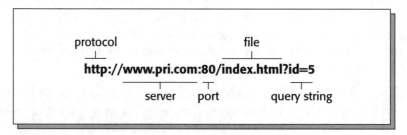

Figure 1.1   A URL.

resource, the user's request is mapped to a program that generates the response, which the Web server then forwards to the client.

The communication link between the server and the programs that generate content is called the *Common Gateway Interface* (CGI). The programs that use CGI to work with the server are called *CGI scripts*. Remember, a user's request for a URL can occur several ways. The two most common ways for CGI scripts to be initiated are these: The user submits a form on an HTML page, or the user clicks on a link to a script that displays an HTML page containing a resource. The HTML page is really a CGI script, that is, a script that provides an image. When the Web server receives a request for a CGI script, it runs the script as a child process. The server sends to the script the user's input, if there is any, and the script sends the server a reply that the server forwards to the client (Figure 1.2).

CGI scripts are used to provide the logic behind a Web page. This logic might be used to compile user entries from a Web form into a report or insert the same data into a relational database. Both of these examples represent the reactive

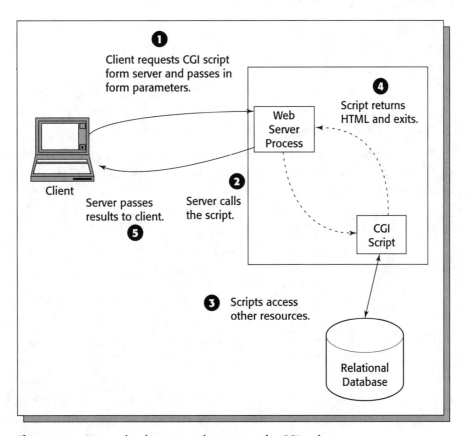

Figure 1.2 Interaction between a browser and a CGI script.

side of CGI scripting. *Reactive scripts* take input from the user and act on the provided data. Writing this type of script involves decoding the data provided to the script by what is called the HTTP or Web server. This HTTP server is the contact point for the Web browsers used by clients.

CGI scripts can also provide data to a client browser. An example of this behavior is a script that displays different Web pages based on a user's security level. When combined with the reactive portion of a script, the data-providing portion might submit a database query based on user input and display the results of the query to the user. Creating output is a partnership between the HTTP server and the CGI script.

As users of Web applications demand more functionality it is often necessary to create groups of scripts that work together. This requires the scripts to share data. The result is the creation of Web applications like the one pictured in Figure 1.3.

This project uses several CGI scripts written in Perl to dynamically generate Web pages. The design for this project uses three scripts and one plain HTML page. The scripts are as follows:

- index.pl
- display.pl
- insert.pl

The page is named insert_form.html. Users access the application via the index.pl page, which generates an HTML page containing the contents of the online catalog. This page is pictured in Figure 1.4.

When the user selects a link on the catalog page, specific information about that product is displayed using the display.pl script. The script produces a page like the one in Figure 1.5.

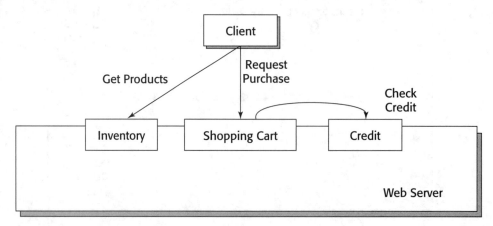

Figure 1.3   Web applications.

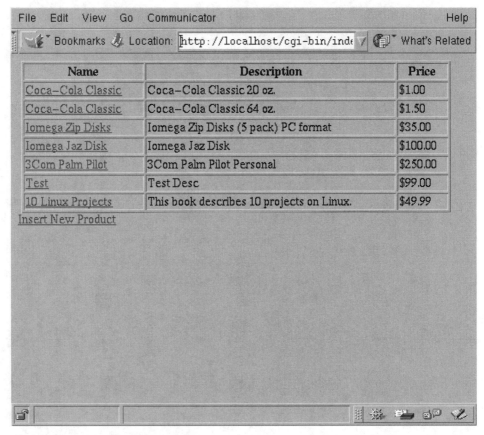

Figure 1.4   Opening catalog page.

Finally, the insert new product link on the index page will take the user to an HTML form like the one shown in Figure 1.6. If the user fills in this form, the new item is inserted in the database and the index page is redisplayed.

This project will give you an idea of how a collection of scripts and pages can be used to create an online application. Also, this project could form the basis of your own online catalogs.

NOTE

For this project, I assume that you have some experience programming in Perl. If you don't, but you have programmed in another language like C or Java, you should be able to work through the code. Keep in mind that everything in the book is also on the CD-ROM, so that you don't have to type anything in to try it out.

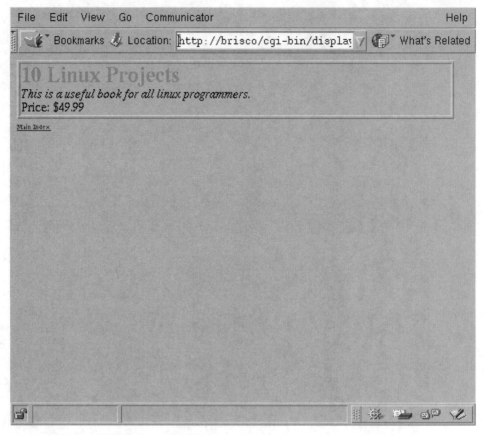

Figure 1.5   Detail page for a product.

Step 1: Building the Database

Because we are using the MySQL database in this project, you will need to install it on your computer. The Appendix includes some helpful tips for this installation. Once you have installed MySQL, you are ready to create the repository for your catalog data.

MySQL separates data into databases. Each MySQL database can contain multiple tables. The databases are separated for security and performance reasons. Security and other configuration information is stored in a database called mysql. Access to data is controlled by user and network address. So, for example, an administrative user could have permission to add tables to a database from within the company network, while a regular user could look at data from any computer on the Internet.

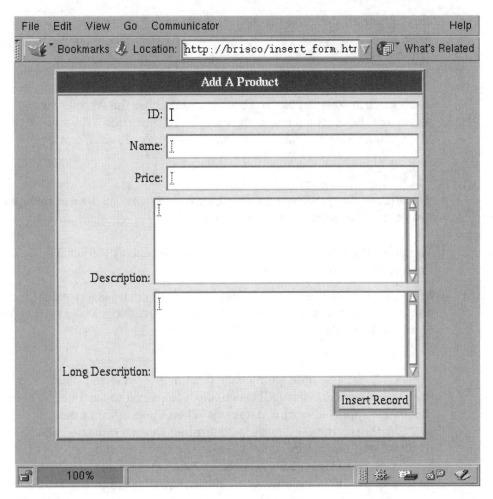

Figure 1.6   Insert form.

Use the mysqladmin program to create a database called products. If you are logged in as root, you should be able to use the command line:

```
#mysqladmin create products
```

This creates an empty database.

The next step is to make the products database available for use. Open the security for the products database by logging into the MySQL configuration database called mysql and adding permissions for a user named stephen to access bugs. To connect to the database use the command line:

```
#mysql -u root mysql
```

Next, grant all permissions for all of your MySQL databases to stephen, or some other user name. Restrict access to the local machine using the following syntax:

```
mysql> GRANT ALL PRIVILEGES ON *.* TO stephen@localhost
```

You are able to keep access to the local host because the Web server and MySQL server will be on the same computer. In a production environment, use the MySQL reference manual to configure a more secure environment.

NOTE

If MySQL and the Web server are on different computers you need to configure the security to allow access from the other computer.

The products database contains a single table called product. This table is defined with five columns, listed in Table 1.1.

In order to make the project more interesting, create a script that builds the database and provides a few default items in the catalog. Make a new file called builddb.pl and start it off like a Perl program:

```
#!/usr/bin/perl -w
```

The Perl Database Interface module (DBI) is the preferred method for accessing a database with Perl. DBI is actually a front end to a collection of modules that each support a specific database. When the program attempts to connect to the database, the DBI module determines the appropriate "driver" for that database and returns the database-specific connection object. As you can see from the code that follows, the connection string for this project is dbi:mysql:products and means use the mysql driver to connect to the products database. Check the Appendix for information on installing DBI and specifically the MySQL DBI module.

```
use DBI;

$dbhandle = DBI->connect("dbi:mysql:products", "stephen", "")
|| &error("Couldn't connect to DB. ".$?);
```

Table 1.1 Product Table Columns

COLUMN	DESCRIPTION
id	A string that uniquely identifies the product
name	The name of the product displayed to the buyer
description	A short description of the product
long_description	A longer text description of the product
price	The price of the product in dollars

Next, get rid of the table if it already exists. This ensures that a new, clean database is created each time you run the script. To get rid of a table, use the DROP TABLE command from SQL. Executing raw SQL with DBI is easy. Just use the database handle returned by the connect and ask it to "do" some SQL, as shown here:

```
$dbhandle->do("DROP TABLE product")
|| print "Already dropped product.\n";
```

NOTE

If you want to keep the existing data, use a program like the one created in Project 6 to back up the database before running this script.

Create the product table, assigning the ID column as a primary key. Depending on your database you generate this primary key automatically. In this project, the user will assign the primary key. Again, use the do method to execute the SQL once you define it.

```
$sql = "CREATE TABLE product (id char(12) not null primary key, name
varchar(80) null, description text null, longDescription text, price
float null)";
$dbhandle->do($sql) || &error($dbhandle->errstr);
```

Insert a few products into the database for testing. Like the DROP TABLE and CREATE TABLE statements, INSERT statements can be executed using the do method of the database handle.

```
$sql = "INSERT INTO product (id, name, description, longDescription,price)
VALUES ('coke20oz', 'Coca-Cola Classic', 'Coca-Cola Classic 20 oz.', 'Coca-
Cola Classic 20 oz. Plastic bottle', 1.00)";
$dbhandle->do($sql) || &error($dbhandle->errstr);

$sql = "INSERT INTO product (id, name, description, longDescription,price)
VALUES ('coke64oz', 'Coca-Cola Classic', 'Coca-Cola Classic 64 oz.', 'Coca-
Cola Classic 64 oz. Plastic bottle', 1.50)";
$dbhandle->do($sql) || &error($dbhandle->errstr);

$sql = "INSERT INTO product (id, name, description, longDescription,price)
VALUES ('iozippc5pk', 'Iomega Zip Disks', 'Iomega Zip Disks (5 pack) PC
format', '100MB Iomega Zip Disks in a convenient 5 pack package - PC
formatted', 35.00)";
$dbhandle->do($sql) || &error($dbhandle->errstr);

$sql = "INSERT INTO product (id, name, description, longDescription,price)
VALUES ('iojaz', 'Iomega Jaz Disk', 'Iomega Jaz Disk', '1000MB Iomega Jaz
Disk. Never run out of disk space again', 100.00)";
$dbhandle->do($sql) || &error($dbhandle->errstr);

$sql = "INSERT INTO product (id, name, description, longDescription,price)
VALUES ('palmpilot', '3Com Palm Pilot', '3Com Palm Pilot Personal', 'Stay
connected with the connected organizer from 3Com', 250.00)";
$dbhandle->do($sql) || &error($dbhandle->errstr);
```

Upon completion, disconnect from the database by telling the database handle to disconnect.

```
$dbhandle->disconnect();
```

Next, define the small subroutine called error used previously.

```
sub error
{
    my($errmsg) = shift;

    print $errmsg;

    exit;
}
```

By running this script you can build the database for the project and provide some sample data for testing:

```
>perl builddb.pl
```

Step 2: Displaying the Catalog

When clients come to the online catalog, the first page that they encounter is a table showing the contents of the catalog. A screen shot of this page is pictured in Figure 1.7. A CGI script called index.pl generates the index page.

The code for this script, shown below, performs a select on the product table in the database. Then the data returned by the select statement is used to create an HTML table that is sent to the client's browser. As always, start the Perl script off right:

```
#! /usr/bin/perl -w
```

Use the DBI module to connect to the database.

```
use DBI;
```

To make the script easy to move between servers, the server name and CGI directories can be stored in variables, $SERVER and $CGI_URL, that can be changed easily.

```
$SERVER = "http://brisco";
$CGI_URL = "$SERVER/cgi-bin";
```

Connect to the database to create a database handle.

```
$dbh = DBI->connect("dbi:mysql:products", "stephen", "");
```

Use that handle to retrieve data from the database. In this case, we want the ID, name, description, and price for all of the elements in the product table. To execute a select statement with DBI, use the database handle's prepare method to

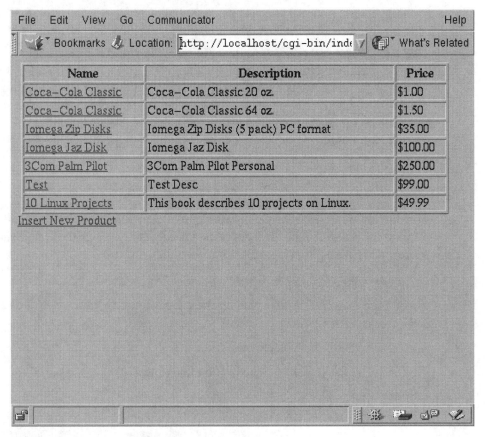

Figure 1.7   Web page generated by index.pl.

generate a statement handle using a provided SQL string. Then tell this statement handle to execute. The execute method returns a value that indicates the number of rows affected by the select statement. The statement handle can be used like a cursor on the data returned by the select statement. In the next block of code you use the statement to access each of these rows of data that the database has returned.

```
$sth = $dbh->prepare("SELECT id, name, description, price FROM product");
$rows = $sth->execute();
```

To build an HTML table that contains the product listing, define a string that contains the HTML for the table header. You could also output HTML here and then output the HTML for each row individually. I decided to build up one string of HTML and print it all at one time, so the code shown here creates a single string of HTML that contains the table and then prints that string to the client in one action.

```
$html_table = "<table border=1 width=500><tr><th>Name</th><th>"
              ."Description</th><th>Price</th></tr>\n";
```

Use a for loop to iterate over all of the rows returned by the select statement. Use the statement handle's fetchrow_array method to get the data for that row. Fetchrow_array returns an array of values, one value for each column in the current row. Each time fetchrow_array is called, it moves to the next row in the database, so you want to call it only once per row. Therefore, store the data returned from fetchrow_array in local variables.

```
for($i=0; $i<$rows; $i++)
{
    ($id, $name, $description, $price) = $sth->fetchrow_array;
```

Format the name and ID as a link using the subroutine link_product defined at the end of this step. This link accesses a second CGI script that takes the ID of a product and displays information about that product.

```
    $name = &link_product($name, $id);
```

Format the price into a string using the subroutine to_dollars defined with the link_product routine.

```
    $price = &to_dollars($price);
```

Append the HTML for the row in the table to the html_table variable.

```
    $html_table .=
"<tr><td>$name</td><td>$description</td><td>$price</td></tr>\n";
}
```

When all of the rows have been added, conclude the HTML for the table.

```
$html_table .= "</table>\n";
```

Conclude the select statement using the finish method. This cleans up any rows left in memory, if you didn't read them all already, and performs any other database-specific house-keeping duties. Once the statement is finished, disconnect from the database using the database handle's disconnect method.

```
$sth->finish();
$dbh->disconnect();
```

Now that you have the data to send to the user, begin the CGI script's response to the client. Start by returning a content type that tells the client what kind of document it is about to receive. This content type is part of the server's response to the browser and should use the Multipurpose Internet Mail Extension (MIME) types to associate the data you are about to send with a known data format. In this case, the client will receive HTML, so use the text/html MIME type string. If you were sending a JPG image you would use the type image/jpeg. The content types available to a CGI script are the standard MIME types plus the experimental, or x-, extensions. MIME types are split into two parts, a general type and a specific type. For example, html has the general type *text* and the specific type *html*. Determine the types for your script by finding the general type, then the specific type. Some example types are listed in Tables 1.2 and 1.3.

The content type is included in the header of the CGI script's response. Because the browser uses a blank line to separate the header of the response from its body, it is necessary to include a blank line after the Content-type statement, as shown here:

```
print "Content-type: text/html\n\n";
```

Using redirection, send the client the HTML for this page. Include a link to the insert_form.html file created later in the project. This page can be used to insert items into the database.

```
print << "EOD";

<HTML>
<BODY>
<CENTER>
$html_table
</CENTER>
<A HREF="$SERVER/insert_form.html">Insert New Product</A>
</BODY>
</HTML>

EOD
```

That concludes the main script. Use the exit command to explicitly end the script.

```
exit;
```

Now, define the link_product and to_dollars subroutines. The link_product routine takes the name and ID of a product and generates a link to the dis-

Table 1.2 General MIME Types

MAJOR TYPE	DESCRIPTION
application	Data for a particular application
text	Textual data
multipart	Multiple independent types, common for mail that contains embedded files and for file uploads to a Web server
image	Image data
audio	Sound/audio data
Video	Video data

Table 1.3 Specific MIME Types

MAJOR TYPE	MINOR TYPES	DESCRIPTION
application		Data types associated with a specific application
	octet-stream	Executable/binary files
	postscript	PostScript data
	rtf	Rich text data
	x-compress	Compressed data, standard Unix compression
	x-gzip	Gnu zipped data
	x-tar	Tar'd data, standard Unix tar
text	Text data types	
	html	HTML
	plain	Plain ASCII text
multipart		Specific to the MIME standard
	rfc822	A MIME mail message
image		Image data types
	gif	gif file data
	jpeg	jpg or jpeg file data
	tiff	tiff or tif file data
	x-xbitmap	Xbm file data
audio		Sound data types
	basic	au or snd file data
	x-aif	aif file data
	x-wav	Wav file data
video		Video, multimedia data types
	mpeg	An mpeg or mpg file/movie
	quicktime	A quicktime movie

play.pl script created in the next step. The URL for the link includes information about the ID to be passed to the display.pl script. Because the ID for a product is an arbitrary string, it must be URL encoded before it is included in link. Encoding a string involves converting nonalphanumeric characters to hexidecimal equivalents of the form %A4. Then all spaces are converted to pluses (+) to prevent spaces in the link. The following code performs this conversion, with comments to indicate each step.

```
sub link_product
{    my($name, $id) = @_;

     # change all % signs in the input to the character code %25
     $id =~ s/%/%25/g; # hardcoded

     # Convert all nonalphanumerics to character codes
     $id =~ s/([^a-zA-Z0-9_ %])/'%'.sprintf("%x", ord($1));/eg;

     # convert spaces to '+'
     $id =~ s/ /+/g;

     $url = "<A HREF=\'$CGI_URL/display.pl?id=$id\'>$name</A>";

     return $url;
}
```

The to_dollars routine formats a price into a number with two digits containing commas every third number. Create another subroutine called commify to perform the comma step, and use sprintf to format the number to two digits.

```
sub to_dollars
{
     my($amount) = shift;

     return (&commify (sprintf("%.2f", $amount)));
}

sub commify
{
     local $_  = shift;
     1 while s/^(-?\d+)(\d{3})/$1,$2/;
     return "\$$_";
}
```

That concludes the index.pl script. When accessed, the script creates a page like the one pictured in Figure 1.7. As new products are added, the page is updated automatically each time it is reloaded.

Step 3: Displaying Item Details

The next script in this project is the display.pl file that is linked to from the index.pl page. This script displays information about an individual product. Begin the script like all Perl scripts, as shown here.

```
#!/usr/bin/perl -w
```

Perhaps one of the main differences between this script and the index.pl one is that display.pl expects input from the client. In this case, the input is the ID of the product to display. In order to read this input, use the CGI module provided with Perl. The CGI module can be used to access information passed to the script including the contents of HTML forms submitted to the script.

```
use DBI;
use CGI;
```

Again, use variables to define the server and CGI directory to allow easy updates if the script is moved.

```
$SERVER = "http://brisco";
$CGI_DIR = "$SERVER/cgi-bin";
```

Unlike the DBI module, the CGI module is used to create a CGI object. This ob-
ject contains data and procedures that can be used to interact with the client.
To create the CGI object, use the keyword new. This creates a reference to the
CGI entity that can be stored in a scalar variable.

```
$query = new CGI;
```

When you created the links for products in the index.pl page, they included
their ID as part of the link. When the user clicks on the link, the display.pl page
knows which product the user selected. Information submitted to a script can
be provided two ways. In this case, the data is appended to the link with a ?,
and it is in the form of a name-value pair. Using the CGI object's param method
you can get the value for the ID of the item to display by asking for the value
passed in with the name "id".

```
$id = $query->param('id');
```

If no ID is returned, then it wasn't provided and the script should fail. You create a subroutine called error to print an error message to the user. Use this subroutine if the ID is not defined.

```
if(! defined($id))
{
    &error("This program expects a parameter that was not supplied.");
}
```

If the ID was provided, connect to the database and get the information about
that product. Use a where clause in your select statement to limit the data returned to the information about the single product.

```
$dbh = DBI->connect("dbi:mysql:products", "stephen", "");

$sql = "SELECT name, longDescription, price FROM product"
    ." WHERE id=\'$id\'";


$sth = $dbh->prepare($sql);
$rows = $sth->execute;
```

Next, make sure that there was data returned by the query statement by testing the value of $rows in an if statement. If no data was returned $rows will be
0 so you could return an error page, or you could do nothing and let the script
fail.

```
if ($rows)
{
```

As you did in Step 1, use the fetchrow_array method to get the data for the requested product and store it in variables.

```
($name, $description, $price) = $sth->fetchrow_array;
```

Use the to_dollars method defined earlier, and included in this script, to convert the price to a nice format.

```
$price = &to_dollars($price);
```

The CGI object can be used to generate the HTTP header and HTML head for a CGI script, so I have included that technique here. You can either use this technique or write things out by hand as in Step 1, based on your personal preference. The header method returns the content-type string, with a default type of text/html. The start_html method returns a string containing the HEAD and TITLE sections of an HTML page.

```
print $query->header;
print $query->start_html($name);
```

Once the header has been sent, use a table to display the information about this product. Also provide a link back to the index.pl page.

```
print << "EOD";

<CENTER><TABLE WIDTH=100% BORDER=1><TR><TD>
<P><FONT COLOR='red' size=+6><B>$name</B></FONT>
<BR><I>$description</I>
<BR>Price: $price
</TD></TR></TABLE></CENTER>
</CENTER>
<FONT SIZE="-2"><A HREF="$CGI_DIR/index.pl">Main Index</A></FONT>
</BODY>
</HTML>
```

In order to use print redirection, the end indicator, EOD in this case, must be on a line by itself, and it must start the line, so the indenting shown above for readability can't be used before the indicator itself.

```
EOD

}
```

Define subroutines to abstract the process of converting prices to formatting strings and to display an error page if an error occurs.

```
sub error
{
    my($errmsg) = shift;

    print $query->header;
```

```
    print $query->start_html("Error");

    print $errmsg;

    print $query->end_html;
    exit;
}

# Formats a number as money
sub to_dollars
{
    my($amount) = shift;

    return (&commify (sprintf("%.2f", $amount)));
}

# Adds commas to thousands
sub commify
{
    local $_  = shift;
    1 while s/^(-?\d+)(\d{3})/$1,$2/;
    return "\$$_";
}
```

When accessed, this script will return a page like the one in Figure 1.8.

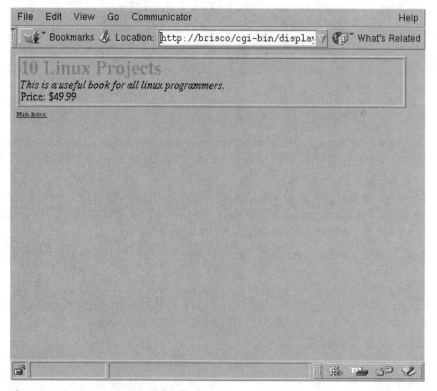

Figure 1.8   Page generated by display.pl.

For fun, you might consider extending this project to support images for each item. Then the display.pl page should return a page that includes an IMG tag. One way to design this addition is to create another script that also takes the ID of a product, but instead of returning HTML it returns a gif. Use the image/gif type instead of text/html in the header of that request to indicate that results are not HTML.

Step 4: Inserting New Items

Inserting data items into the catalog requires two files. First, you need an HTML page that contains a form for describing the product. Second, you need a CGI script to handle this form when it is submitted to the server and to insert the new product in the database.

The HTML shown here, and pictured in Figure 1.9, defines a form that sends information to a CGI script called insert.pl.

```
<HTML>
<HEAD>
<TITLE>Insert Product</TITLE>
</HEAD>

<BODY>

<CENTER>
<TABLE bgColor=006666 BORDER=2 CELLSPACING=1 CELLPADDING=4><TR><TD
ALIGN="center">
<FONT COLOR="white"><B>Add A Product</B></FONT></TD></TR>
<TR bgColor=F0F0F0><TD ALIGN="right">

<FORM ACTION="/cgi-bin/insert.pl" METHOD="POST">
ID: <INPUT TYPE=text NAME="id" SIZE=40><BR>
Name: <INPUT TYPE=text NAME="name" SIZE=40><BR>
Price: <INPUT TYPE=text NAME="price" SIZE=40><BR>
Description: <TEXTAREA NAME="description" COLS=40 ROWS=6
WRAP=virtual></TEXTAREA><BR>
Long Description: <TEXTAREA NAME="longDescription" COLS=40 ROWS=6
WRAP=virtual></TEXTAREA><BR>
<INPUT TYPE=submit VALUE="Insert Record">
</FORM>

</TD></TR></TABLE>
</CENTER>

</BODY>
</HTML>
```

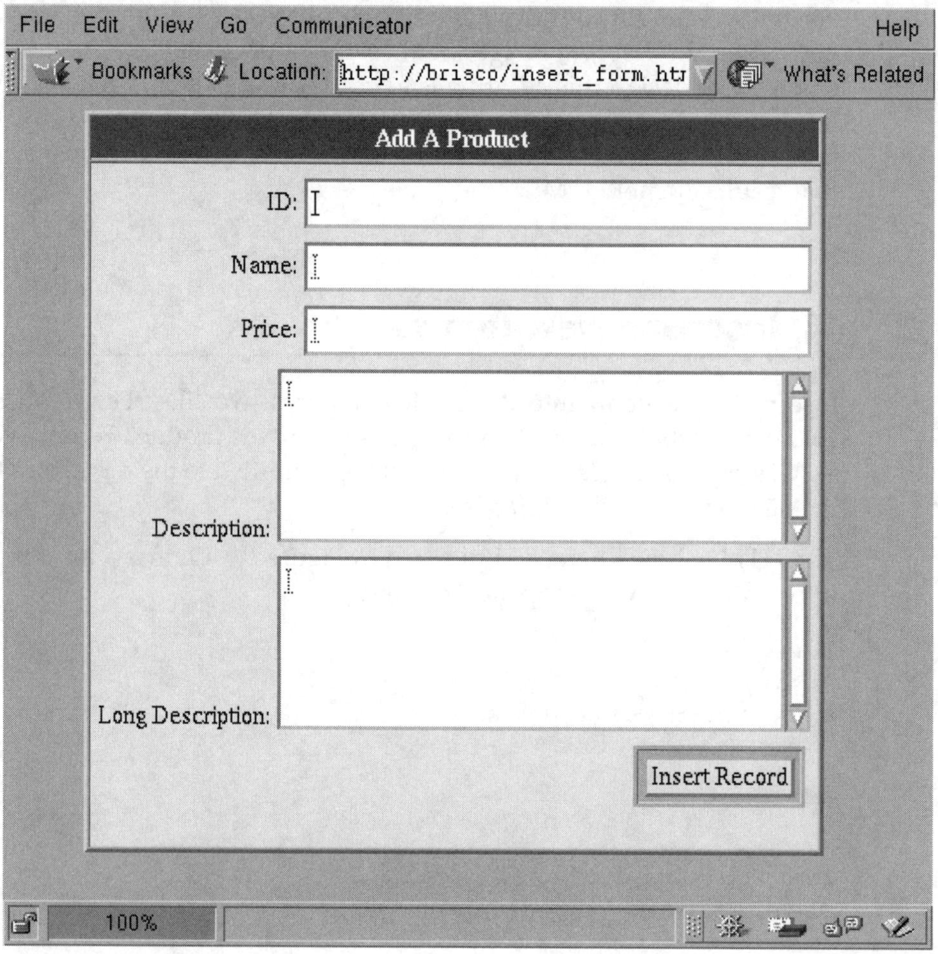

Figure 1.9 Insert HTML page.

The final CGI script for this project is insert.pl. This file is similar to the display.pl script because it uses the CGI module to read information submitted to the script. This information is used to define a new product in the database.

```perl
#! /usr/bin/perl -w

use DBI;
use CGI;

$SERVER = "http://brisco";
$CGI_DIR = "$SERVER/cgi-bin";

# this is a template for the required data and formats
%REQUIRED_DATA = ( 'price' => "number", 'id' => "string", 'name' =>
"string", 'description' => "string", 'longDescription' => "string");
```

```
# create a new CGI object
$query = new CGI;
```

To make accessing the form data easier, create a subroutine to store the form data in an associative array.

```
%data = &query_hash($query);
```

Because this script expects all of the form elements to be filled in, you need to verify that the data is complete. Use an associative array to define the required data, defined previously as REQUIRED_DATA, and a subroutine called verify_data, defined here, to perform the check.

```
%data = &verify_data(%data);
```

If the data verifies, connect to the database and insert the new product data.

```
$dbh = DBI->connect("dbi:mysql:products", "stephen", "");

$sql = "INSERT INTO product (id, name, description, longDescription, price)
VALUES (\'$data{id}\', \'$data{name}\', \'$data{description}\',
\'$data{longDescription}\', $data{price})";
```

The insertion could fail, especially if the ID is already in use. In this case, display an error page using a subroutine similar to the one defined in previous scripts.

```
$dbh->do($sql) || &error($dbh->errstr);
```

Upon successful completion of the insert, disconnect from the database.

```
$dbh->disconnect();
```

Then redirect the client back to the index.pl page so that it can see that the product was inserted successfully. The CGI object knows how to perform the redirection. Under the covers, the redirect method causes the CGI object to send a special header field to the client. The client then will load a new page instead of this one.

```
print $query->redirect("$CGI_DIR/index.pl");
```

As in previous scripts, the error subroutine for this script should display an error message in an HTML page and exit the script.

```
sub error
{
    my($errmsg) = shift;

    print $query->header;
    print $query->start_html("Error");

    print $errmsg;

    print $query->end_html;
    exit;
}
```

The query_hash subroutine is supposed to take all of the form data submitted to the script and put it into an associative array. To perform this task, get a list of names for the data using the param method. This returns an array of names that correspond to the names of the form elements on the HTML page. Then for each element name, get the value for that element and put the name and value in an associative array. Finally, return the array to the caller.

```
sub query_hash
{
    my($query) = shift;
    my(%FORM, $field);

    my(@fields) = $query->param();

    foreach $field(@fields)
    {
        $FORM{$field} = $query->param($field);
    }
    return %FORM;
}
```

The verify_data subroutine takes an associative array as an argument. Make an array that contains the list of required values. This will correspond to the names of the form elements on the HTML page. Then check that each of the required elements is in the associative array passed to the subroutine.

```
sub verify_data
{
    my(%data) = @_;

    # Build a list of required fields
    my(@required) = keys(%REQUIRED_DATA);

    # initialize this to empty so we don't raise errors
    my($html_message) = '';

    foreach $req(@required)
    {
        if(defined($data{$req}) && $data{$req})
        {
```

If the value is there, make sure that numeric data contains only digits and decimals. If it is a string, make sure that the quotes are correct.

```
            if($REQUIRED_DATA{$req} eq "number")
            {
                if($data{$req} =~ /[^0-9\.]/)
                {
                    $html_message .=
                     "<LI>The field $req contains non-numeric data\n";
                }
            }
            else
```

```
        {
            $data{$req} =~ s/'/''/g;
            $data{$req} =~ s/"/""/g;
        }
    }
    else
    {
        $html_message .=
            "<LI>The field <B>$req</B> is required.\n";
    }
}
```

If there was a problem, use an HTML message to define it, and then send this message to the user as an error.

```
if($html_message ne '')
{
    $html_message = "<P><B>The form submission had errors</B><BR>Please
click your back button and correct them:<UL>$html_message</UL>";

    &error($html_message);
}
```

Otherwise, return the data, indicating success.

```
    return %data;
}
```

This script demonstrates how you can use server-side programs to validate forms and request that the user fill in specific information. The solution for Project 3 shows the complementary idea of using JavaScript on the client to require that fields be filled in. Keep in mind that a product program could actually use both techniques. By checking on the client, the user sees a responsive interface; by checking on the server, the CGI script ensures that the correct information was provided.

Wrap Up

It is fairly easy to create an online, database-driven application using Perl and HTML. The key to any Web application is the collection of scripts and pages, as well as the connection between them. In this case, the index.pl script generates pages with links to other scripts and other pages. The insert.pl script uses redirect to send the user back to the index page when an insertion succeeds. This sort of interconnectedness is common in Web applications and forms the complexity of a Web application in the same way that multiple windows would add complexity to a GUI application. In the next project, you create an engine for creating a Web application with Java that allows you to embed Java in HTML.

Java-based Web Page Scripting Engine

Project Objectives

In this project, you will learn how to:

- Prepare the Apache server to run Java servlets
- Create and install a Java servlet
- Create and access JHTML pages
- Parse JHTML files
- Define a custom Class loader for a Java program

 ## YOU WILL NEED

✔ A Web server that runs servlets

✔ JDK 1.2 (JDK 1.1 will work also with some installation modifications)

✔ Java programming experience

✔ Web programming experience

✔ Experience with Apache modules is helpful

I have used the Apache server for my explanation and begin with a discussion of how to add servlet support to the server. You may already have a Web server that supports servlets, in which case you will be able to skip Step 1.

Memo

To: Stephen
From: The Manager

Stephen, what type of server technology would you suggest for our development team? We are creating Web applications that output dynamic HTML pages and handle form submissions.

The Manager

Memo

To: The Manager
From: Stephen

Manager, I prefer to create this type of application using JHTML. JHTML files can combine Java and HTML to create dynamic Web programs. I have attached an engine for interpreting these files.

Stephen

About This Project

If you completed Project 1, or if you have ever done CGI scripting for Web applications, you probably are familiar with the amount of work it takes to create Web pages and separate scripts that work together to form a unified application. Well, you aren't the first person to get that feeling. Almost as soon as the Web started to grow, people were thinking of new ways to create Web applications. Their motivation was twofold. First, make applications easy to write. Second, try to improve on the performance degradation caused by the CGI scripts running separately from the Web server. Initially, two techniques were added to Web programming: server plugins and applets. That gave rise to three programming models:

CGI. Using the common gateway interface (CGI), you could write an application that handles an HTML form request. This requires a graphics person to lay out the HTML form and then a programmer to write the CGI script, separately. If the layout of the table returned from the CGI script needs to be modified then most of the work will be done in the CGI script.

Server plugin. Using the API of the specific server, a similar solution to CGI could be created. The only difference is that the solution would work only with the server for which the plugin was created.

Applet. You could create an applet that contains the form. The applet could connect to a server process or directly to the database and return the results. This puts most of the layout burden on the developer and can have significant security considerations, such as interacting through a firewall.

Consider the example that uses CGI. You could create a CGI script that sits on the server and waits for requests from the HTML form. When the Web client sends a request, the CGI script can process the form, access the database, and then output HTML back to the client. This would require you to create a script that generates HTML based on dynamic content. As the developer of the script, you would be responsible for the visual appearance of the data on the page since the HTML would have to be "hard-coded" in the CGI script. It's not reasonable to expect a graphic layout person to learn how to write CGI scripts, so what choice do you have? This means that you'll need an expensive engineering resource if you just want to change the font in your table. If this sounds unreasonable to you, you're not alone.

Server-side plugins have the same problems, if not worse. To write a plugin you probably have to write C code that must be compiled and installed by the server administrator. This makes it a far cry from something that a Web designer is likely to want to do. Server plugins do solve some performance problems by putting the code for an application in the Web server's process. That also means, however, that bugs in the plugin affect the Web server as well.

Applets provided a great way to improve the client's view of a Web application, but they still often require a server component, and they are very programmer intensive.

In other words, none of these solutions really meets the goal of being simple to use and improving server performance. Another solution was found in the form of *server-side scripting*. The idea behind server-side scripting is that rather than embedding the presentation code (HTML in this case) inside the application (the CGI script in this case) it would be better if the business logic could simply be referred to from the presentation. In other words, a graphic layout expert could put together a complex HTML page that included a table. He or she would have server-side scripting tools that made it possible to simply specify what values need to display in the table at specific locations in the Web page. These tools would refer to more complex business rules created by the developer that actually did the work of processing the form, accessing data sources, logging the transaction, and returning values. The graphic layout person simply uses special tags to identify placeholders for values in the Web page. When this special HTML page is requested, the server executes the business logic created by the developer and inserts the values dynamically in the HTML template created by the graphic layout person. This way you could change the font, color, and alignment without recompiling the code. The developer focuses on the business process, and the graphics person focuses on the presentation of the results.

Project 2 builds a Web page scripting engine based on Sun's Java in HTML format, *JHTML*. JHTML allows a programmer to insert Java code into an HTML page. Like other server scripting engines, this JHTML engine works like a server plugin, which reduces the separation of server and Web application. At the same time, it is simple to use for designers because they just write HTML. For programmers it is powerful, providing all of the functionality of a Java application. Project 3 discusses a Web application implemented in CGI and JHTML so that you can compare these two technologies.

The JHTML engine is a servlet, meaning that it is a Java program plugged into the Web server. It also generates other servlets for the JHTML pages that you create. By converting from JHTML to servlet, the Java in a JHTML page can reference all of the resources that a Java servlet can. Namely, the JHTML code can access databases with JDBC, services with JNDI, Enterprise JavaBeans, and all of the other Java APIs. By its very nature, the servlet is also a safe server plugin because it relies on garbage collection to protect the Web server from memory leaks due to the JHTML programmer's code.

NOTE

This is an intermediate to advanced project that relies on a strong Java and Web programming background to complete from scratch. The pages you create to use this scripting engine, however, are approachable to the newest Java developer. If you haven't done any Web programming, you may want to look at Project 1 before working on this one.

JHTML scripting allows you to combine logic and presentation for a dynamic Web page while still keeping them separate enough for more than one person to maintain. This scripting engine also provides you with access to all of the standard Java libraries, making it a very powerful and extensible environment.

To give you a basic idea of what you will create in this project, here is a simple .jhtml file:

```
<HTML>
<HEAD>
<TITLE>Sample1 JHTML File</TITLE>
</HEAD>

<BODY>
Hello
<java>
    String name;
    if ((name = request.getParameter("name")) != null)
        out.print(name);
</java>

<!—
    Note that for simplicity the form calls the same file
    with the value for the name text field filled in
—>
<FORM METHOD=POST ACTION="sample1.jhtml">
  Enter your name and press submit
  <INPUT TYPE=TEXT NAME=name>
  <BR><BR><INPUT TYPE=SUBMIT>
</FORM>

<java>
    for(int i=1;i<6; i++)
        out.print("<H"+ i +"> Heading " + i );
</java>

</BODY>
</HTML>
```

Figure 2.1 illustrates what this file looks like before and after submitting a name.

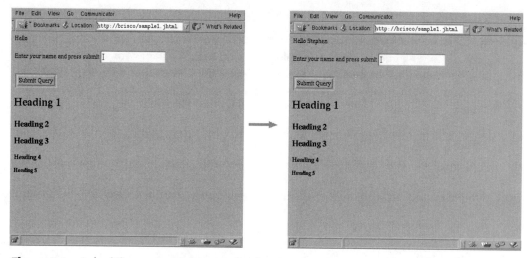

Figure 2.1 Submitting a request for sample1.jhtml.

The first time that the file sample1.jhtml is requested by a client, the JHTML engine, a servlet, is called by the Web server. The JHTML engine generates and compiles a servlet called _sample1.java. The servlet is called from then on whenever the sample1.jhtml file is requested. If the .jhtml file is changed, then the whole process repeats, and a new servlet is created for that page. The advantage of this model is that the servlet does not need to be recompiled every time it is requested. Think of the JHTML engine as being responsible for all client requests for a JHTML file. The servlet that implements the engine handles requests by delegating them to a servlet associated with a particular file. If the servlet doesn't exist, one is compiled. The JHTML servlet is basically a manager, delegating requests from each client to the appropriate JHTML-generated servlet.

NOTE

The code for this project was originally developed at Paradigm Research and released under the GNU public license. As a result, you are free to use the code or finished project as you see fit within the terms of that license.

As part of this project I cover three main tasks:

1. Preparing the Web server to run servlets
2. Defining the scripting language
3. Implementing the scripting engine

Keep in mind that the format for your scripted pages is based on an existing standard. This standard, called JHTML, is being supplanted by a more HTML-like format called Java Server Pages (JSP). JSP is an interesting format for HTML programmers because it uses HTML and JavaBeans to do work. JHTML requires more Java programming experience for the logic, but it is also more flexible. Based on my experience building a large Web site with JHTML, this scripting engine will be a powerful tool for you to create highly dynamic Web sites.

Basic Concepts and Design

Before diving into this project, you need to understand some of the basics about how Web servers work and how to write servlets. Servlet programming is particularly important because the JHTML engine is implemented as a servlet, and because it also generates servlets. Basically, servlets represent the extension of applet style programming onto the Web server. In the same way that an applet is a Java program plugged into a Web browser, a servlet is a Java program plugged into a Web server. Like applets, servlets are written by extending an existing class and implementing one or two key methods.

The first step to define a servlet is to create an object that implements the javax.servlet.Servlet interface. Once this class is defined, you can implement methods that handle client requests. There are two standard ways to implement the Servlet interface. The first is to subclass javax.servlet.GenericServlet. GenericServlet implements all of the methods of the Servlet interface, as listed in Table 2.1, and provides a few convenience methods. The second way to implement the servlet is to subclass javax.servlet.http.HttpServlet. Implementing the servlet in this way provides more methods for dealing with servlets that interact with a Web server. Objects can also implement Servlet directly, although

Table 2.1   Servlet Interface Methods

METHOD	DESCRIPTION
`void destroy()`	Cleans up whatever resources are being held
`ServletConfig getServletConfig()`	Returns a servlet config object, in particular the configuration object passed to init
`String getServletInfo()`	Returns a string containing information about the servlet, such as its author, version, and copyright
`void init(ServletConfig)`	Initializes the servlet
`void service (ServletRequest, ServletResponse)`	Called each time a request is made to the servlet

this technique is normally reserved for cases where it is necessary for the object to belong to a specific inheritance hierarchy.

Once a servlet is programmed and compiled, it is installed on a Web server. This installation process requires four things. First, the server has to be told about the servlet. Second, the servlet's class files must be placed correctly, so that the server can access them. Third, the installer can assign installation parameters for the servlet. These parameters will be passed to the servlet when it is used.

Finally, the server must be told to associate the servlet with a URL. Often this URL is based on the name of the servlet's class or on an alias. For example, a servlet named hello might be accessed at:

```
http://www.pri.com/servlet/hello
```

The server can also allow a servlet to be associated with a complete type of URL. For example, the JHTML pages you create in this project are compiled by a servlet, the scripting engine, that handles all requests to ".jhtml" files. In other words, the JHTML engine's servlet handles a file request type, rather than a particular URL.

When the user accesses a URL represented by a servlet, the Web server first checks to see if it has loaded the code for that servlet. Some Web servers provide an administrative tool for preloading servlets; others wait until the first user request before loading the servlet. Loading the servlet is a two-step process. First, an instance of the servlet's class is created using the default constructor, based on the class name provided when the servlet was configured to a particular URL. Second, the servlet is notified of its loading.

Like applets, servlets are notified of their instance creation and destruction by the servlet host. In particular, the servlet is sent the message "init" when it is first loaded and "destroy" when it is unloaded from the server. These specific messages are used, instead of relying on the constructor and finalize method, to give the Web server control over when and how it notifies the servlet. In fact, a server could send init and destroy to the same servlet object several times, assuming that it is unloaded before being initialized again.

In the servlet model, only one object is created to service each URL. This object receives the init, service, and destroy messages for that URL. In other words the init method is called once, regardless of the number of requests, and the destroy method is called once when the servlet is unloaded. The service method is called on the same servlet object every time any client accesses that URL on the server.

The init method, as declared next, takes a ServletConfig object as its argument. For servlets that extend GenericServlet, the configuration object is stored by the servlet for later use in the GenericServlet's implementation of init. When subclassing GenericServlet and overriding the init method, you should call super.init() in the init method to inherit this behavior.

```
public void init(ServletConfig config) throws ServletException
```

Using the provided configuration, init should prepare the servlet for work. This initialization could involve creating a network connection, loading a file into memory, or any other potentially lengthy operation. The server guarantees that it will send init once on load and wait to send any service messages to the servlet until init has returned. This means that init is basically thread safe, and it will be called only once per servlet load.

If an error occurs during initialization, the servlet should throw an exception. The package that contains the servlet also defines the ServletException and UnavailableException classes. UnavailableExceptions are thrown during init if the initialization cannot complete. There are two types of unavailable servlets: A servlet can be permanently unavailable and a servlet can be temporarily unavailable. A permanently unavailable servlet cannot be recovered. A temporarily unavailable servlet can recover after some condition is met. An example of a permanently unavailable servlet would be a servlet configured to use a file that doesn't exist. A temporarily unavailable servlet could be one that uses a database that is currently unavailable. The key differentiation is that permanently unavailable servlets require administrative action. Temporarily unavailable servlets can become available later without administrative action, or they can be self-correcting. The scripting engine in this project uses these exceptions to notify the server if it is not configured correctly.

Table 2.2 shows the UnavailableException methods that provide information to the servlet host or Web server. The most important method for truly self-correcting servlets is getUnavailableSeconds. Servlets use this method to tell

Table 2.2   UnavailableException Methods

METHOD	DESCRIPTION
public boolean isPermanent()	Returns true if the servlet requires administrative intervention before becoming available
public Servlet getServlet()	The servlet in question
public int getUnavailableSeconds()	The number of seconds that the servlet expects to be unavailable

the server how long the servlet needs to correct the current problem. All of these values are set by arguments in the constructor for UnavailableException.

Servlets implement the destroy method to clean up any outstanding resource. For example, a servlet might close a network connection or file that it is holding open. The servlet's host will try to wait on all service requests to be fulfilled before destroy is sent to the servlet.

Keep in mind that most servlets should perform reasonably short operations, in order to provide user responsiveness. In those cases it is not necessary to plan too extensively around calling destroy too early. Servlets that do not require open resources, created in init and closed in destroy, may not even need to implement the method.

Once a servlet is initialized, the key method used to interact with it is service, declared here:

```
public void service(ServletRequest request,
    ServletResponse response) throws ServletException
```

This service method is made up of a simple interface that includes an object that contains information about the request and an object that encapsulates the response. Whenever a request arrives at the server for a particular servlet, the server wraps up information about the request, creates a response object to contain information relevant to the response, and calls service. The service method uses a ServletException, a special type of Exception object, to indicate when an exception has occurred.

An example of the service method appears next in the form of the classic HelloWorld program. The results of accessing this servlet are pictured in Figure 2.2. The bold code shows that the service method is sent a request object that contains the details of the client request and a response object that is used to return values to the client. The method writes "Hello World" to a Web page on the client browser.

Figure 2.2 Hello World.

```
import java.io.*;
import java.util.*;
import javax.servlet.*;
import javax.servlet.http.*;

public class HelloWorldServlet extends GenericServlet
{
    public void service(ServletRequest request,
                        ServletResponse response)
                        throws ServletException,
                        IOException
    {
        PrintWriter out;

        response.setContentType("text/html");

        out = response.getWriter();

        out.println("<HTML><HEAD><TITLE>");
        out.println("Hello World");
        out.println("</TITLE></HEAD><BODY>");
        out.println("<H1>Hello World</H1>");
        out.println("</BODY></HTML>");

        out.close();
    }
}
```

Other servlets can have similar versions of service or implementations that are more complex. The important point is that service is the Web server's interface to the servlet. You, as the servlet writer, can do anything you want, as long as

Java supports it, inside the service method. This could include using the Java Naming and Directory Interface (JNDI) to look up the e-mail address in an LDAP directory or finding inventory items in a database through the Java Database Connectivity packages (JDBC).

The servlet you create in this project generates other servlets from scripted JHTML pages. As a result, the servlets created from these pages can do anything that a normal servlet could do.

Step 1: Preparing the Web Server

This project leverages the servlet programming model to create a Web page scripting engine. As a result, the Web server that you use to implement this project must support servlets. If you purchase a Web server commercially, you can ask the sales or support staff about servlet support. On the other hand, if you use the Apache server, common to most Linux distributions, you can add servlet support using an open source tool called JServ.

JServ is a module that can be plugged into the Apache Web server. You can get this module in source code or binary form from the Java Apache project at http://java.apache.org. This URL also has other resources related to programming Apache with Java. See the Appendix for information on installing JServ on your machine.

Once the installation is successful, you can configure the servlet created in this project. The code for the servlet is included in the file jhtml.jar in a directory called Project2, which also can be accessed with CVS from the main repository on the CD-ROM. To install this servlet perform the following updates:

1. Create a directory to hold your compiled JHTML servlets. On my machine this is /root/jserv/pageCompile. Change the permissions on this directory to make it writable by the Web server. Your Web server may run as the user nobody, so this directory could need to be writable by everyone. If the server runs as a specific user, like apache or httpd, you can open the directory to only that user.

2. Tell the server to associate the jhtml servlet with .jhtml files by updating jserv.conf to include:

```
ApJServAction .jhtml
/example/com.pri.servlets.jhtml.JHTMLServlet
```

3. Copy the jhtml.jar file into your JServ installation directory; in my case this was /root/jserv.

4. Copy the jhtml.jar file into the extensions folder for Java 2. My path is:

```
/root/jdk1.2/jre/lib/ext/jhtml.jar
```

5. Update the jserv.properties file to include this new directory in the class path. Also add the jhtml.jar file to the class path. Make sure that the JServ and JSDK files are in this path as well. Add them if they are not already.

```
wrapper.classpath=/root/jserv/jhtml.jar
wrapper.classpath=/root/jserv/pageCompile
```

6. Update the example.properties file to include the following initialization parameters. You should update the initArgs values to reflect your installation paths and the directory you created above. The initialization parameters themselves are described next.

```
servlet.jhtml.initArgs=compileCommand=/stephen/jdk1.2/bin/javacì\,
workingDir=/root/jserv/pageCompile
```

You will need to restart the Web server to see these changes take effect.

The JHTMLServet, like any other, can be configured by the administrator. The parameters for the scripting engine, as we will implement it, are listed in Table 2.3.

Table 2.3 Scripting Engine Configuration Parameters

PROPERTY	DESCRIPTION
WorkingDir	The directory for storing generated .java and .class files. *Our engine requires this value to be set.*
DefaultEncoding	Defines the default encoding to use for servlets. Any encoding name that is supported by the java.io package is a valid encoding string value for this property. The default value of null causes PageCompileServlet to treat the file as an array of bytes. *The current implementation ignores this parameter.*
Verbose	If true, prints a message when compiling a .jhtml file. The default value is false.
DefaultPageClassName	The name of the class to use as a base class for pages that do not explicitly specify it. The default value is set to HttpServlet.
PackagePrefix	The package name to prepend onto the name of the generated class. The default value is set to pagecompile.
CheckURI	Test the URL for the requested page and make sure that the user is not trying to trick the servlet into returning JHTML code instead of the servlet's output.
CompileCommand	The command for compiling the JHTML-generated servlets. The default value is: javac -d *buildDirectory sourceFile* When executed, the value of the workingDir property is substituted for the string *buildDirectory* and the absolute path of the source file is substituted for the string *sourceFile*.

Use one of the example pages from the Project2/examples directory on the CD-ROM to make sure that the installation works. Copy this file to the Web server's document root and try to access it from a browser. Be sure to restart the server after configuring it and before trying to access files. If an error occurs, try reloading the page. If that fails, check your configurations, especially the class path, and double-check that the directory you created for the compiler to use is writable by the user that the Web server runs as.

Step 2: Defining the Scripting Language

JHTML pages are defined by combining HTML and Java code inside <java> and </java> tags. These tags can contain attributes, as defined in Table 2.4. The <java type=code> is the same as <java>, so the type=code attribute will often be left out for clarity.

The Java code inside the <java> tags will be included in the server page's servlet as is. For example, if you perform a simple update to your Hello World page as follows:

```
<HTML>
<HEAD>
<TITLE>
Hello World
</TITLE>
</HEAD>
<BODY>
```

Table 2.4 Java Tag Attributes

ATTRIBUTE	PURPOSE
<java type=code></java>	Code that should be included as is in the servlet generated for this JHTML page. Performs same function as <java></java>.
<java type=import></java>	Defines the name of a class to import.
<java type=extends></java>	Defines the name of a class to extend the servlet from.
<java type=print></java>	Defines an expression in Java to send to the output stream.
<java type=implements></java>	Defines a list of interfaces the servlet must implement.
<java type=class></java>	Describes member variables and defining methods of the page class directly.

```
<java>
    out.println("<H1>Hello Java World!</H1>");
</java>
</BODY>
</HTML>
```

and have the PageCompileServlet compile your new dynamic JHTML into a servlet, the result is code like this:

```java
package pagecompile;

import javax.servlet.*;
import javax.servlet.http.*;
import java.io.*;
import java.util.*;
import com.pri.utils.*;

public class _HelloWorld
extends javax.servlet.http.HttpServlet
{

    static
    {
    }

    public void service (HttpServletRequest request,
            HttpServletResponse response)
        throws ServletException, IOException
    {
        ServletOutputStream out=response.getOutputStream();
        RandomAccessBuffer fileData = FileCache.getRandomBufferForFile(
            "/home/httpd/html/HelloWorld.jhtml");
        String __tmp;

        response.setContentType("text/html");

        try
        {
            out.write(__fileData.read(0,58));

                out.println("<H1>Hello Java World!</H1>");

            out.write(__fileData.read(119,17));
        }
        catch(Exception jhtml_exp)
        {
            log(jhtml_exp.toString());
        }
        finally
        {
            if(__fileData != null) __fileData.close();
        }
    }

}
```

Notice that the regular HTML is output directly from the file to the client, while the Java code is executed in place. A cached copy of the file is used to maximize performance while still allowing the servlet to read the HTML directly rather than duplicating it in the servlet code. The example uses the automatic definition of the variable out, to represent the stream back to the client. This allows the JHTML writer to return output easily without dealing with the response object.

The straight <java> tags indicate code that will be included verbatim in the generated service method. This means that variable definitions are scoped according to the code that surrounds them in the JHTML, but they can exist beyond a single set of <java> tags. As an example of how scoping works, I have created three JHTML pages. The first page contains two sets of <java> tags. The first set defines a variable name and prints it. The second set reassigns the name and prints it, showing what happens when you try to redeclare a variable. The third page shows what the servlet looks like when you define two Java code blocks. Here is the code for the first Web page.

```
<HTML>
<HEAD>
<TITLE>
Try Reassign
</TITLE>
</HEAD>
<BODY>
<H2>Java Block One</H2>
<java>
    String name = "Mister Zero";
    out.println(name);
</java>
<H2>Java Block Two</H2>
<java>
    name = "Master Blaster";
    out.println(name);
</java>
</BODY>
</HTML>
```

Notice the assignments in the bolded code in the previous HTML. The second set of tags doesn't need to redefine the variable because it is already defined in the first set. The separate <java> blocks are combined into the single service method with only a single line of code between them writing out the HTML that separated the </java> and <java> tags ending and beginning the two blocks.

This means that the HTML code in the following page will not work because it tries to redefine a variable in a scope that already defines it.

```
<HTML>
<HEAD>
<TITLE>
```

```
Try Redeclare
</TITLE>
</HEAD>
<BODY>
<H2>Java Block One</H2>
<java>
    String name = "Mister Zero";
    out.println(name);
</java>
<H2>Java Block Two</H2>
<java>
    String name = "Master Blaster";
    out.println(name);
</java>
</BODY>
</HTML>
```

The page defined here will not compile because of the redefintion of the name variable. Instead the client is sent a message indicating the error, as pictured in Figure 2.3.

If you want the <java> blocks to have separate scopes in the resulting servlet code, use curly brackets to delimit them, as in the following file:

```
<HTML>
<HEAD>
<TITLE>
Two Code Blocks
</TITLE>
</HEAD>
<BODY>
```

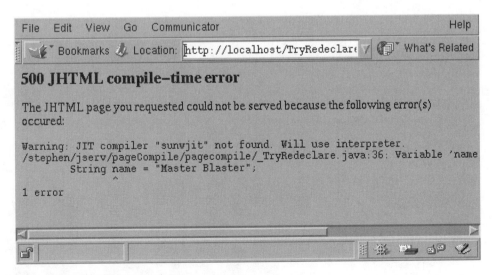

Figure 2.3   Attempt to redefine error page.

```
<H2>Java Block One</H2>
<java>
{
    String name = "Mister Zero";
    out.println(name);
}
</java>
<H2>Java Block Two</H2>
<java>
{
    String name = "Master Blaster";
    out.println(name);
}
</java>
</BODY>
</HTML>
```

This file creates separate blocks for each variable and compiles appropriately. Essentially, Java uses { and } to define a scope. When you compile this code, the first and second declarations of the name variable appear in different {} blocks and therefore different scopes. Because each scope gets its own copy of the variable, they do not conflict.

Keeping in mind the simple inclusion mechanism used to create the Java code for a JHTML page, you can create loops and conditionals as well. In this case, the code block for the if portion of a conditional can begin in one <java> block and conclude in another. By combining these <java> tags and curly brackets indicating Java blocks you can create conditional HTML, as in the following example. This example sets a variable called test and prints the string "True" if test is true, or it displays "False" if test is false.

```
<HTML>
<HEAD>
<TITLE>
Conditional HTML
</TITLE>
</HEAD>
<BODY>
<H2>Setting Value to False</H2>
<java>
    boolean test = false;
</java>
<H2>The value is:
<java>
if(test)
{
</java>
True
<java>
}
```

```
else
{
</java>
False
<java>
}
</java>
</H2>
</BODY>
</HTML>
```

Note the multiple <java>-</java> blocks surrounding the if-else statement and the HTML it displays. The if-else block has been turned into an if-else statement in the servlet. The HTML outside the <java> tags is sent to the client conditionally, based on the if-else statement.

The same technique can be used to create a loop over a piece of HTML, as demonstrated in the following code. This JTHML page loops through an array of names and prints them using the implicit variable out. In this example, out is the servlet's output stream or PrintWriter as appropriate. The variable called out and the other resources available in a JTHML page are discussed in detail in a moment.

```
<HTML>
<HEAD>
<TITLE>
Looping HTML
</TITLE>
</HEAD>
<BODY>
<java>
    String names[]={"Tommy"
                    ,"Kristan"
                    ,"Cheryl"
                    ,"Stephen"};

    int i,max;

    max = names.length;

    for(i=0;i<max;i++)
    {
</java>
I see <java>out.println(names[i]);</java>.<BR>
<java>
    }
</java>
</BODY>
</HTML>
```

The result is shown in Figure 2.4.

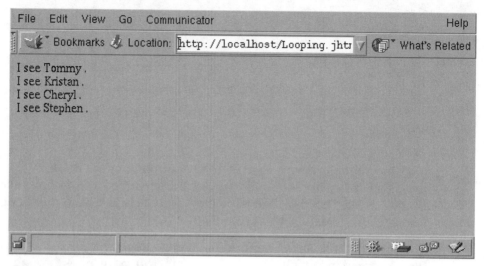

Figure 2.4 Looping HTML.

Using loops and conditionals that operate on regular HTML is a powerful technique that allows HTML designers to fill in the contents of a dynamic page, while still relying on Java code to perform complex business and application logic. For example, in the case of a database query, the programmer can use Java code to fetch data and loop over the query results, relying on HTML from the designer to display each result. In this same query example, the programmer can branch based on the number of results, and the designer can provide different pages to the client based on whether data exists.

Accessing Servlet Information

By default, the expected encoding for JHTML servlets is regular ASCII HTML. In this case, HTML is returned to the client as bytes that match their character equivalent. As discussed previously, the scripting engine automatically creates a stream for accessing the pipe to the client and calls it out.

Besides out, the JSP has access to two variables, as defined in the generated service method. These values are request, an HttpServletRequest object, and response, an HttpServletResponse object. Both values can be referred to by name between the <java> and </java> tags. The following example uses the request object to print information about the client.

```
<HTML>
<HEAD>
<TITLE>
Print Environment
```

```
</TITLE>
</HEAD>
<BODY>
<H1>Requested URL</H1>

<java>
out.println(HttpUtils.getRequestURL(request).toString());
</java>

<BR>
<H1>Headers</H1>

<java>
        Enumeration headers;
        String curHeader;

        headers = request.getHeaderNames();

        while(headers.hasMoreElements())
        {
            curHeader = (String) headers.nextElement();

out.println(curHeader+"="+request.getHeader(curHeader)+"<BR>");
        }
</java>

<BR>
<H1>Request Information</H1>

<java>
        try
        {
            out.println("AuthType="+request.getAuthType()+"<BR>");
            out.println("Scheme="+request.getScheme()+"<BR>");
            out.println("Method="+request.getMethod()+"<BR>");
            out.println("Request URI="
               +request.getRequestURI()+"<BR>");
            out.println("Request protocol="
               +request.getProtocol()+"<BR>");
            out.println("Servlet path="
               +request.getServletPath()+"<BR>");
            out.println("Path Info="+request.getPathInfo()+"<BR>");
            out.println("Path Translated="
               +request.getPathTranslated()+"<BR>");
            out.println("Query String="
               +request.getQueryString()+"<BR>");
            out.println("Content length="
               +request.getContentLength()+"<BR>");
            out.println("Content type="
               +request.getContentType()+"<BR>");
            out.println("Server name="
               +request.getServerName()+"<BR>");
            out.println("Server port="
               +request.getServerPort()+"<BR>");
```

```
        out.println("Remote user="
           +request.getRemoteUser()+"<BR>");
        out.println("Remote address="
           +request.getRemoteAddr()+"<BR>");
    }
    catch(Exception exp)
    {
        out.println("Exception: "+exp+"<BR>");
    }
</java>

<BR>
<H1>Parameter Information</H1>

<java>
    Enumeration parameters;
    String[] values;
    String curParam;
    String value;
    int i,max;

    parameters = request.getParameterNames();

    while(parameters.hasMoreElements())
    {
        curParam = (String) parameters.nextElement();

        values = request.getParameterValues(curParam);
        value = request.getParameter(curParam);
        out.println(curParam+"=<BR><UL>");

        if((values != null)&&(values.length>1))
        {
            max = values.length;

            for(i=0;i<max;i++)
            {
                out.println("<LI>"+values[i]);
            }
        }
        else if(value != null)
        {
            out.println("<LI>"+value);
        }

        out.println("</UL>");
    }
</java>

</BODY>
</HTML>
```

When compiled and accessed, this page displays the results shown in Figure 2.5.

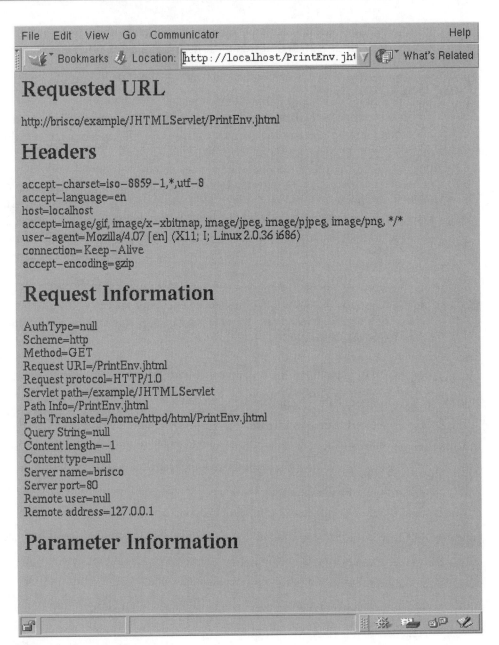

Figure 2.5 PrintEnv.jhtml.

The JHTML page above has access to the client's query string and request information. In the preceding example, you actually access the page using the URL:

```
http://localhost:8080/printenv.jhtml?yes=no&ray=sun&ray=beam
```

where localhost is the name of the machine containing the Web server you are using for testing. Notice that this URL includes a query string for testing.

Using Backquotes

To preserve the strict distinction between <java> blocks and HTML you are not allowed to embed <java> blocks inside another HTML tag. For example, the code:

```
<font size=<java>out.print(i)</java>>Hello</font>
```

is incorrect. Instead, you can use backquote characters (`) to indicate a value that you want to print to the client. This value can be any object or primitive type. If it is a primitive type it is converted to a string using the wrapper classes. If it is an object, the toString method is used. In the case that a null value is provided, then the empty string is inserted where the backquotes appear.

 NOTE

Outside of a tag, the backquotes act as normal backquotes and are not interpreted by the PageCompileServlet.

The following example shows how you can use these quotes to change font size in a looping construct. Notice how the Java block sets up a for loop but doesn't close it. This is followed by HTML code that is generated as part of the loop. A second Java block closes the for loop.

```
<HTML>
<HEAD>
<TITLE>
Backquotes in Tags
</TITLE>
</HEAD>
<BODY>
<java>
    int i,max;

    max = 8;

    for(i=1;i<max;i++)
    {
</java>

<font size=`i`>`Hello World`</font><BR>
<java>
    }
</java>
</BODY>
</HTML>
```

When accessed, this page looks like the one in Figure 2.6.

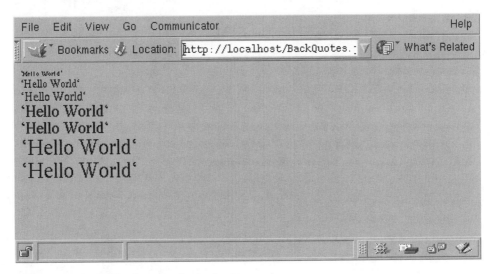

Figure 2.6 Using backquotes in the font tag.

Notice that the backquotes around the Hello World string remain intact because they are not inside an HTML tag.

Printing Values

For situations outside of HTML tags where you want to print the value of a Java construct, you can use the <java type=print> and </java> tags to indicate a Java expression that you want to have sent to the client. This is a shortcut for using out.print. The contents of the two tags can be any Java value, any object or primitive, that could be sent to the String.valueof method. As with backquotes, the objects are toString'ed and wrapper classes convert the primitive values like ints and floats.

 NOTE
Keep the conversion of data to strings in mind during your study of the scripting engine. The engine will have to implement this conversion.

The following example modifies the previous one to use the <java type=print> and </java> tags to print the value font size as part of the HTML.

```
<HTML>
<HEAD>
<TITLE>
Printing Values
</TITLE>
</HEAD>
```

```
<BODY>
<java>
    int i,max;

    max = 8;

    for(i=1;i<max;i++)
    {
</java>

<font size=`i`>
Font Size = <java type=print>i</java>
</font>
<BR>

<java>
    }
</java>
</BODY>
</HTML>
```

When displayed, this looks like the page in Figure 2.7.

As you can see in this JHTML page, the print attribute provides the same functionality outside an HTML tag as the backquote does inside a tag.

Changing the Page's Servlet Class Definition

A JHTML page can configure the output of the scripting engine by using special <java> tags. There are three variations of the <java> tag for changing the code that the engine generates. First, you can specify new import statements so

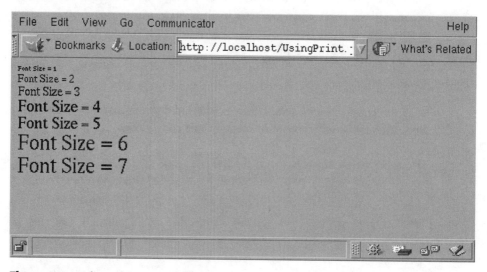

Figure 2.7 Using print.

that you can include custom Java code or nondefault packages. Second, you can specify the servlet's superclass, although the class you specify must subclass HttpServlet. Third, you can specify code that is not part of the service method. All of these variations on the standard tag are implemented as types.

The first type is import. Use tags of the form:

```
<java type=import>java.net.*</java>
```

to import other packages or classes into the JHTML page's associated servlet. By default, the servlet packages as well as java.io and java.util are imported in your generated servlet. The engine also imports several packages that provide special classes for the generated code. A good example of using this tag is to import java.sql into a page that uses JDBC to access a database.

The second type of <java> tag that changes the class definition is extends. Use the tag:

```
<java type=extends>SuperclassName</java>
```

to specify a new superclass for the servlet. The superclass for your servlet must be in the Web server's class path. For example, with the JServ engine you can add these classes to the class path as configured in the properties files.

CAUTION

Be sure to import the class you are extending. Because the code generated from the JSP is in a package, this import statement is required to get to classes not in the page compiler's package.

Using extends can make your Web sites easier to maintain by grouping reusable code into a servlet for extending. This way each JHTML page can reuse rather than reimplement code for the site. For example, your site could use a servlet super class that provides data validation or formatting functions to the scripted pages. You could even implement the super class to implement some form of resource pooling. This pooling would depend on the Web server's willingness to share a class between servlets.

NOTE

If you change the code for the parent class of a JHTML page and recompile it, you may need to restart the Web server to see the changes.

The final type of <java> tag for altering the generated code uses the type class. This tag takes the form:

```
<java type=class>java code</java>
```

The information in this block is treated as part of the servlet's class definition. It is not included in the service method, but it is included in the class. This type of <java> block can be used to define methods and instance variables.

That completes the definition of the scripting language. Basically, it contains the <java> tag with its various types. Now let's look at how the scripting engine is implemented to convert these pages into Java code, compile the code, and configure the serlvets to handle user requests.

Step 3: Implementing the Scripting Engine

The scripting engine is accessed via a single Java servlet called com.pri .servlets.jhtml.JHTMLServlet. This servlet actually has a simple job: It converts a JHTML page into Java, compiles it, and executes it. The only real decision making that goes on occurs when the servlet decides to recompile the page. This decision is affected by a number of values, as diagrammed in Figure 2.8. First the servlet checks if the page has previously been compiled. If not, it compiles the page. If the page has been compiled but the compiled version is out of date, the page is recompiled.

The page is recompiled the first time it is accessed after it changes, or the administrator can configure the servlet to wait for a minimum amount of time before checking if the recompile needs to occur. In situations where the page doesn't change often, increasing this minimum time improves performance slightly because the check will be done less frequently. Recall that the page compiler has to compile the Java code the first time a JHTML page is accessed. This means that the very first user to access the page could experience a delay that others, accessing the page later, will not encounter. If an error occurs during the compilation process, the scripting engine formats it and returns the error information to the client. This allows the developer to see errors during testing.

In order to implement the servlet a number of classes are used. The classes are defined in two packages:

- com.pri.servlets.jhtml
- com.pri.utils

First and foremost is the class com.pri.servlets.jhtml.JHTMLServlet. This class defines the servlet that is installed into the Web server to handle JHTML pages. The JHTMLServlet uses a com.pri.servlets.jhtml.JHTMLCompiler object to compile the page and a com.pri.servlets.jhtml.JHTMLClassLoader to load the servlet class into the Web server process. Each of these classes is described in detail later in this chapter.

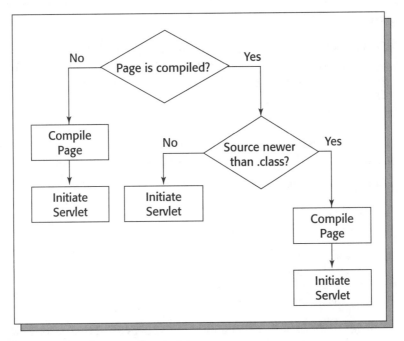

Figure 2.8 Page compiler decision tree.

Along with the main servlet classes, a number of classes are used from the package com.pri.utils. These classes are available on the CD-ROM and are described in Table 2.5, but they are not described in the text of this chapter to save space.

Table 2.5 Utility Classes

CLASS	DESCRIPTION
FileCache	Stores files in memory so that they can be read more quickly. Can return a RandomAccessBuffer for the file to be used by the JHTML servlets.
RandomAccessBuffer	Provides a read-write collection of bytes that can be accessed like a RandomAccessFile, including seek and position.
StringUtils	Generic string utility methods, including escaping strings and splitting a string into an array.
TagParser	Parses tag-based files, like HTML or JHTML.
TagHandler	An interface for working with the TagParser, discussed more later.
UrlClassLoader	Loads a class file from a URL into memory.
URLDecoder	Decodes URL encoded data, the mirror to the java.net.URLEncoder class.

JHTMLServlet

JHTMLServlet is the primary class in the scripting engine; it defines the servlet that is registered with the Web server to handle JHTML pages. The following code defines JHTMLServlet. Like all of the code in this book, this class is available on the CD-ROM.

First, JHTMLServlet.java includes the package definition and import statements, shown next. This class uses some of the standard packages as well as the servlet libraries from Sun and the utils package discussed in the previous section:

```
package com.pri.servlets.jhtml;

import java.io.*;
import java.lang.reflect.*;
import java.util.*;
import javax.servlet.*;
import javax.servlet.http.*;
import com.pri.servlets.jhtml.*;
import com.pri.utils.*;
```

JHTMLServlet extends javax.servlet.http.HttpServlet. This parent class provides some of the basic structure used to define a servlet that handles Web requests.

```
public class JHTMLServlet extends HttpServlet
{
```

The JHTMLServlet requires a number of configuration parameters, as described in Table 2.3. The value of each parameter is stored in an instance variable, as defined here, for easy access. Instance variables are also defined to store a JHTMLClassLoader, the servlets generated from JHTML pages, and a mapping between the servlets the engine has generated and the times that those pages were tested for changes. Note that the current implementation of this servlet accepts the defaultEncoding parameter but doesn't use it. You should consider implementing this feature as a challenge.

```
    private File workingDir;
    private String compileCommand;
    private boolean checkUri;
    private JHTMLClassLoader jhtmlClassLoader;
    private Hashtable jhtmlServlets;
    private String pageBase;
    private String defaultEncoding;
    private boolean verbose;
    private int pageCheckSeconds;
    private String defaultPageClassName;
    private String packagePrefix;
    private Hashtable lastCheck;
```

For convenience, static variables are used to define the file extension expected by the scripting engine and the version of this implementation. These variables are defined as follows:

```
public static final String jhtmlExtension = ".jhtml";
public static final String VERSION = "1.0";
```

The server invokes a servlet's init method when the servlet is loaded. JHTMLServlet uses this opportunity to cache the values of its configuration parameters, as shown next. The only code of note in this example are the lines where the JHTML compiler class is configured with the new compile command, and the line that checks to be sure a working directory is provided. If no working directory is assigned, the init method will throw an exception, causing the serlvet loading process to fail and making the JHTML engine unavailable. Both of these sections are highlighted.

Before returning, the init method also initializes the other instance variables.

```
public void init(ServletConfig config) throws ServletException
{
    super.init(config);

    String tmp;

    compileCommand = config.getInitParameter("compileCommand");

    if((compileCommand != null) && (compileCommand.length()>=1))
    {
        JHTMLCompiler.setCompileCommand(compileCommand);
    }

    defaultEncoding = config.getInitParameter("defaultEncoding");

    if((defaultEncoding != null) && (defaultEncoding.length()>=1))
    {
        JHTMLCompiler.setDefaultEncoding(defaultEncoding);
    }

    defaultPageClassName =
        config.getInitParameter("defaultPageClassName");

    if((defaultPageClassName != null)
          && (defaultPageClassName.length()>=1))
    {
        JHTMLCompiler.setDefaultPageClassName(defaultPageClassName);
    }

    packagePrefix = config.getInitParameter("packagePrefix");

    if((packagePrefix != null) && (packagePrefix.length()>=1))
    {
        JHTMLCompiler.setPackagePrefix(packagePrefix);
    }
```

```java
tmp = config.getInitParameter("pageCheckSeconds");

lastCheck = new Hashtable();
if((tmp != null) && (tmp.length()>=1))
{
    try
    {
        pageCheckSeconds = Integer.parseInt(tmp);
    }
    catch(Exception exp)
    {
        pageCheckSeconds = 0;
    }
}

tmp = config.getInitParameter("verbose");

if((tmp != null) && tmp.equalsIgnoreCase("true"))
{
    verbose = true;
}
else
{
    verbose = false;
}

tmp = config.getInitParameter("workingDir");

if(tmp == null)
{
    throw new
      ServletException("no workingDir init parameter specified");
}

workingDir = new File(tmp);

tmp = config.getInitParameter("checkuri");

if(tmp != null && tmp.equalsIgnoreCase("true"))
{
    checkUri = true;
}
else
{
    checkUri = false;
}

 tmp = config.getInitParameter("pagebase");

if(tmp != null)
{
    pageBase = tmp;
}
else
{
```

```
            pageBase = "";
        }

        jhtmlClassLoader = new JHTMLClassLoader(workingDir);
        jhtmlServlets = new Hashtable();
    }
```

The service method, as discussed earlier, is called each time a request is made to a servlet. In the case of the JHTML servlet, the service method is called each time a client attempts to access a page with the .jhtml extension. The arguments to service are standard and include an HttpServletRequest object to provide information about the client's request and an HttpServletResponse object that the servlet can use to respond to the client.

The service method for JHTMLServlet, shown next, defines variables for managing a loop, the JHTML file, the servlet generated from the JHTML file, and the compiler used to generate the servlet. Several strings are also declared for use in creating the JHTML file's File object.

All of the code for service is included in one of several try-catch blocks to handle any exceptions that occur.

```java
protected void service(HttpServletRequest request,
                       HttpServletResponse response)
  throws IOException, ServletException
{
    int i, j;
    File jhtmlFile;
    String s, className, jhtmlPath;
    Servlet srv;
    JHTMLCompiler jhtmlCompiler;

    try
    {
```

Depending on the configuration, the servlet checks the URL that was used to request it to see if that URL is an attempt to reference the servlet directly by passing in a file name as the path info of an HTTP request. This check assumes that the servlet is registered under the alias jhtml.

```java
        // check URI for security
        if(checkUri)
        {
            s = URLDecoder.decode(request.getRequestURI());
            i = s.indexOf("/servlet/");
            j = s.indexOf("/jhtml/");

            if(i >= 0 && j >= 0 && i < j)
            {
                throw new JHTMLException("Direct requests to "
                        +"/servlet/jhtml are not allowed.");
            }
        }
```

Assuming that the checkURI code is successful, the next step is to create a file that points to the JHTML file on the disk. Creating this file object requires several steps. First, the path is obtained by asking the request object for the servlet path. This will be the part of the URL containing the path to the JHTML file. Second, the file is tested to ensure that it has the correct extension. Third, the page base initialization parameter is used to create the real file path in the situation that aliases are used to locate the files on disk. These three steps are shown here.

```
// determine jhtml file and class name
jhtmlPath = request.getServletPath();

if((jhtmlPath != null) &&
    jhtmlPath.endsWith(jhtmlExtension))
{
    jhtmlFile =
        new File(getServletContext().getRealPath(jhtmlPath));
}
else
{
    jhtmlPath = request.getPathTranslated();

    if(jhtmlPath == null)
    {
        throw new JHTMLException("No JHTML page specified");
    }

    if(!jhtmlPath.endsWith(jhtmlExtension))
    {
        throw new JHTMLException("The requested file"
        + " does not have the required extension "
        + jhtmlExtension);
    }

    jhtmlFile = new File(pageBase +
                        URLDecoder.decode(jhtmlPath));

    //path is just the extra, not the full path
    jhtmlPath = request.getPathInfo();
}
```

Finally, the servlet checks for the file, as shown here. If the file does not exist, an error message is sent to the client and the service method returns immediately.

```
if(!jhtmlFile.exists())
{
    response.sendError(HttpServletResponse.SC_NOT_FOUND);
    return;
}
```

Given the file path for the JHTML file, the servlet uses the JHTMLCompiler class to generate a class name for that file. This process, discussed next, uses the path of the file and the package prefix configured in init to create a class, plus package name.

```
className =
    JHTMLCompiler.getClassNameForJHTMLFile(jhtmlPath);
```

The first time a JHTML file is requested, the JHTMLServlet converts it to a servlet and stores that servlet, by class name, in a Hashtable called jhtmlServlets. The next section of code checks to see if that servlet exists. If the servlet was already created, the script engine checks for changes in the page since the last compilation. If the page has changed the servlet is unloaded, the class loader is reset to notify it that the servlet class is no longer valid, and the servlet is created as new. If the servlet exists and the page hasn't changed, the servlet is used as is. If the servlet has never been created, the engine tries to load it. This load will succeed if the JHTML file was used earlier but the Web server has been restarted since the time it was cached.

```
// try to load jsp servlet from cache or class file
srv = (Servlet) jhtmlServlets.get(className);

if(srv == null)
{
    srv = loadServlet(className);
}
else if(needsReload(jhtmlFile,className))
{
    unloadServlet(srv);
    refreshClassLoader(srv.getClass());
    srv = null;
}
```

If a servlet was unloaded, you create it using the JHTMLCompiler class. A compiler object is created and initialized before it is instructed to load the servlet. Once created, the compiler is told to compile the code it creates and the servlet is loaded. If this process fails, an exception is thrown and handled in the surrounding try-catch block. In verbose mode, a message is logged each time the compiler is run.

```
// compile & load jsp servlet if we haven't loaded it yet
if(srv == null)
{
    jhtmlCompiler = new JHTMLCompiler(workingDir,
                    jhtmlFile,
                    className,request);

    if(verbose)
    {
        log("Compiling "+jhtmlFile);
    }

    jhtmlCompiler.compile();
```

```
        srv = loadServlet(className);

        if(srv == null)
        {
            throw new JHTMLException("Could not load jhtml ú+
                        servlet class " + className);
        }
    }
}
```

Whenever an exception occurs, a hard-coded HTML page is returned to the user, and the return status for the client's request is set to internal server error.

```
catch(Exception jspexc)
{
    response.setStatus(
            HttpServletResponse.SC_INTERNAL_SERVER_ERROR
        , "JHTML compile-time error");
    response.setContentType("text/html");

    PrintWriter out = response.getWriter();

    out.println("<HTML><HEAD><TITLE>"
            + HttpServletResponse.SC_INTERNAL_SERVER_ERROR
            + " JHTML compile-time error"
            +"</TITLE></HEAD><BODY>"
            +"<H2>"
        +HttpServletResponse.SC_INTERNAL_SERVER_ERROR
            + " JHTML compile-time error</H2>"
            +"The JHTML page you requested could not be"
            +" served because the following error(s) "
            +"occured:<BR><PRE>");

    out.println(jspexc.getMessage());

    out.println("</PRE></BODY></HTML>");

    out.close();

    return;
}
```

Assuming that the servlet for this JHTML page is loaded, the JHTML engine calls its service method and prints an error page if any exceptions occur. This step forwards the current request from the client through the JHTMLServlet to the servlet associated with the JHTML page.

```
// run JHTML servlet
try
{
    srv.service(request, response);
}
catch(Exception jspexc)
{
```

```
                    response.setStatus(
                        HttpServletResponse.SC_INTERNAL_SERVER_ERROR
                    , "JHTML run-time error");
                response.setContentType("text/html");

                PrintWriter out = response.getWriter();

                out.println("<HTML><HEAD><TITLE>"
+ HttpServletResponse.SC_INTERNAL_SERVER_ERROR
+ " JHTML run-time error</TITLE></HEAD><BODY>"
+ "<H2>"
+ HttpServletResponse.SC_INTERNAL_SERVER_ERROR
+ " JHTML run-time error</H2>"
+ "The JHTML page you requested could not be served because the following
error(s) occured:<BR><PRE>");

                out.println(jspexc.getMessage());

                out.println("</PRE></BODY></HTML>");

                out.close();

                return;
        }
    }
```

When the Web server unloads servlets, it calls their destroy method. In this servlet, use the destroy method to unload any of the servlet classes that have been used.

```
public void destroy()
{
    super.destroy();

    Enumeration        e;
    Servlet            srv;

    e = jhtmlServlets.elements();

    while(e.hasMoreElements())
    {
        srv = (Servlet) e.nextElement();
        unloadServlet(srv);
    }
}
```

Web servers query the servlet for its origin and usage via the getServletInfo method. The implementation provides minimal information, but it is useful to the caller.

```
public String getServletInfo()
{
    return "JHTML page compile servlet, modified from GNUJSP by PRI";
}
```

In the service method, you encountered a call to the needsReload method shown here. This method takes the name of the servlet class and the File object for a JHTML file and checks to see if the file is newer than the servlet that has been loaded for it. The current time is stored in a Hashtable so later tests can wait for a specified number of seconds to perform this test. A Boolean is returned to indicate whether the file needs to have its servlet regenerated.

```
private boolean needsReload(File jhtmlFile,String className)
{
      File classFile =
JHTMLCompiler.getFileForClass(workingDir,className,".class");
      long classMod,jhtmlMod;
      boolean retVal = false;
      boolean doCheck = true;

      if(classFile.exists())
      {
          if(pageCheckSeconds != 0)
          {
              String jhtmlPath = jhtmlFile.getAbsolutePath();
              Long lastCheckTime =
                  (Long) lastCheck.get(jhtmlPath);
              long now,then;

              now = System.currentTimeMillis();

              if(lastCheckTime != null)
              {
                  then = lastCheckTime.longValue();

                  if((now-then)<(pageCheckSeconds*1000))
                  {
                      doCheck = false;
                  }
                  else
                  {
                      lastCheckTime = new Long(now);
                      lastCheck.put(jhtmlPath,lastCheckTime);
                  }
              }
              else
              {
                  lastCheckTime = new Long(now);
                  lastCheck.put(jhtmlPath,lastCheckTime);
              }
          }

          if(doCheck)
          {
              jhtmlMod = jhtmlFile.lastModified();
              classMod = classFile.lastModified();
```

```
            if(jhtmlMod > classMod) retVal = true;
        }
    }
    else
    {
        retVal = true;
    }

    return retVal;
}
```

The JHTMLServlet uses a JHTMLClassLoader to manage the servlet classes it generates. The first step in this process is to load the servlet's class. The class loader, discussed next, will cache class references as they are created to ensure that future references are correct. If the servlet class is loaded, an instance is created. Once created, the servlet is initialized, cached, and returned. Any exceptions cause the method to forward the exception object to the caller or to return null, indicating failure.

Notice that a subclass of ServletConfig is used. This class, discussed here, is a proxy for the real configuration information and translates calls appropriately for the JHTML servlets.

```
private Servlet loadServlet(String className) throws JHTMLException
{
    Class c;
    Field fld;
    Servlet srv;

    // load servlet class
    try
    {
        c = jhtmlClassLoader.loadClass(className);

        if(c == null) return null;

    }
    catch(ClassNotFoundException cnfexc)
    {
        return null;
    }
    // instantiate servlet
    try
    {
        srv = (Servlet) c.newInstance();
    }
    catch(IllegalAccessException iaexc)
    {
        throw new JHTMLException(
            "Could not instantiate jhtml servlet class "
```

```
                    + className
                    + " because of an illegal access exception");
            }
            catch(InstantiationException iexc)
            {
                throw new JHTMLException(
                 "Could not instantiate jhtml servlet class "
                + className
                + " because it is an interface or an abstract class");
            }

            // init servlet
            try
            {
                srv.init(new SubServletConfig(this));
            }
            catch(Exception exc) {}

            jhtmlServlets.put(className, srv);

            return srv;
        }
```

When required, the JHTML servlet can unload servlets by notifying them to destroy and removing them from the cache. To request an unload, use the unloadServlet method shown here.

```
        private void unloadServlet(Servlet srv)
        {
            try
            {
                srv.destroy();
            }
            catch(Exception exc) { }

            jhtmlServlets.remove(srv.getClass().getName());
        }
```

When a class is reloaded, the class loader is told to refresh to ensure that the cache is cleaned up. This prevents reuse of an existing implementation.

```
        private void refreshClassLoader(Class c)
        {
            jhtmlClassLoader.refresh(c);
        }
    }
```

The servlet configuration proxy class called SubServletConfig is shown here. This class implements all of the ServletConfig methods and forwards them appropriately.

```
class SubServletConfig implements ServletConfig
{
```

```
       JHTMLServlet serv;

        public SubServletConfig(JHTMLServlet s)
        {
            serv = s;
        }

       public ServletContext getServletContext()
       {
           return serv.getServletContext();
       }

       public String getInitParameter(String name)
       {
           return null;
       }

       public Enumeration getInitParameterNames()
       {
           return (new Vector()).elements();
       }
   }
```

That's it for the code for the JHTML servlet that acts as the primary focus of the scripting engine. As you read over and study the code, keep in mind the basic process for this engine. When a JHTML page is requested, the JHTMLServlet is notified. The servlet checks to see if that page has been requested before. If it has, a servlet exists for it and is forwarded the request. If the page is newly requested, a servlet is created and then forwarded the request.

The majority of the work for this project is in managing the servlet classes and in caching information to improve performance. In use, PRI has tested this engine with a range of JHTML pages and found that they can be processed in milliseconds once the servlet is generated. Depending on the compiler you use, the initial page compilation can take up to several seconds. I highly suggest looking into optimized compilers, like IBM's jikes, for deployment of this servlet. In my experience, these fast compilers can speed up the processing of a JHTML page by at least one order of magnitude.

JHTMLCompiler

While the JHTMLServlet class is the front end to the scripting engine, the JHTMLCompiler class performs most of the work in converting the JHTML page into a Java servlet. In order to parse the JHTML file, the TagParser class from the com.pri.utils package is used. This class parses the file and makes callbacks to the JHTMLCompiler object when prespecified tags are encountered. The callbacks are discussed in the text that follows, but the parser itself is provided on the CD-ROM without discussion here to save space. Basically, the parser reads the files looking for < and > characters. When these are encountered, the parser looks for the tag they contain and uses a callback to notify you that a tag was found.

JHTMLCompiler defines a number of instance variables. Most of these are used to store information about the location of the JHTML file, the location of the Java file created in the process, and the information gained from the parsing process. In particular, a string buffer is used to store up the service method as it is generated, and another is used to keep track of code outside the service method. Remember that the compiler's job is to create a servlet, so these buffers hold code to define that servlet. Vectors and hashtables are used to keep information about the parsed items, such as import statements and interfaces. Each variable is commented in the code that follows to indicate its use.

 NOTE

As implemented, this class provides minor support for server-side includes that refer to other servlets. This code is optional and is not discussed in detail. For more information on server-side includes, use Sun's Web site at java.sun.com.

Class variables are used to store configuration information and to define the types of java tags that can exist in a JHTML file.

The following code begins the definition for JHTMLCompiler.

```
package com.pri.servlets.jhtml;

import java.io.*;
import java.util.*;
import javax.servlet.http.HttpServletRequest;
import com.pri.utils.*;

public class JHTMLCompiler implements TagHandler
{
    private File classFilesDir; //where class files go
    private File jhtmlFile; //the jhtml file we are compiling
    private File javaFile; //the Java file created from the JHTML
    private String className; //the class for this JHTML file
    private HttpServletRequest servletRequest; //the request object
    private TagParser parser; //A parser for reading the JHTML
    private StringBuffer serviceMethod; //Stores the service method
    private StringBuffer classCode; //Code in <java type=class> tags
    private Hashtable params; //For Server side includes
    private Hashtable servletAtts; //For Server side includes
    private Vector imports; //packages in <java type=import>
    private Vector interfaces; //interfaces in <java type=implements>
    private String extendsDirective; //Class name in <java type=extends>

    //Holders for tracking data between tags
    private long start,end;
    private long actualStart,actualEnd;
```

```
    private static String compileCommand; //Parameter set by servlet
    private static String defaultEncoding; //Parameter set by servlet
private static String defaultPageClassName; //Parameter set by servlet
    private static String packagePrefix; //Parameter set by servlet

    //Constants that represent java tag types, and server side includes
    public final static String CODE="code";
    public final static String IMPORT="import";
    public final static String EXTENDS="extends";
    public final static String PRINT="print";
    public final static String IMPLEMENTS="implements";
    public final static String CLASS="class";
    public final static String PARAM="param";
    public final static String SERVLET="servlet";
    public final static String END_SERVLET="/servlet";
```

A static initializer, shown next, is used to set up the configuration variables. By default the javac compiler is used, all servlets subclass javax.servet.http .HttpServlet, normal encoding is used, and all classes are placed inside the pagecompile package for identification.

```
static
{
    compileCommand = "javac";
    defaultEncoding = null;
    defaultPageClassName = "javax.servlet.http.HttpServlet";
    packagePrefix = "pagecompile";
}
```

In order to allow access to the configuration parameters, provide the class methods shown here.

```
public static void setCompileCommand(String cc)
{
    compileCommand = cc;
}

public static void setDefaultEncoding(String cc)
{
    defaultEncoding = cc;
}

public static void setDefaultPageClassName(String cc)
{
    if(cc == null)
        defaultPageClassName = "javax.servlet.http.HttpServlet";
    else
        defaultPageClassName = cc;
}

public static void setPackagePrefix(String cc)
{
    packagePrefix = cc;
}
```

When a JHTMLCompiler object is created, using the constructor shown here, it should cache the information provided about the JHTML file to compile. The servlet request is included in the initialization to allow the compiler to get information about the client request.

The method getFileForClass converts the information about general class file locations and the class name into an actual location for the Java file that this compiler will create. This method is discussed later in this chapter.

```java
public JHTMLCompiler(File classFilesDir, File jhtmlFile
                        , String className
                        , HttpServletRequest servletRequest)
{
    this.classFilesDir = classFilesDir;
    this.jhtmlFile = jhtmlFile;
    this.javaFile
        = getFileForClass(classFilesDir, className, ".java");

    this.className = className;
    this.servletRequest = servletRequest;
}
```

When the compiler is told to compile, it makes sure that a class file is not already in place. If a class file does exist, it is destroyed to prevent versioning problems. Next, the compiler performs three tasks, implemented as three methods. First, the compiler parses the JHTML file, parseHTMLFile. Next, the compiler generates the Java file that defines the new servlet, generateJavaFile. Finally, the compiler compiles the Java file into a .class file, compileJavaFile. Keep in mind that the servlet generated from a JHTML file will use a cached copy of the file to return HTML and will generate Java code only for text between the <java> and </java> tags. Regular HTML will result in calls to print from the cached copy of the file.

```java
public void compile() throws JHTMLException
{
    try
    {
        File classFile = JHTMLCompiler.getFileForClass(classFilesDir
                                        ,className,".class");

        if(classFile.exists())
        {
            classFile.delete();
        }

        parseJHTMLFile();
        generateJavaFile();
        compileJavaFile();
    }
```

```
            catch(JHTMLException e)
            {
                throw e;
            }
            catch(Exception exp)
            {
                throw new JHTMLException(exp.toString());
            }
    }
```

The JHTMLCompiler uses a TagParser from com.pri.utils to do the actual work of reading the JHTML file and identifying the important tags. All of the variables used to store information throughout the parsing are initialized at the top of parseJHTMLFile, as shown next. Also, a buffered reader is created using the FileCache class. This class caches the data for the JHTML file in memory and creates read-only access to the file. The FileCache is also smart, and it will reload the cache if the file has changed since it was originally loaded.

```
    private void parseJHTMLFile() throws JHTMLException
    {
        Reader reader;//For reading the file

        parser = new TagParser();
        registerWith(parser);
        parser.setIgnoreTrailingEnd(true);
        //need true for servlet tags parser.setNotifyInsideTags(false);

        start = 0;
        end = 0;

        reader = FileCache.getBufferedReaderForFile(jhtmlFile);

        serviceMethod = new StringBuffer();
        classCode = new StringBuffer();
        imports = new Vector();
        interfaces = new Vector();
        params = new Hashtable();
```

When the parser is told to parse, it will read the entire file and make callbacks to the compiler when it encounters registered tags. These callbacks store information from the file into the variables initialized previously. At the end of the file, there could still be some plain HTML of which the parser didn't notify the compiler. In this case, code is added to the service method that will write out the remaining HTML. Notice that the location of the HTML in the JHTML file is used to identify it. The data for the JHTML file will be available in the service method, thanks to the same FileCache copy that you used here.

```
        try
        {
            parser.parse(reader);
```

```
            //Clean up the end of the file.
            end = parser.getCurrentPosition();

            if(actualStart == -1) actualStart = start;

            actualEnd = end;

            if((actualStart >= 0)&&((actualEnd-actualStart)>0))
            {
                serviceMethod.append("\t\tout.write(__fileData.read(");
                serviceMethod.append(actualStart);
                serviceMethod.append(",");
                serviceMethod.append(actualEnd - actualStart);
                serviceMethod.append("));\n");
            }
        }
        catch(Exception exp)
        {
            throw new JHTMLException(exp.toString());
        }
```

As a final step, the compiler checks to see if a super class was defined in the JHTML file using the <java type=extends> tag. If not, the default is used.

```
        if((extendsDirective==null)||(extendsDirective.length() == 0))
        {
            extendsDirective = defaultPageClassName;

            if(extendsDirective == null)
                extendsDirective ="javax.servlet.http.HttpServlet";
        }
    }
```

The Java file for a JHTML page's servlet is generated in the generateJavaFile method, shown here, using the information cached during the parsing process. Try-catch blocks are included in the generated code to handle exceptions that occur in the JHTML file's Java. Local variables, packageName and actClassName, are used to store the package and class names for the new class. The packageDir variable stores the directory for the file, based on its package. A PrintWriter called out is used to write to the new Java file.

```
    private void generateJavaFile() throws JHTMLException
    {
        String packageName;
        String actClassName;
        int i,max; //for loops
        PrintWriter out;
        File packageDir;

        try
        {
```

Get the location of the last . in the full class name.

```
i = className.lastIndexOf(".");
```

Get the directory in which this Java file should be placed. Use mkdirs to ensure that it exists.

```
packageDir = new File(javaFile.getParent());
packageDir.mkdirs();
```

Create a PrintWriter for the new Java file.

```
out = new PrintWriter(new FileWriter(javaFile));
```

Using the location of the last . in the class name, get the package name and the actual class name. Store them in packageName and actClassName.

```
if(i>0)
{
    packageName = className.substring(0,i);
    actClassName = className.substring(i+1);
}
else
{
    packageName = null;
    actClassName = className;
}
```

If there is a package name, start the new Java file with the appropriate package statement.

```
if(packageName != null)
{
    out.print("package ");
    out.print(packageName);
    out.println(";\n");
}
```

Insert the standard import statements into the file.

```
out.println("import javax.servlet.*;");
out.println("import javax.servlet.http.*;");
out.println("import java.io.*;");
out.println("import java.util.*;");
out.println("import com.pri.utils.*;");
```

Add any import statements that the JHTML file requested using <java type=import> tags.

```
max = imports.size();

for(i=0;i<max;i++)
{
    out.print("import ");
```

```
            out.print((String)imports.elementAt(i));
            out.println(";");
      }

      out.println();
```

Begin the class definition, using the actual class name and the super class defined by <java type=extends> or the default.

```
      out.print("public class ");
      out.println(actClassName);
      out.print("extends ");
      out.println(extendsDirective);
```

Declare any interfaces that the JHTML page should implement based on the <java type=implements> tags. These are stored in the interface's vector.

```
      max = interfaces.size();

      if(max > 0) out.print("implements ");

      for(i=0;i<max;i++)
      {
            if(i!=0) out.print(",");

            out.print((String)interfaces.elementAt(i));
      }

      if(max>0) out.println();//new line after interfaces
```

Declare a static block for compatibility with Sun's JHTML implementation.

```
      out.println("{");
      out.println();
      out.println("\tstatic");
      out.println("\t{");
      out.println("\t}");
      out.println();
```

Output the service method. This method starts by providing the out local variable. Next a RandomAccessBuffer is obtained from the FileCache for the JHTML file. This buffer is stored in the __fileData variable. A temporary variable called __tmp is declared for use throughout the method.

```
      out.println("\tpublic void service (HttpServletRequest
request,");
      out.println("\t\t\tHttpServletResponse response)");
      out.println("\t\tthrows ServletException, IOException");
      out.println("\t{");
      out.println("\t\tServletOutputStream "
                  +"out=response.getOutputStream();");
      out.println("\t\tRandomAccessBuffer __fileData = "
                  +"FileCache.getRandomBufferForFile(");
      out.print("\t\t\t\"");
      out.print(StringUtils.escape(jhtmlFile.getAbsolutePath()));
```

```
                     out.println("\");");
                     out.println("\t\tString __tmp;");
                     out.println();
```

The servlet generated from the JHTML page returns HTML by default so it outputs the appropriate header. This content type is discussed in detail in Project 1.

```
                     out.println("\t\tresponse.setContentType(\"text/html\");");
                     out.println();
```

You cached the contents of the service method in the serviceMethod StringBuffer. Output them here, inside a try-catch block.

```
                     out.println("\t\ttry\n\t\t{");
                     out.println(serviceMethod.toString());
                     out.println();
                     out.println("\t\t}");

                     if(serviceMethod.length()>0)
                     {
                         out.println("\t\tcatch(Exception jhtml_exp)\n\t\t{");
                         out.println("\t\t\tlog(jhtml_exp.toString());");
                         out.println("\t\t}");
                     }
```

In the final part of the block, close the file buffer.

```
                     out.println("\t\tfinally\n\t\t{");
                     out.println("\t\tif(__fileData != null) __fileData.close();");
                     out.println("\t\t}");
                     out.println("\t}");
```

Output any code that was defined in <java type=class> tags.

```
                     out.println(classCode.toString());
```

Complete the class definition and this method.

```
                     out.println("}");
                     out.close();
                 }
             catch(Exception exp)
             {
                 throw new JHTMLException(exp.toString());
             }
         }
```

In order to compile the Java file, a command-line string is created and executed. Success is based on the lack of response from the command-line process. Any output from this process is treated as error messages, and they are returned to the client in place of the JHTML page.

```
     private void compileJavaFile() throws JHTMLException
     {
```

```
StringBuffer cmdLine = new StringBuffer();
Process compile;
InputStream in,err,realIn = null;
int cur;

try
{
    cmdLine.append(compileCommand);
    cmdLine.append(" -d ");
    cmdLine.append(classFilesDir.getAbsolutePath());
    cmdLine.append(" ");
    cmdLine.append(javaFile.getAbsolutePath());

    compile = Runtime.getRuntime().exec(cmdLine.toString());

    err = compile.getErrorStream();
    in = compile.getInputStream();

    while(true)
    {
        if(err.available()!=0) realIn = err;
        else if(in.available()!=0) realIn = in;

        if(realIn != null) break;

        try
        {
            compile.exitValue();
            break;
        }
        catch(Exception exp)
        {
        }

        Thread.sleep(50);//don't just poll over and over
    }

    cmdLine.setLength(0);

    if(realIn != null)
    {
        while((cur=realIn.read()) >= 0)
        {
            cmdLine.append((char)cur);
        }

        realIn.close();
    }
}
catch(Exception exp)
{
}

if(cmdLine.length()>0)
    throw new JHTMLException(cmdLine.toString());
}
```

JHTMLCompiler defines the standard mapping between a JHTML file's name and its class name. This mapping converts directories to packages and prepends the package prefix to ensure a standard parent package for all classes. Spaces and other invalid characters in the path are converted to underscores (_) for readability. To access the map between name and class use the static method getClassNameForJHTMLFile.

```
public static String getClassNameForJHTMLFile(String jhtmlFile) throws
JHTMLException
    {
        int                i,max = jhtmlFile.lastIndexOf(".jhtml");
        StringBuffer       buf = new StringBuffer(max+10);
        char               c;

        if(max<0) max = jhtmlFile.length();

        if(packagePrefix != null) buf.append(packagePrefix);

        for(i=0;i<max;i++)
        {
            c = jhtmlFile.charAt(i);

            if(Character.isJavaIdentifierPart(c))
            {
                buf.append((char) c);
            }
            else if((c=='/')||(c=='\\'))
            {
                if(buf.length()>0) buf.append("._");
                else buf.append("_");
            }
            else
            {
                buf.append((char) '_').append(Integer.toHexString(c));
            }
        }

        return buf.toString();
    }
```

The opposite of converting files to class names is converting the class name to a file through string concatenation. The getFileForClass method, shown here, implements this process.

```
public static File getFileForClass(File classFilesDir, String
className, String suffix)
    {
        return new File(classFilesDir, className.replace('.',
File.separatorChar) + suffix);
    }
```

The core of the JHTMLCompiler class is in the handleTag callback used by the Tag parser to notify the compiler when tags are encountered. This method receives information about the tag, any end tag, the attributes in the tag, and the actual text data between the start and end tags as arguments. An arbitrary rendezvous object is also provided but is not used here. The TagParser code has been used for a number of applications, and this rendezvous is provided for the generic case.

```
public String handleTag(String tag,String data
                       ,String etag,Hashtable atts
                       ,Object rendezvous)
    throws ParsingException
{
    String type=null; //The value of the type attribute
    String actTag=tag; //The tag encountered
    String retVal = ""; //The code to return
    String urlString = null;
    String val,name,value; //Used for parsing name-value pairs

    if(atts!=null)
    {
        type = (String) atts.get("TYPE");
        actTag = (String) atts.get("TAG");
    }
```

The first thing the compiler has to do when a tag is encountered is to figure out if there was some HTML between the last call to this method and the current call. If so, the code to send this HTML to the client is added to the servlet's service method, as shown here:

```
end = parser.getCurrentPosition();

if(actTag==null)//HTML
{
    if(actualStart == -1) actualStart = start;

    actualEnd = end;
}
else
{
   if((actualStart >= 0)&&((actualEnd-actualStart)>0))
   {
        serviceMethod.append("\t\tout.write(__fileData.read(");
        serviceMethod.append(actualStart);
        serviceMethod.append(",");
        serviceMethod.append(actualEnd - actualStart);
        serviceMethod.append("));\n");
   }

    actualStart = actualEnd = -1;
```

Next the compiler checks to see which tag was encountered and caches the appropriate information. Code is included in the service method buffer, class code goes in the class buffer, and information about imports and other tags are included in vectors and hashtables. Of special note are the print tag and back-quotes. These use a conditional statement and the com.pri.util.ServletUtils class to convert any form of Java data into a string for output to the client.

If a FORM is encountered, update the ACTION to include any URL encoding that the servlet should use. This will ensure that servlet sessions and other server-provided services are supported by your new page.

```
if("FORM".equalsIgnoreCase(actTag))//rewrite URL
{
    if(atts != null)
        urlString = (String) atts.get("ACTION");

    if(urlString != null)
    {
        urlString = urlString;//no URL encoding
        serviceMethod.append(
            "\t\t__tmp=response.encodeUrl(\"");
        serviceMethod.append(urlString);
        serviceMethod.append("\");\n");
        atts.put("ACTION","\"+__tmp+\"");

        serviceMethod.append("\t\tout.println(\"");
        serviceMethod.append(reconstructTag(atts));
        serviceMethod.append("\");\n");
    }
}
```

Perform the same encoding update for links in the HTML.

```
else if("A".equalsIgnoreCase(actTag))//rewrite URL
{
    if(atts != null)
        urlString = (String) atts.get("HREF");

    if(urlString != null)
    {
        urlString = urlString;//no URL encoding

        serviceMethod.append(
            "\t\t__tmp=response.encodeUrl(\"");
        serviceMethod.append(urlString);
        serviceMethod.append("\");\n");
        atts.put("HREF","\"+__tmp+\"");

        serviceMethod.append("\t\tout.println(\"");
        serviceMethod.append(reconstructTag(atts));
        serviceMethod.append("\");\n");
    }
}
```

Text in backquotes and <java type=print> tags should be turned into a string and output. To get a string from any value, use the ServletUtil class, included in this project. This class provides a valueOf method for all of the primitive types as well as Objects. In the case that a null value is encountered, print an empty string in its place.

```
else if("`".equals(actTag) || PRINT.equalsIgnoreCase(type))
{
    val = data.replace('`',' ');

    serviceMethod.append("\t\t__tmp=ServletUtil.valueOf(");
    serviceMethod.append(val);
    serviceMethod.append(
        ");\n\t\t__tmp=(__tmp==null)?\"\":__tmp;\n");
    serviceMethod.append("\t\tout.print(__tmp);\n");
}
```

The <param>, <servlet>, and </servlet> tags are used for server-side includes.

```
else if(PARAM.equalsIgnoreCase(actTag))
{
    name = (String) atts.get("NAME");
    value = (String) atts.get("VALUE");

    if((name!=null)&&(value!=null))
        params.put(name,value);
}
else if(SERVLET.equalsIgnoreCase(actTag))
{
    servletAtts = atts;
    params.clear();
}
else if(END_SERVLET.equalsIgnoreCase(actTag))
{
    createServletCode(servletAtts,params);

    params.clear();
    servletAtts = null;
}
```

Any text between <java> and </java> tags or <java type=code> tags belongs in the service method, so append it to the serviceMethod string buffer.

```
else if((type==null)||(CODE.equalsIgnoreCase(type)))
{
    serviceMethod.append(data);
}
```

Code in <java type=import> tags should be converted to package names, by splitting any lines into single strings. Add these package names to the imports array.

```
else if(IMPORT.equalsIgnoreCase(type))
{
    Vector statements = StringUtils.splitLines(data);
```

```
        int i,max;

        max = statements.size();

        for(i=0;i<max;i++)
        {
            imports.addElement(statements.elementAt(i));
        }
    }
```

Convert <java type=implements> tags into interface names and add them to the interfaces instance variable.

```
        else if(IMPLEMENTS.equalsIgnoreCase(type))
        {
            Vector statements = StringUtils.splitLines(data);
            int i,max;

            max = statements.size();

            for(i=0;i<max;i++)
            {
                interfaces.addElement(statements.elementAt(i));
            }
        }
```

Append any code in <java type=class> tags to the classCode string buffer.

```
        else if(CLASS.equalsIgnoreCase(type))
        {
            classCode.append(data);
        }
```

Capture the class name in a <java type=extends> tag in the extendsDirective instance variable. Note that if this tag appears more than once, the last occurrence is used.

```
        else if(EXTENDS.equalsIgnoreCase(type))
        {
            extendsDirective = data;
        }
    }
```

Keep track of where you are in the file to write out the HTML appropriately.

```
    start = end;
```

The parser wants us to return a string; just return "".

```
    return retVal;
}
```

The TagParser requires its user to register the tags it wants to handle. The registerWith method performs these initializations and indicates for the parser which tags should be checked for attributes and which should not. The parser can also use a default handler for PLAINTEXT, as registered by name, and it will ignore tags inside other tags if told to do so. In this case, the <java> tag is registered with an end tag of </java>, and all tags inside those are ignored. This ensures that a < or > in the Java code is not treated as part of a tag.

```java
public void registerWith(TagParser parser)
{
    parser.registerTagHandler("JAVA",this);
    parser.registerTagHandler("SERVLET",this);
    parser.registerTagHandler("/SERVLET",this);
    parser.registerTagHandler("PARAM",this);
    parser.registerTagHandler("PLAINTEXT",this);
    parser.registerTagHandler("FORM",this);//handle URL rewriting
    parser.registerTagHandler("A",this);//handle URL rewriting

    parser.registerForBackquotes(this);

    parser.registerForAtts("JAVA");
    parser.registerForAtts("A");
    parser.registerForAtts("FORM");
    parser.registerForAtts("SERVLET");
    parser.registerForAtts("PARAM");

    parser.registerEndTag("JAVA","</JAVA>");
    parser.suppressNotifyInside("JAVA");
}
```

The compilation process alters form and link tags. The reconstructTag shown here can be used to create a tag from a hashtable of name-value pairs. The value of the TAG attribute is expected to be the tag itself.

```java
public String reconstructTag(Hashtable atts)
{
    Enumeration keys;
    String key,value;
    StringBuffer retVal = new StringBuffer();

    key = (String) atts.get("TAG");

    retVal.append("<");
    retVal.append(key);

    keys = atts.keys();

    while(keys.hasMoreElements())
    {
        key = (String) keys.nextElement();
        value = (String) atts.get(key);

        retVal.append(" ");

        if(key.equals("TAG"))
        {
            //do nothing
```

```
        }
        else if(key.equals(value))
        {
            retVal.append(key);
        }
        else
        {
            retVal.append(key);
            retVal.append("=\\\"");
            retVal.append(value);
            retVal.append("\\\"");
        }
    }

    retVal.append(">");

    return retVal.toString();
    }
}
```

That's it for the JHTMLCompiler class. This class includes a lot of code for parsing and generating other files.

JHTMLClassLoader

The JHTMLCLassLoader is a special class loader that caches the class objects for servlets as they are loaded. Because class loaders automatically perform some caching, this loader uses another class called ProxyClassLoader to perform the actual class-loading work and really just manages the cache.

```
package com.pri.servlets.jhtml;

import java.io.*;
import java.util.*;
import com.pri.servlets.jhtml.*;
import com.pri.utils.*;

public class JHTMLClassLoader extends ClassLoader
{
    private File classFilesDir;
    private Hashtable classCache;

    public JHTMLClassLoader(File classFilesDir)
    {
        this.classFilesDir = classFilesDir;
        this.classCache = new Hashtable();
    }

    public Class loadClass(String name) throws ClassNotFoundException
    {
        return loadClass(name,true);
```

```
    }

    protected Class loadClass(String className, boolean resolve)
     throws ClassNotFoundException
    {
        Class c;

        try
        {
            c = (Class) classCache.get(className);

            if(c == null)
            {
                ProxyClassLoader loader =
                    new ProxyClassLoader(classFilesDir);
                c = loader.loadClass(className,resolve);

                if(c!=null) classCache.put(className,c);
            }
        }
        catch(Exception exp)
        {
            c =null;
        }
        catch(Error er)
        {
            c =null;
        }

        return c;
    }

    public void refresh(Class c)
    {
        classCache.remove(c.getName());
    }
}
```

ProxyClassLoaders are really temporary objects created to load a class and then forgotten about so that their cache is ignored.

```
class ProxyClassLoader extends ClassLoader
{
    private File        classFilesDir;

    public ProxyClassLoader(File classFilesDir)
    {
        this.classFilesDir = classFilesDir;
    }

    protected Class loadClass(String className, boolean resolve)
     throws ClassNotFoundException
```

```
{
    Class c;
    byte[] classData = loadClassData(className);

    if(classData != null)
    {
        c = defineClass(className, classData
                        , 0, classData.length);
    }
    else
    {
        c = findSystemClass(className);

        if(c == null)
        {
            return null;
        }
    }
    if(resolve)
    {
        resolveClass(c);
    }

    return c;
}
```

As shown next, the code for a class is obtained using the JHTMLCompiler's ability to map class names back to the file that they represent.

```
private byte[] loadClassData(String className)
{
    File                classFile;
    DataInputStream     in;
    byte[]              classData;

    classFile =
        JHTMLCompiler.getFileForClass(classFilesDir
                        , className, ".class");

    try
    {
        in = new DataInputStream(
                    new FileInputStream(classFile));

        try
        {
            classData = new byte[(int) classFile.length()];
            in.readFully(classData, 0, classData.length);
            return classData;
        }
        finally
        {
```

```
            in.close();
        }
    }
    catch(IOException ioexc)
    {
    }

    return null;
    }
}
```

These two class loaders work together to ensure that servlets can be loaded and cached to maximize performance while still ensuring that a new copy of the class can be loaded if necessary.

Wrap Up

This project gives you some idea of the power of servlets and also of the JHTML scripting technology. The next project will use JHTML pages to create a bug-tracking system. Keep in mind that you don't have to understand all of the JHTMLServlet code to use JHTML pages. Just install the servlet on your Web server and write JHTML pages as needed. The code is provided and discussed here in case you want to better understand the page compilation process, add features, or fix any problems that you find.

Web-based Bug Tracker

Project Objectives

In this project, you will learn how to:

- ■ **Create a new database in MySQL**
- ■ **Create the JHTML pages or create the Perl CGI scripts**
- ■ **Access MySQL using JDBC or Perl**

 YOU WILL NEED

- ✔ **A Web server with the scripting engine from Project 2 installed, including the JDK for that engine**
- ✔ **MySQL database**
- ✔ **A JDBC driver to connect to the database**
- ✔ **Java programming experience**
    - **Or**
- ✔ **A Web server with support for CGI**
- ✔ **Perl**
- ✔ **The MySQL Perl modules, discussed in Project 1**
- ✔ **Perl programming experience**
    - **Optional**
    - ✔ **Web programming experience with CGI**
    - ✔ **SQL experience**

Although this project is implemented using the MySQL database server, you could easily port it to other database available on Linux, including Postgres and mSQL. Both projects will require you to use a browser to access the final application. You should be able to use any browser. A JavaScript enabled browser will also allow the form validation code to run.

Memo

To: Stephen
From: Marketing Guru

Stephen, during the beta cycle, our customers want to be able to vote on the importance of various bugs and feature requests. Can you create a Web site that allows them to enter new requests and gives them the ability to vote for various features, ranking their importance?

Marketing Guru

Memo

To: Marketing Guru
From: Stephen

Guru, try out the URL http://bugs/index.html. Let me know if that is what you are looking for. I used a relational database back end so that we can use multiple tools with the same bug database. Also, I created versions in Perl and JHTML, so that the project manager for the final deployment can pick which technology he or she wants to use.

Stephen

About This Project

This project creates a basic bug-tracking program using the Java scripting engine from Project 2 or Perl, plus a relational database. The program created in this project stores information about bugs in a database. Users of the system can submit bugs using a Web form or search for bugs by key word. Along with the bugs themselves, a set of votes is kept for each bug. These votes are used to determine the severity of the bug. For example, the person who submitted a bug can mark it as critical, while others who find the bug in the database think it is a cosmetic change. The overall severity of the bug is an average of each person's vote.

Although the final solution to this project is not a professional-level bug-tracking system, it is likely a sufficient bug-tracking system for small projects, and it can certainly form the foundation for a more complete application. I included this project so that you could use it as the basis for your own bug tracking and as a chance to compare JHTML, a server-scripting technology, with CGI. You will end up comparing Perl and Java as well, but that wasn't my focus, just a byproduct.

Basic Concepts and Design

At the heart of the bug-tracking application is a relational database that stores information about bugs. This database is a server program called MySQL, http://www.tcx.se/, which runs separately from the tracking system. It is optimized to store data of varying types for fast retrieval. MySQL in particular has been written to make reading data very fast. Because MySQL is a free (or close to free) product, it does not contain every feature of a commercial database. For an application such as this one, however, many of the features in a larger database are unnecessary and can even reduce performance. I chose MySQL for this project because it is fast and available, and because it supports Java, Perl, and C programming access.

In general, a relational database stores information as entries in tables, where a table is a set of rows and columns. The columns define the types of data for each entry. The rows represent the entries themselves. This project uses two tables. The first is called BUGS, shown in Table 3.1. BUGS contains seven columns. Rows in the BUGS table represent individual bugs. For each bug submitted to the system, a row is added to the BUGS table.

The second table is called VOTES and contains two columns. The first column, ID, is used to reference a bug in the BUGS table. The second, severity, indicates

Table 3.1 BUGS Table

COLUMN	DESCRIPTION
id	A unique ID number
shortdesc	A one-line description of the bug
description	A multiline, complete description of the bug
workaround	Suggested workarounds
date_reported	When the bug was reported
environment	The user's computing environment when he or she reported the bug
category	The seriousness of this bug

a single person's vote for the importance of this bug. Many users might vote on the severity of a bug to indicate their opinion of its importance.

Access to the database relies on a language called the *Structured Query Language (SQL)*. SQL provides syntax for obtaining data from tables and putting data into tables. At the fundamental level, SQL provides commands to insert, update, delete, and select data, where select is the querying functionality of a database. If you are unfamiliar with SQL you may want to look at the reference manual for MySQL to get an idea of the various functionalities it supports.

For the Java version of this project, the Java Database Connectivity (JDBC) library is used to access the MySQL database in this project. JDBC is designed to provide a generic database access library. Drivers are plugged into the library to access specific databases. The driver used in this project is available under the GNU public license at www.worldserver.com/mm.mysql. One of the major advantages of this driver is that it is written in Java and uses standard socket code to access MySQL. This means that it works over networks and will run as part of any Java application, assuming that the application has access to the standard JDBC libraries that have been part of the JDK since version 1.1. The home page for Matthew's MySQL JDBC driver also contains some rather impressive performance information that should satisfy most project evaluators.

The Perl version of this project uses a DBI module to access MySQL. DBI is similar to JDBC in that it provides a standard interface to databases and uses drivers to access each particular vendor's database server.

The user interface for this project is composed of HTML pages. These pages are created in the Java version using the scripting engine described in Project 2. For

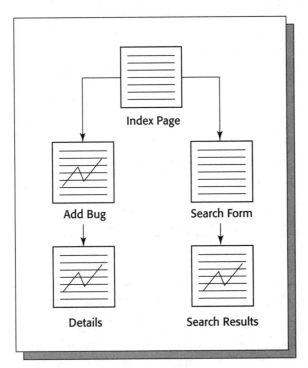

Figure 3.1 Tracking system design.

the Perl version, the dynamically generated pages are created using Perl CGI scripts. The bug-tracking program uses five Web pages. Figure 3.1 shows the structure of the bug-tracking system and the user's interaction with it.

Here's how the system will work: The user starts at the index page. A link on the index page takes the user to the search page where the user can search for a bug. A form on this page allows the user to input the search parameters, the characteristics of the bug. When the search is submitted, the search results page displays the bugs that match the search parameters as a set of links. Each link takes the user to the detail page for the specific bug, which describes the bug that he or she selected. All of the pages include a menu that returns the user to the submission or search page.

 NOTE

All of the following steps of the project assume that you have a Web server installed. If you don't, see the Appendix for information on installing the Apache Web server.

Step 1: Create the Database

In order to create the database you will need to complete the following steps:

1. Install MySQL.
2. Create the bugs database.
3. Grant permissions on the database.
4. Create the database tables using a Java or Perl program.

Install MySQL

The first step in this project is to install MySQL. MySQL is available as standard Linux RPM packages for easy installation on Linux. Two packages are required to use the database. The first package contains the server, and the second the client. Without both applications, you won't be able to store data and administer the database. See the Appendix for more information on installing MySQL.

MySQL separates data into databases. Each MySQL database can contain multiple tables. The databases are separated for security and performance reasons. Security and other configuration information is stored in a database called mysql. The user and network address control access to data. For example, an administrative user might have permission to add tables to a database from within the company network, while a regular user would have permission only to look at data, but the user could do so from any computer on the Internet.

For the purposes of this project, you should install MySQL on the same computer as the Web server that you plan to use.

Create the Bugs Database

Use the mysqladmin program to create a database called bugs. If you are logged in as root, you should be able to use the command line:

```
#mysqladmin create bugs
```

This will create an empty database.

Grant Permissions to the Database

Next, make the database available for use. To do this, open the security for the bugs database by logging into the MySQL configuration database called mysql and adding permissions for a user named stephen to access bugs. To connect to the database, use the command line:

```
#mysql "u root mysql
```

Next, grant all permissions for the bugs database to stephen and restrict access to the local machine using the following command on the mysql promp:

```
GRANT ALL PRIVILEGES ON *.* TO stephen@localhost
```

You can maintain access to the local host because the Web server and MySQL server will be on the same computer. In a production environment with more complex security restrictions, such as having the Web server and MySQL on different computers, use the MySQL reference manual to configure a more secure environment.

NOTE

If MySQL and the Web server are on different computers you need to configure the security to allow access from the Web server's computer. Also, check with your Web server vendor for any security issues from that perspective.

Create the Database Tables

Create the database tables. Rather than create the tables by hand, you can create a JDBC or Perl program to do it. This allows you to test your Java/ JDBC/Perl environment.

Creating the Tables in Java

First, add the MySQL JDBC driver to your class path. The file will be called mysql.jar, and it contains all of the class files necessary to access MySQL locally or over the network. As we did in Project 2, add the mysql.jar file to the class path in your JServ configuration file and in the compileCommand configuration variable for the JHTML servlet.

Second, you create a script that will create the database tables in the bugs database. The following Java class definition, called BugDBBuilder, is one example of how you might do this. All of the database connectivity for this example uses a file called db.properties to provide information about the database. This makes the program more flexible and able to deal with different installations. At the beginning of the builder program the properties are loaded into the resources variable for use.

```
import java.sql.*;
import java.util.*;
import java.io.*;

public class BugDBBuilder
```

```
{
    public static void main(String[] args)
    {
        System.out.println("BugDBBuilder starting");

        try
        {
            ResourceBundle resources;
            InputStream in=null;
            ResourceBundle newResources;

            in = ClassLoader.getSystemResourceAsStream("db.properties");

            resources = new PropertyResourceBundle(in);

            in.close();
```

JDBC expects drivers to register themselves with the DriverManager for access by programs. This application loads the class, by name, using the value of jdbc.driver in the properties files:

```
            Class.forName(resources.getString("jdbc.driver"));
            System.out.println("Loaded the JDBC driver");
```

When the driver class is loaded, it registers with DriverManager. Programs can then connect to a database by specifying it with a URL. In this case, the URL is available from a properties file.

```
            Connection conn = DriverManager.getConnection(
                            resources.getString("jdbc.url")
                ,resources.getString("jdbc.user")
                ,resources.getString("jdbc.password"));
            System.out.println("Connected to DB");
```

A database connection is represented by a Connection object. In this example, the connection is stored in the conn variable. This connection updates the database each time an SQL statement is executed. To postpone updates, set the autocommit flag to false. This forces the connection to wait for you to tell it to commit changes before the changes take effect:

```
            conn.setAutoCommit(false);
```

SQL statements are executed in JDBC using a Statement object. In this example, the statement is stored in the variable named *s*:

```
            Statement s = conn.createStatement();
```

Next, tell the database to remove the table called BUGS because you can't create the same table twice, as shown in the code below. By deleting the table first, this script has the side effect that it purges an existing database and creates a new clean one. This is useful for testing, but in a production environment you might want to use a backup utility like the one in Project 8 before destroying the existing tables. It is important to wrap any code in try-catch blocks because the statement will throw an exception if the SQL fails. In this case, the SQL will fail if the table doesn't exist, which is what happens the first time you run the program. I hope that you will run the program only once, so this step is optional but a good programming habit.

```
try
{
    s.executeUpdate("drop table BUGS");
}
catch(SQLException exp)
{
    System.out.println("Already dropped BUGS");
}
```

To create the BUGS table, use the SQL command CREATE TABLE. MySQL supports automatically incremented columns, and I have used one in this project to uniquely identify each bug. The other columns store text and a date.

```
s.execute("CREATE TABLE BUGS("
            +"id int AUTO_INCREMENT PRIMARY KEY"
            +", shortdesc varchar(255)"
            +", description text"
            +", workaround text"
            +", date_reported date"
            +", category varchar(64)"
            +", environment text)");
System.out.println("Created table BUGS");
```

Repeat the last two steps to create the VOTES table.

```
try
{
    s.executeUpdate("drop table VOTES");
}
catch(SQLException exp)
{
    System.out.println("Already dropped VOTES");
}

s.execute("CREATE TABLE VOTES(id int"
            +", severity int)");
System.out.println("Created table VOTES");
```

Close the statement to clean up resources.

```
            s.close();
            System.out.println("Closed statement");
```

Commit the changes to the database and close your connection to it. This cleans up database resources and makes the tables available for other programs.

```
            conn.commit();
            conn.close();
            System.out.println("Committed transaction "+
                                    "and closed connection");

        }
        catch (Throwable e)
        {
            System.out.println("exception thrown:");

            if (e instanceof SQLException)
                printSQLError((SQLException)e);
            else
                e.printStackTrace();
        }

        System.out.println("DBBuilder finished");
    }

    static void printSQLError(SQLException e)
    {
        while (e != null) {
            System.out.println(e.toString());
            e = e.getNextException();
        }
    }
}
}
```

The db.properties file contains information about connecting to the database. As I mentioned previously, the database you want to connect to is called bugs and you can use the user named stephen with no password to connect to it. The URL for this connection indicates that it is a JDBC URL for the mysql database on localhost at port 3306, the default, for the bugs database. This URL is highlighted in the context of the full properties file.

```
jdbc.driver=org.gjt.mm.mysql.Driver
jdbc.url=jdbc:mysql://127.0.0.1:3306/bugs
jdbc.user=stephen
jdbc.password=
```

Finally, update the properties file to match your installation and run BugDB-Builder to build your database. If this program fails, check your class path and MySQL installation. Especially pay attention to the error messages provided to determine if there is a security problem, indicating that you didn't grant permissions for stephen on your current machine to the bugs database.

Creating the Database Tables in Perl

Creating the database in Perl is slightly easier than the Java version because you side step the properties file. To access MySQL in Perl, you need to have the MySQL DBI driver installed. See the Appendix for information on this driver. You'll use the DBI module to connect to the database, so include it at the top of a script called bugdbbuilder.pl.

```
#! perl -w

use DBI;
```

Next, create a connection to the bugs database. Specify the database with a configuration string of the form, dbi:vendor:database. In this case, use the string dbi:mysql:bugs. Also, provide the user name and password to the DBI module's connect method. This returns a database handle. If the connection fails, print an error message.

```
$dbhandle = DBI->connect("dbi:mysql:bugs", "stephen", "") ||
&error("Couldn't connect to DB. ".$?);
```

Tell the database to drop the table called BUGS. As mentioned previously, by dropping the table first, you ensure a clean version of the database after running this script.

```
$dbhandle->do("DROP TABLE BUGS") || print "Already dropped BUGS.\n";
```

Now, create the SQL statement used to build the BUGS table, as described in Table 3.1. Then execute the SQL, printing an error message if an error occurs.

```
$sql = "CREATE TABLE BUGS(id int AUTO_INCREMENT PRIMARY KEY";
$sql .= ", shortdesc varchar(255)";
$sql .= ", description text";
$sql .= ", workaround text";
$sql .= ", date_reported date";
$sql .= ", category varchar(64)";
$sql .= ", environment text)";

$dbhandle->do($sql) || &error($dbhandle->errstr);
```

Repeat the drop-create process with the VOTES table.

```
$dbhandle->do("DROP TABLE VOTES") || print "Already dropped VOTES.\n";

$sql = "CREATE TABLE VOTES(id int";
$sql .= ", severity int)";

$dbhandle->do($sql) || &error($dbhandle->errstr);
```

Finally, disconnect from the database.

```
$dbhandle->disconnect();
```

You may want to use a subroutine to manage errors, so that you can do more than print a message. Or you could update the code shown to just call print directly when an error occurs.

```
sub error
{
    my($errmsg) = shift;

    print $errmsg;

    exit;
}
```

Run this script on the machine with the database to create the tables for this project.

Step 2: Create the Index Page

The first page a user encounters in this bug-tracking application is the index page. This is a simple HTML page, shown in Figure 3.2, that provides links to the submission and search pages.

Here's the HTML code for the Java version of this page:

```
<html>
<head>
<title> Bug Tracker</title>
</head>
```

Figure 3.2 Index page.

```
<body bgcolor="#ffffff" link="#006699" vlink="#006699">

<center>
<table border=0 cellpadding=0 cellspacing=0 width=600><tr><td>

<font face="Verdana,Arial,Helvetica" size=+3>
<b>
Welcome to MiniBug Tracker...
</b>
</font>

<blockquote>
<font face="Verdana,Arial,Helvetica" size=+1>

<a href="addbug.jhtml">Submit a Bug</a><br>
<a href="searchbug.jhtml">Search Bug Database</a>

</font>
</blockquote>

</td></tr></table>

</center>
</body>
</html>
```

The HTML for this page is almost the same for the Java and Perl versions. If you are completing the Perl version of the project, replace the reference to add-bug.jhtml with /cgi-bin/addbug.pl. Basically, the Perl scripts are accessed from the cgi-bin directory, while the JHTML pages can live anywhere on the server.

Step 3: Create the Submission Page

The next step in this project is to create the page used to submit bugs to the database. This page could be implemented a number of ways. First, you could create an HTML page that references a JHTML scripted page. Second, you could create a plain HTML page that accesses a Perl CGI script. Third, you could combine the page that displays the form with the script that handles it. This final version is the one I chose. In Java, this means that the form for submitting bugs is on a page scripted to handle the submission process. In Perl, the page form is displayed with HTML dynamically created by a CGI script. This same script handles the form submission and performs the bug insertion. By combining the two functions you can improve the maintainability of this project through modularity.

The steps that follow walk through the creation of the Java page and Perl script. Both versions have two components. First, the script figures out if it is handling

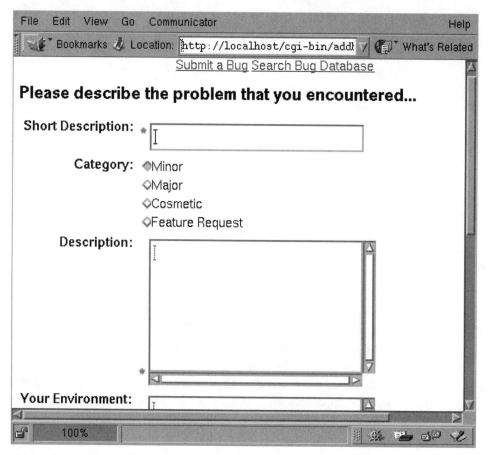

Figure 3.3 Add bug Web page.

a form submission and, if so, inserts the new bug. Second, the script displays the Web page from Figure 3.3.

Create the Java addbug.jhtml Page

The Java version of the submission page is called addbug.jhtml. This page performs two tasks. First, it displays a form that the user fills out to submit a bug. Second, when the form is submitted, it is sent to the JHTML page to be processed. After addbug.jhtml processes the new submission, the user is redirected to the details page for that bug. Using the page to process its own forms is great for development time and maintenance.

Handle the Submission Process

At the top of addbug.jhtml, you declare the variables you will need to store information from the form. There are six form elements: a short description, a description, a suggested workaround, the user's environment, the severity of the bug, and the category to which it is assigned. Remember that the scripting engine for these JHTML pages takes the code between <JAVA> tags and uses it to create the service method for a servlet. In this case, the first part of this method should handle the request and redirect the user if necessary:

```
<JAVA>
String shortdesc=null,description=null,workaround=null,environment=null;
String severity=null,category=null;
boolean firstTime=false;
String id=null;
String error = "";
```

Check if the page is being accessed from a link or if the user submitted the form to the page with the following:

```
shortdesc = request.getParameter("shortdesc");

if((shortdesc!=null)&&(shortdesc.length()>0)) firstTime = true;
```

If the user submitted the form, process it; otherwise, simply let the HTML be displayed:

```
if(firstTime)
{
```

Using the built-in request variable, access the data submitted to this page. Request is an HTTPServletRequest object, and its value is passed into the service method generated from this JHTML page. Each form element submitted to the page shows up as a parameter. The name of the parameter corresponds to the name of the form element.

```
    description = request.getParameter("description");
    workaround = request.getParameter("workaround");
    environment = request.getParameter("environment");
    severity = request.getParameter("severity");
    category = request.getParameter("category");

    if(workaround==null) workaround = "";
    if(environment==null) environment = "";
```

This application requires that when someone submits a bug it at least has a severity, category, and description. Use an if statement to check that these were submitted. JavaScript is used on the client side to help the user be sure to fill in these fields, so this step is a second check.

```
if((description!=null)
   &&(category!=null)&&(severity!=null))
{
```

Rather than include the code for connecting to the database inside this part of the page, relegate it to another method. In the solution, this method, called createDBConnection, is defined at the bottom of the JHTML page.

```
java.sql.Connection conn = createDBConnection();
java.sql.Statement s = conn.createStatement();
```

Next, use a StringBuffer to build the SQL necessary to add this new bug to the database. Create a calender to access information about the submission day, and use a try-catch block to handle any errors that could occur when you communicate with the database server.

```
try
{
    StringBuffer sql = new StringBuffer();
    java.util.GregorianCalendar now
        = new java.util.GregorianCalendar();

    sql.append("insert into BUGS ");
    sql.append(" (shortdesc,description,workaround,date_reported");
    sql.append(",category,environment) ");
    sql.append("values ('");
    sql.append(shortdesc);
    sql.append("','");
    sql.append(description);
    sql.append("','");
    sql.append(workaround);
    sql.append("','");
    sql.append(now.get(Calendar.YEAR)
                +"-"+(now.get(Calendar.MONTH)+1));
    sql.append("-"+now.get(Calendar.DAY_OF_MONTH));
    sql.append("','");
    sql.append(category);
    sql.append("','");
    sql.append(environment);
    sql.append("')");
```

For debugging, a string called error is used to track exceptions and the SQL being submitted. You don't need to include this variable, but it may help if you extend the project beyond the solution.

```
error = sql.toString();
```

Tell the JDBC statement to execute the SQL and update the BUGS database. If this is successful, update the VOTES database as well.

```
if(s.executeUpdate(sql.toString()) != 0)
{
```

The MySQL driver provides access to the autoincrement fields in the database via a custom method called getLastInsertID. If the statement is the correct type, get this value and use it as the ID for the new bug. This, with this ID, and the submitted severity value update the VOTES database.

```
if(s instanceof org.gjt.mm.mysql.Statement)
{
    id = String.valueOf(
      ((org.gjt.mm.mysql.Statement)s).getLastInsertID());

    sql.setLength(0);

    sql.append("insert into VOTES (id,severity)");
    sql.append("values (");
    sql.append(id);
    sql.append(",");
    sql.append(severity);
    sql.append(")");
    s.executeUpdate(sql.toString());
}
else
{
    throw new Exception("Couldn't get id.");
}
    }
}
catch (Exception exp)
{
    error += exp.toString();
}
```

At the end of the database code, close the statement and connection to clean up any database resources. The finally statement is used to ensure that the cleanup occurs even if an exception is thrown.

```
finally
{
    try
    {
        s.close();
        conn.close();
    }
    catch(Exception exp)
    {
        error += exp.toString();
    }
    }
}
```

Finally, in the case that a new bug was added, the ID variable is initialized. Use it to redirect the user to the bugdetails.jhtml page created in the next step. Use return to conclude the service method generated from this JHTML page. This prevents any rogue HTML from going to the browser before or after the redirect statement.

```
if(id!=null)
{
    response.sendRedirect("bugdetails.jhtml?id="+id);
    return;
}
}

</JAVA>
```

Output the HTML

Next define the HTML for your submissions form. This HTML will be sent, as is, to the client when the JHTML page is submitted. The HTML shown next and pictured in Figure 3.3 uses JavaScript to validate the form and targets addbug.jhtml with the form submission. The JavaScript for this version of the page is available on the CD-ROM in a file called formutils.js.

```
<html>
<head>
<title> Bug Tracker - Report a Bug</title>
</head>
<body bgcolor="#ffffff" link="#006699" vlink="#006699">

<center>
<java type="print">error</java>

<table border=0 cellpadding=0 cellspacing=0 width=600><tr><td>

<center>
<font face="Verdana,Arial,Helvetica" size=+1>
<a href="addbug.jhtml">Submit a Bug</a>
<a href="searchbug.jhtml">Search Bug Database</a>
</font>
</center>
<br>

<font face="Verdana,Arial,Helvetica" size=+3>
<b>
Please describe the problem that you encountered...
</b>
</font>
<script src="formutils.js">
</script>

<form name="buginfo" action="addbug.jhtml" method="post"
    onSubmit="return verifyForm(this);">
```

```
<table border=0>
<tr>
<td align=right valign=top>
<font face="Verdana,Arial,Helvetica" size=+1>
<b>
Short Description:
</b>
</font>
</td>
<td>
<img name="shortdesc" src="images/star.gif">
<font face="Verdana,Arial,Helvetica" size=+1>
<input type="text" name="shortdesc" onChange="isFilled(this)" size=26>
</font>
</td>
</tr>

<tr>
<td align=right valign=top>
<font face="Verdana,Arial,Helvetica" size=+1>
<b>
Category:
</b>
</font>
</td>
<td>
<font face="Verdana,Arial,Helvetica" size=+1>
<input type="radio" name="category" value="minor" checked>Minor<br>
<input type="radio" name="category" value="major">Major<br>
<input type="radio" name="category" value="cosmetic">Cosmetic<br>
<input type="radio" name="category" value="feature">Feature Request<br>
</font>
</td>
</tr>

<tr>
<td align=right valign=top nowrap>
<font face="Verdana,Arial,Helvetica" size=+1>
<b>
Description:
</b>
</font>
</td>
<td valign=top>
<img name="description" src="images/star.gif">
<font face="Verdana,Arial,Helvetica" size=+1>
<textarea name="description" onChange="isFilled(this)" rows=8 cols=26>
</textarea>
</font>
</td>
</tr>
```

```
<tr>
<td align=right valign=top nowrap>
<font face="Verdana,Arial,Helvetica" size=+1>
<b>
Your Environment:
</b>
</font>
</td>
<td>
<img src="images/blank.gif">
<font face="Verdana,Arial,Helvetica" size=+1>
<textarea name="environment" rows=4 cols=26>
</textarea>
</font>
</td>
</tr>


<tr>
<td align=right valign=top nowrap>
<font face="Verdana,Arial,Helvetica" size=+1>
<b>
Workaround:
</b>
</font>
</td>
<td>
<img src="images/blank.gif">
<font face="Verdana,Arial,Helvetica" size=+1>
<textarea name="workaround" rows=8 cols=26>
</textarea>
</font>
</td>
</tr>

<tr>
<td align=right valign=top>
<font face="Verdana,Arial,Helvetica" size=+1>
<b>
Severity:
</b>
</font>
</td>
<td valign=top>
<font face="Verdana,Arial,Helvetica" size=+1>
<input type="radio" name="severity" value="2" checked>Next Version<br>
<input type="radio" name="severity" value="3">Fix Immediately<br>
<input type="radio" name="severity" value="1">Cosmetic<br>
<input type="radio" name="severity" value="0">Don't Bother<br>
</font>
</td>
</tr>
```

```
<tr>
<td align=right valign=top>
<br>
</td>
<td align=left valign=top>
<font face="Verdana,Arial,Helvetica" size=+1>
<img src="images/blank.gif">
<input type="submit" name="Submit" value="Submit Bug">
</font>
</td>
</tr>

</form>
</table>

</td></tr></table>

</center>

</body>
</html>
```

As an organizational tool, the code for the createDBConnection method and the import statements form this JHTML page; they are included at the bottom of the file.

```
<JAVA type=class>
private java.sql.Connection createDBConnection()
{
    java.sql.Connection conn=null;

    try
    {
        Class.forName("org.gjt.mm.mysql.Driver");
        conn = java.sql.DriverManager.getConnection("jdbc:mysql: "+
                           "//127.0.0.1:3306/bugs?user=stephen");
    }
    catch(Exception exp)
    {
    }

    return conn;
}
</JAVA>

<JAVA type=import>
java.sql.*
java.util.*
org.gjt.mm.mysql.*
</JAVA>
```

Now install this page on the Web server and access it using the index.html page. You should be able to see the form, indicating that the JHTML compile process was successful. Submitting the form adds bugs to the database, but the redirect fails until you complete the next step.

Create the Perl Submission Script

Like the Java version of the submission script, the Perl version, called add-bug.pl, starts by checking if this script was called as the result of the user submitting the form on the page this script generates. Start the script by including the DBI module for database access, the CGI module for interpretting HTML form data, and the file stringutils.pl, included on the CD-ROM, for escaping strings sent to the database.

```perl
#!/usr/bin/perl

use DBI;
use CGI;
require "stringutils.pl";
```

Handle the Submission Process

Use a string called $error to store any error messages. Include these in the HTML sent to the user.

```perl
$error = "";
```

Create a CGI object to manage connectivity with the client.

```perl
$query = new CGI;
```

Use the short description field in the HTML form to determine if the script is being run to handle a bug submission or just to display the form.

```perl
$shortdesc = $query->param('shortdesc');

if(defined($shortdesc))
{
```

If this is a submission, get all of the elements from the form. Define a variable for each element, initializing the $environment and $workaround variables to "" if no value was provided by the user.

```perl
    $description = $query->param("description");
    $workaround = $query->param("workaround");
    $environment = $query->param("environment");
    $severity = $query->param("severity");
    $category = $query->param("category");

    $workaround = "" if (!defined($workaround));
    $environment = "" if (!defined($environment));
```

Check that the user provided the required fields before performing the insert.

```
if($description&&$category&&$severity)
{
```

Connect to the database and create a database handle.

```
$dbh = DBI->connect("dbi:mysql:bugs", "stephen", "");
```

Get the current time, so that you can store it as the submission time for this bug.

```
($sec,$min,$h,$day,$month,$year) = localtime(time());
```

Create the SQL to insert the bug. Use the escape function from stringutils.pl, provided on the CD-ROM, to convert any special characters. This function takes characters like ' and replaces them with \' so that the database can accept them.

```
$sql = "insert into BUGS (shortdesc,description";
$sql .= ",workaround,date_reported,category,environment)";
$sql .= "values (\'";
$sql .= &escape($shortdesc);
$sql .= "\',\'";
$sql .= &escape($description);
$sql .= "\',\'";
$sql .= &escape($workaround);
$sql .= "\',\'";
$sql .= "$year-$month-$day";
$sql .= "\',\'";
$sql .= $category;
$sql .= "\',\'";
$sql .= &escape($environment);
$sql .= "\')";
```

Perform the insertion.

```
if($dbh->do($sql))
{
```

If it works, use a select statement and the MySQL function LAST_INSERT_ID to get the ID of the new bug. Because this ID is generated by the database, you have to get it from there.

```
$sth = $dbh->prepare("select LAST_INSERT_ID()");
$rows = $sth->execute();
```

Use the new ID and the submittor's severity level to insert the first vote for this bug in the VOTES table. If this insertion fails, store an error message in the $error variable.

```
if($rows)
{
    ($id) = $sth->fetchrow_array();

    $sql = "insert into VOTES (id,severity)";
    $sql .= "values ($id,$severity)";
```

```
                    if(!$dbh->do($sql))
                    {
                        $error="Couldn\'t insert vote.";
                    }
                }
                else
                {
                    $error = "Couldn\'t get id.";
                }
            }
            else
            {
                $error = "Failed to insert bug.";
            }
```

Disconnect from the database.

```
            $dbh->disconnect();
    }
```

If you were able to perform the insertion and get the resulting ID, redirect the client to the details page for that bug.

```
    if($id!=null)
    {
        print $query->redirect("/cgi-bin/bugdetails.pl?id=".id);
        return;
    }
}
```

Output the HTML

Next output the HTML for your submissions form using print redirection. This HTML is sent, as is, to the client when the JHTML page is submitted. The HTML shown here and pictured in Figure 3.3 uses JavaScript to validate the form and targets addbug.jhtml with the form submission. The JavaScript for this version of the page is available on the CD-ROM in a file called formutils.js. Start the output with the HTTP header expected by the client.

```
print $query->header();
print << "EOD";

<html>
<head>
<title> Bug Tracker - Report a Bug</title>
</head>
<body bgcolor="#ffffff" link="#006699" vlink="#006699">

<center>
$error
```

```html
<table border=0 cellpadding=0 cellspacing=0 width=600><tr><td>

<center>
<font face="Verdana,Arial,Helvetica" size=+1>
<a href="/cgi-bin/addbug.pl">Submit a Bug</a> <a
href="/searchbug.html">Search Bug Database</a>
</font>
</center>
<br>

<font face="Verdana,Arial,Helvetica" size=+3>
<b>
Please describe the problem that you encountered...
</b>
</font>
<script src="/formutils.js">
</script>

<form name="buginfo" action="/cgi-bin/addbug.pl" method="post"
onSubmit="return verifyForm(this);">

<table border=0>
<tr>
<td align=right valign=top>
<font face="Verdana,Arial,Helvetica" size=+1>
<b>
Short Description:
</b>
</font>
</td>
<td>
<img name="shortdesc" src="/images/star.gif">
<font face="Verdana,Arial,Helvetica" size=+1>
<input type="text" name="shortdesc" onChange="isFilled(this)" size=26>
</font>
</td>
</tr>

<tr>
<td align=right valign=top>
<font face="Verdana,Arial,Helvetica" size=+1>
<b>
Category:
</b>
</font>
</td>
<td>
<font face="Verdana,Arial,Helvetica" size=+1>
<input type="radio" name="category" value="minor" checked>Minor<br>
<input type="radio" name="category" value="major">Major<br>
<input type="radio" name="category" value="cosmetic">Cosmetic<br>
```

```
<input type="radio" name="category" value="feature">Feature Request<br>
</font>
</td>
</tr>

<tr>
<td align=right valign=top nowrap>
<font face="Verdana,Arial,Helvetica" size=+1>
<b>
Description:
</b>
</font>
</td>
<td valign=top>
<img name="description" src="/images/star.gif">
<font face="Verdana,Arial,Helvetica" size=+1>
<textarea name="description" onChange="isFilled(this)" rows=8 cols=26>
</textarea>
</font>
</td>
</tr>

<tr>
<td align=right valign=top nowrap>
<font face="Verdana,Arial,Helvetica" size=+1>
<b>
Your Environment:
</b>
</font>
</td>
<td>
<img src="/images/blank.gif">
<font face="Verdana,Arial,Helvetica" size=+1>
<textarea name="environment" rows=4 cols=26>
</textarea>
</font>
</td>
</tr>

<tr>
<td align=right valign=top nowrap>
<font face="Verdana,Arial,Helvetica" size=+1>
<b>
Workaround:
</b>
</font>
</td>
<td>
<img src="/images/blank.gif">
<font face="Verdana,Arial,Helvetica" size=+1>
```

```
<textarea name="workaround" rows=8 cols=26>
</textarea>
</font>
</td>
</tr>

<tr>
<td align=right valign=top>
<font face="Verdana,Arial,Helvetica" size=+1>
<b>
Severity:
</b>
</font>
</td>
<td valign=top>
<font face="Verdana,Arial,Helvetica" size=+1>
<input type="radio" name="severity" value="2" checked>Next Version<br>
<input type="radio" name="severity" value="3">Fix Immediately<br>
<input type="radio" name="severity" value="1">Cosmetic<br>
<input type="radio" name="severity" value="0">Don't Bother<br>
</font>
</td>
</tr>

<tr>
<td align=right valign=top>
<br>
</td>
<td align=left valign=top>
<font face="Verdana,Arial,Helvetica" size=+1>
<img src="/images/blank.gif">
<input type="submit" name="Submit" value="Submit Bug">
</font>
</td>
</tr>

</form>
</table>

</td></tr></table>

</center>

</body>
</html>
EOD
```

Don't forget to include a blank line after the EOD tag indicating the end of your print redirection statement. Install this script in your Web server's cgi-bin directory. On my computer this is /home/httpd/cgi-bin.

Step 4: Create the Details Page

Both the submissions and search processes use the same script to display information about a particular bug. This page performs two tasks. First, it displays a read-only copy of the information for a bug. Second, it allows the viewer to vote for the severity of that bug. When a vote occurs, the details page handles the form submission itself and redisplays. The solution on the CD-ROM, and included below, looks like Figure 3.4 when accessed by a client.

Create the Java Version of the Details Page

The Java version of this page is called bugdetails.jhtml. Start off by declaring variables to hold information about a bug. Use the existence of an input param-

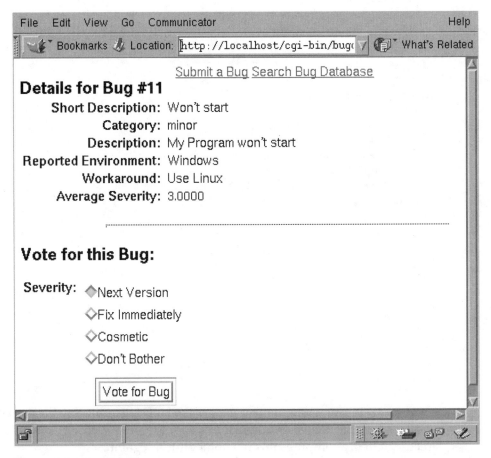

Figure 3.4   Bug details page.

eter called severity to determine if the user accessed the page by submitting a vote, or if the user was just accessing the page. In either case, the ID parameter must be set to the ID of a bug in the database in order to identify it.

```
<JAVA>
String shortdesc=null,description=null,workaround=null,environment=null;
String severity=null,category=null;
boolean voting=false;
String id=null;
String error = "";

id = request.getParameter("id");
severity = request.getParameter("severity");

if((severity!=null)&&(severity.length()>0)) voting = true;
```

Next, create a database connection and statement:

```
java.sql.Connection conn = createDBConnection();
java.sql.Statement s = conn.createStatement();

try
{
    StringBuffer sql = new StringBuffer();
    java.sql.ResultSet rs;
```

If the user submitted a vote, start by inserting the new vote into the VOTES table:

```
    if(voting)
    {
        sql.append("insert into VOTES (id,severity)");
        sql.append("values (");
        sql.append(id);
        sql.append(",");
        sql.append(severity);
        sql.append(")");

        s.executeUpdate(sql.toString());
    }
```

Now query the VOTES table and get the average value for the severity of a bug by its ID. If there are many votes for one bug, the VOTES table will contain a row for each vote, all with the same ID but possibly with different levels of severity. The following code asks the database to average those values and return the average:

```
    sql.setLength(0);
    sql.append("select AVG(severity) from VOTES where id=");
    sql.append(id);
```

The results for this query are provided in the form of a ResultSet object. This object provides access to information by column name or index. Indices start at 1, so your average is in column 1. The ResultSet is like a cursor or enumeration, and you use the next method to iterate over the rows returned by a query. In this case, make sure that at least one row is returned and get the value in the first column.

```java
rs = s.executeQuery(sql.toString());

if(rs.next())
{
    severity = rs.getString(1);
}
```

Next, you get all of the columns for the row in the BUGS database that has the ID of your bug. All bugs have a unique ID, so only one row is returned. Because you know the names of the columns in the BUGS table, the columns can be accessed by name instead of index.

```java
sql.setLength(0);
sql.append("select * from BUGS where id=");
sql.append(id);

rs = s.executeQuery(sql.toString());

if(rs.next())
{
    category = rs.getString("category");
    description = rs.getString("description");
    shortdesc = rs.getString("shortdesc");
    workaround = rs.getString("workaround");
    environment = rs.getString("environment");
}
}
catch (Exception exp)
{
    error += exp.toString();
}
```

Next, clean up the database connection.

```java
finally
{
    try
    {
        s.close();
        conn.close();
    }
    catch(Exception exp)
    {
        error += exp.toString();
    }
}

</JAVA>
```

Finally, you define the HTML for the details page. Use the java print tag to include the bug's ID number in the title for the page, as well as the other bug information.

```
<html>
<head>
<title> Bug Tracker -  Bug #<java type="print">id</java></title>
</head>
<body bgcolor="#ffffff" link="#006699" vlink="#006699">

<center>
<table border=0 cellpadding=0 cellspacing=0 width=600><tr><td>

<center>
<font face="Verdana,Arial,Helvetica" size=+1>
<a href="addbug.jhtml">Submit a Bug</a> <a href="searchbug.jhtml">Search
Bug Database</a>
</font>
</center>

<font face="Verdana,Arial,Helvetica" size=+3>
<b>
Details for Bug #<java type="print">id</java>
</b>
</font>

<table border=0>
<tr>
<td align=right valign=top>
<font face="Verdana,Arial,Helvetica" size=+1>
<b>
Short Description:
</b>
</font>
</td>
<td>
<font face="Verdana,Arial,Helvetica" size=+1>
<java type="print">shortdesc</java>
</font>
</td>
</tr>

<tr>
<td align=right valign=top>
<font face="Verdana,Arial,Helvetica" size=+1>
<b>
Category:
</b>
</font>
</td>
<td>
<font face="Verdana,Arial,Helvetica" size=+1>
<java type="print">category</java>
```

```
</font>
</td>
</tr>

<tr>
<td align=right valign=top nowrap>
<font face="Verdana,Arial,Helvetica" size=+1>
<b>
Description:
</b>
</font>
</td>
<td valign=top>
<font face="Verdana,Arial,Helvetica" size=+1>
<java type="print">description</java>
</font>
</td>
</tr>

<tr>
<td align=right valign=top nowrap>
<font face="Verdana,Arial,Helvetica" size=+1>
<b>
Reported Environment:
</b>
</font>
</td>
<td>
<font face="Verdana,Arial,Helvetica" size=+1>
<java type="print">environment</java>
</font>
</td>
</tr>

<tr>
<td align=right valign=top nowrap>
<font face="Verdana,Arial,Helvetica" size=+1>
<b>
Workaround:
</b>
</font>
</td>
<td>
<font face="Verdana,Arial,Helvetica" size=+1>
<java type="print">workaround</java>
</font>
</td>
</tr>

<tr>
<td align=right valign=top>
```

```
<font face="Verdana,Arial,Helvetica" size=+1>
<b>
Average Severity:
</b>
</font>
</td>
<td valign=top>
<font face="Verdana,Arial,Helvetica" size=+1>
<java type="print">severity</java>

</font>
</td>
</tr>

</form>
</table>

<br><hr width=400 size=3><br>

<font face="Verdana,Arial,Helvetica" size=+3>
<b>
Vote for this Bug:
</b>
</font>

<form name="voteform" action="bugdetails.jhtml" method="post">

<input type="hidden" name="id" value="`id`">

<table border=0>

<tr>
<td align=right valign=top>
<font face="Verdana,Arial,Helvetica" size=+1>
<b>
Severity:
</b>
</font>
</td>
<td valign=top>
<font face="Verdana,Arial,Helvetica" size=+1>
<input type="radio" name="severity" value="2" checked>Next Version<br>
<input type="radio" name="severity" value="3">Fix Immediately<br>
<input type="radio" name="severity" value="1">Cosmetic<br>
<input type="radio" name="severity" value="0">Don't Bother<br>
</font>
</td>
</tr>

<tr>
<td align=right valign=top>
<br>
</td>
<td align=left valign=top>
<font face="Verdana,Arial,Helvetica" size=+1>
```

```
<img src="images/blank.gif">
<input type="submit" name="Submit" value="Vote for Bug">
</font>
</td>
</tr>

</form>
</table>

</td></tr></table>

</center>
</body>
</html>
```

Like the addbug.jhtml page, the createDBConnection method and the import statements are at the bottom of bugdetails.jhtml.

```
<JAVA type=class>
private java.sql.Connection createDBConnection()
{
    java.sql.Connection conn=null;

    try
    {
        Class.forName("org.gjt.mm.mysql.Driver");
        conn = java.sql.DriverManager.getConnection("jdbc:mysql: "
                  +"//127.0.0.1:3306/bugs?user=stephen");
    }
    catch(Exception exp)
    {
    }

    return conn;
}
</JAVA>

<JAVA type=import>
java.sql.*
java.util.*
org.gjt.mm.mysql.*
</JAVA>
```

Now install this page on the server and retest the submissions page to be sure that it redirects you appropriately.

Create the Perl Version of the Details Page

The Perl version of the details page is called bugdetails.pl. Like the previous Perl script, this one is broken into two pieces. The first handles voting; the second displays the HTML. Start by including the DBI and CGI packages as well as the stringutils.pl library. In this script, you will use the unescape function from stringutils.pl to replace new line characters with <BR> tags in the HTML.

```
#!/usr/bin/perl

use DBI;
use CGI;
require "stringutils.pl";
```

Declare the $error variable to hold error message, and create a CGI object.

```
$error = "";
$query = new CGI;
```

Output the HTTP header.

```
print $query->header();
```

Get the ID and severity as submitted to the script. If a severity is available, then the script should register a vote before displaying details about the bug with this ID. The version shown here doesn't double-check that the ID is provided. In a commercial application, you should double-check every parameter that you expect from the user.

```
$id = $query->param('id');
$severity = $query->param('severity');

if(defined($severity)&&(length($severity)>0))
{
    $voting = 1;
}
```

Connect to the database.

```
$dbh = DBI->connect("dbi:mysql:bugs", "stephen", "");
```

If a severity was provided, insert a new vote in the VOTES table.

```
if($voting != 0)
{
    $sql = "insert into VOTES (id,severity)";
    $sql .= "values ($id,$severity)";

    if(!$dbh->do($sql))
    {
        $error = "Failed to insert new vote.";
    }
}
```

Create the SQL to select the average severity for this bug from the VOTES table.

```
$sql = "select AVG(severity) from VOTES where id=$id";
```

Execute the select statement and if it returns anything, get the average severity.

```
$sth = $dbh->prepare($sql);
$rows = $sth->execute();

if($rows)
{
    ($severity) = $sth->fetchrow_array();
}
```

Now, get the information about the current bug from the BUGS table. Store the data for each bit of information in a separate variable.

```
$sql = "select * from BUGS where id=$id";

$sth = $dbh->prepare($sql);
$rows = $sth->execute();

if($rows)
{
    ($id,$shortdesc,$description,$workaround,$date,$category,$environment)
     = $sth->fetchrow_array();

    $shortdesc = &unescape($shortdesc);
    $desription = &unescape($description);
    $workaround = &unescape($workaround);
    $date = &unescape($date);
    $category = &unescape($category);
    $environment = &unescape($environment);
}
```

Disconnect from the database.

```
$dbh->disconnect();
```

Output the HTML for the details page using print redirection. Use variable interpolation to include information about the bug in the HTML. These variables are highlighted in the code below. At the bottom of the page is a form to vote on the severity of this bug.

```
print << "EOD";

<html>
<head>
<title> Bug Tracker -  Bug #$id</title>
</head>
<body bgcolor="#ffffff" link="#006699" vlink="#006699">

<center>
<table border=0 cellpadding=0 cellspacing=0 width=600><tr><td>

<center>
<font face="Verdana,Arial,Helvetica" size=+1>
<a href="/cgi-bin/addbug.pl">Submit a Bug</a> <a href="/cgi-
bin/searchbug.pl">Search Bug Database</a>
```

```
</font>
</center>

<font face="Verdana,Arial,Helvetica" size=+3>
<b>
Details for Bug #$id
</b>
</font>

<table border=0>
<tr>
<td align=right valign=top>
<font face="Verdana,Arial,Helvetica" size=+1>
<b>
Short Description:
</b>
</font>
</td>
<td>
<font face="Verdana,Arial,Helvetica" size=+1>
$shortdesc
</font>
</td>
</tr>

<tr>
<td align=right valign=top>
<font face="Verdana,Arial,Helvetica" size=+1>
<b>
Category:
</b>
</font>
</td>
<td>
<font face="Verdana,Arial,Helvetica" size=+1>
$category
</font>
</td>
</tr>

<tr>
<td align=right valign=top nowrap>
<font face="Verdana,Arial,Helvetica" size=+1>
<b>
Description:
</b>
</font>
</td>
<td valign=top>
<font face="Verdana,Arial,Helvetica" size=+1>
$description
```

```
</font>
</td>
</tr>

<tr>
<td align=right valign=top nowrap>
<font face="Verdana,Arial,Helvetica" size=+1>
<b>
Reported Environment:
</b>
</font>
</td>
<td>
<font face="Verdana,Arial,Helvetica" size=+1>
$environment
</font>
</td>
</tr>

<tr>
<td align=right valign=top nowrap>
<font face="Verdana,Arial,Helvetica" size=+1>
<b>
Workaround:
</b>
</font>
</td>
<td>
<font face="Verdana,Arial,Helvetica" size=+1>
$workaround
</font>
</td>
</tr>

<tr>
<td align=right valign=top>
<font face="Verdana,Arial,Helvetica" size=+1>
<b>
Average Severity:
</b>
</font>
</td>
<td valign=top>
<font face="Verdana,Arial,Helvetica" size=+1>
$severity
</font>
</td>
</tr>

</form>
</table>
```

```
<br><hr width=400 size=3><br>

<font face="Verdana,Arial,Helvetica" size=+3>
<b>
Vote for this Bug:
</b>
</font>

<form name="voteform" action="/cgi-bin/bugdetails.pl" method="post">

<input type="hidden" name="id" value="$id">

<table border=0>

<tr>
<td align=right valign=top>
<font face="Verdana,Arial,Helvetica" size=+1>
<b>
Severity:
</b>
</font>
</td>
<td valign=top>
<font face="Verdana,Arial,Helvetica" size=+1>
<input type="radio" name="severity" value="2" checked>Next Version<br>
<input type="radio" name="severity" value="3">Fix Immediately<br>
<input type="radio" name="severity" value="1">Cosmetic<br>
<input type="radio" name="severity" value="0">Don't Bother<br>
</font>
</td>
</tr>

<tr>
<td align=right valign=top>
<br>
</td>
<td align=left valign=top>
<font face="Verdana,Arial,Helvetica" size=+1>
<img src="/images/blank.gif">
<input type="submit" name="Submit" value="Vote for Bug">
</font>
</td>
</tr>

</form>
</table>

</td></tr></table>

</center>


</body>
</html>

EOD
```

Be sure to include a blank line after the EOD string that ends the rediretion.

Install this page on the server in the cgi-bin directory and retest the submissions page to be sure that it redirects you appropriately.

Step 5: Create the Search Page

A form on a simple HTML page is used to submit search requests. The form on this page, pictured in Figure 3.5, targets the searchresults.jhtml page for the Java version of this project, and it should target the /cgi-bin/searchresults.pl script for the Perl version, to perform the search and display the results.

The HTML for this page looks like this:

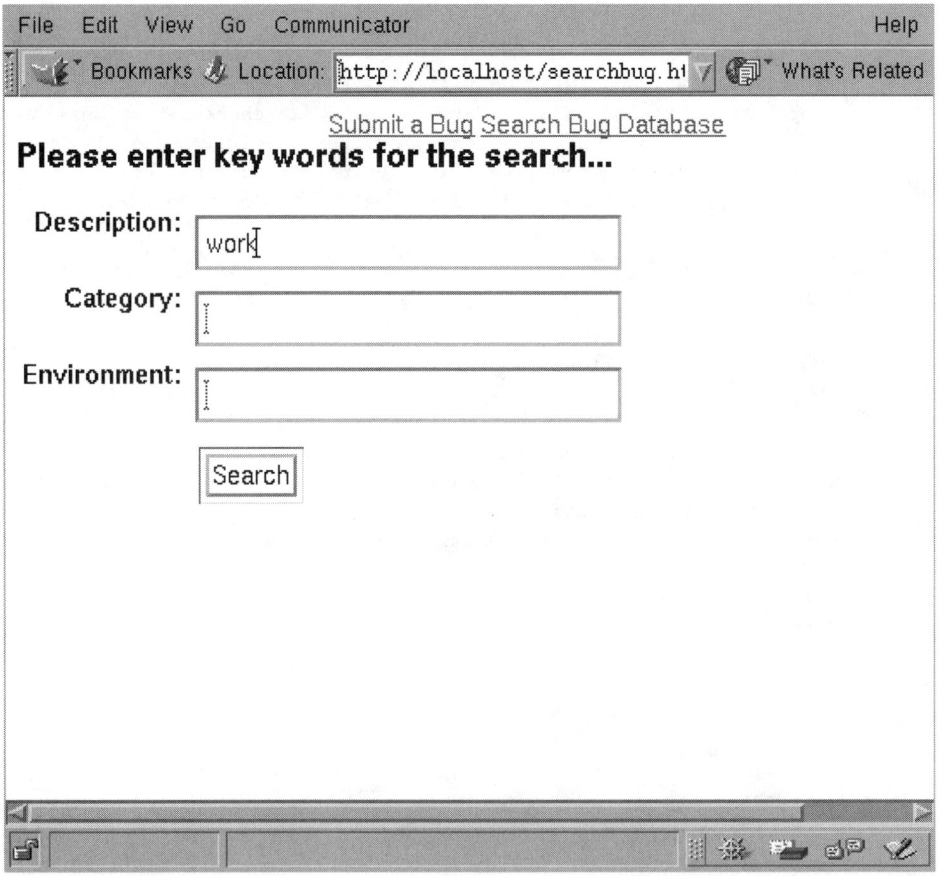

Figure 3.5 SearchBug.jhtml.

```
<html>
<head>
<title> Bug Tracker - Search Bugs</title>
</head>
<body bgcolor="#ffffff" link="#006699" vlink="#006699">

<center>
<table border=0 cellpadding=0 cellspacing=0 width=600><tr><td>

<center>
<font face="Verdana,Arial,Helvetica" size=+1>
<a href="addbug.jhtml">Submit a Bug</a> <a href="searchbug.jhtml">Search
Bug Database</a>
</font>
</center>

<font face="Verdana,Arial,Helvetica" size=+3>
<b>
Please enter key words for the search...
</b>
</font>

<form name="buginfo" action="searchresults.jhtml" method="post">

<table border=0>
<tr>
<td align=right valign=top>
<font face="Verdana,Arial,Helvetica" size=+1>
<b>
Description:
</b>
</font>
</td>
<td>
<font face="Verdana,Arial,Helvetica" size=+1>
<input type="text" name="description" size=26>
</font>
</td>
</tr>

<tr>
<td align=right valign=top>
<font face="Verdana,Arial,Helvetica" size=+1>
<b>
Category:
</b>
</font>
</td>
<td>
<font face="Verdana,Arial,Helvetica" size=+1>
<input type="text" name="category" size=26>
</font>
```

```
</td>
</tr>

<tr>
<td align=right valign=top nowrap>
<font face="Verdana,Arial,Helvetica" size=+1>
<b>
Environment:
</b>
</font>
</td>
<td>
<font face="Verdana,Arial,Helvetica" size=+1>
<input type="text" name="environment" size=26>
</font>
</td>
</tr>

<tr>
<td align=right valign=top>
<br>
</td>
<td align=left valign=top>
<font face="Verdana,Arial,Helvetica" size=+1>
<input type="submit" name="Submit" value="Search">
</font>
</td>
</tr>

</form>
</table>

</td></tr></table>
</center>
</body>
</html>
```

Install this page on your server and make sure that you can access it from the index.html page created in Step 2.

Step 6: Create the Search Results Page

The last script in this project is the search results page. This page, shown in Figure 3.6, displays a list of bugs that meet the search parameters. The search is controlled by three parameters passed in from the search page.

As with the add bug and bug details functionality, there is a different version of this script for Java and Perl.

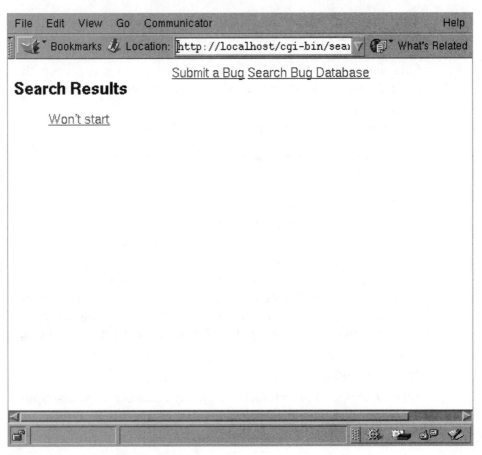

Figure 3.6 Search results page.

Create the Java Search Results Page

Like the other JHTML pages in this project, most of the Java for searchre-sults.jhtml is at the top of the page. This page also makes heavy use of condi-tional and looping HTML where HTML is mixed with Java code. You start by declaring variables to hold the description, environment, and category para-meters submitted from the search page. Initialize these variables:

```
<JAVA>
String description=null,environment=null,category=null;
String id=null;
String error = "";
int matchCount = 0;
```

```
description = request.getParameter("description");
environment = request.getParameter("environment");
category = request.getParameter("category");
```

If the user has provided at least one search parameter, connect to the database and declare a StringBuffer to hold the SQL for our search query.

```
if((description!=null)
    ||(category!=null)||(category!=null))
{
    java.sql.Connection conn = createDBConnection();
    java.sql.Statement s = conn.createStatement();

    try
    {
        StringBuffer sql = new StringBuffer();
        java.sql.ResultSet rs;
```

SQL queries use the where clause to limit the results. In this case, use the where clause with the LIKE operator to test if the parameters provided by the user match some part of the values in the database. For the description, match either the short or full description field in the database. Use | | to indicate or and && to indicate and when creating the compound where clause. For example:

```
(description like %Java% || shortdesc like %Java%)
    && environment like %linux%
```

will find all bugs that contain the word Java in either their description or short description and have the word Linux in their environment description.

```
        sql.append("select * from BUGS where ");

        if(description != null)
        {
            matchCount++;
            sql.append("(description like '%");
            sql.append(description);
            sql.append("%')");

            sql.append("|| (shortdesc like '%");
            sql.append(description);
            sql.append("%')");
        }

        if(environment != null)
        {
            if(matchCount > 0) sql.append(" && ");
            matchCount++;
            sql.append("(environment like '%");
            sql.append(environment);
            sql.append("%')");
        }
```

```java
        if(category != null)
        {
            if(matchCount > 0) sql.append(" && ");
            matchCount++;
            sql.append("(category like '%");
            sql.append(category);
            sql.append("%')");
        }
```

Next, execute the query.

```java
        matchCount = 0;
        rs = s.executeQuery(sql.toString());
</JAVA>
```

Start defining the HTML for this page. The HTML for the search results will be generated in a loop:

```html
<html>
<head>
<title> Bug Tracker - Search Results</title>
</head>
<body bgcolor="#ffffff" link="#006699" vlink="#006699">

<center>
<table border=0 cellpadding=0 cellspacing=0 width=600><tr><td>

<center>
<font face="Verdana,Arial,Helvetica" size=+1>
<a href="addbug.jhtml">Submit a Bug</a> <a href="searchbug.jhtml">Search
Bug Database</a>
</font>
</center>

<font face="Verdana,Arial,Helvetica" size=+3>
<b>
Search Results
</b>
</font>

<blockquote>
<font face="Verdana,Arial,Helvetica" size=+1>
```

Loop over the result set, creating a link to bugdetails.jhtml for each bug, with the ID parameter configured properly. Use the bug's short description as the text of the link. Keep track of the number of bugs found so that an informational message can be printed if no bugs are returned from the query.

```java
<JAVA>
while(rs.next())
{
    matchCount++;
```

```
</JAVA>

<a href="bugdetails.jhtml?id=`rs.getString("id")`">
<JAVA type="print">rs.getString("shortdesc")</JAVA>
</a></br>

<JAVA>
}

if(matchCount == 0)
{
</JAVA>
No Results Found.
<JAVA>
}
</JAVA>

</font>
</blockquote>
</td></tr></table>

</center>

</body>
</html>
```

End the try-catch block around the database access. If an error occurred, notify the user. Finally, close the database connection.

```
<JAVA>
    }
        catch (Exception exp)
        {
            error += exp.toString();
            out.println(error);
        }
        finally
        {
            try
            {
                    s.close();
                    conn.close();
            }
            catch(Exception exp)
            {
                error += exp.toString();
            }
        }
}
</JAVA>
```

Like the addbug.jhtml page, the createDBConnection method and the import statements are at the bottom of searchresults.jhtml.

```
<JAVA type=class>
private java.sql.Connection createDBConnection()
{
    java.sql.Connection conn=null;

    try
    {
        Class.forName("org.gjt.mm.mysql.Driver");
        conn = java.sql.DriverManager.getConnection("jdbc:mysql: "
                +"//127.0.0.1:3306/bugs?user=stephen");
    }
    catch(Exception exp)
    {
    }

    return conn;
}
</JAVA>

<JAVA type=import>
java.sql.*
java.util.*
org.gjt.mm.mysql.*
</JAVA>
```

Let's install the results page on your Web server and test the search engine by submitting a bug and then searching for it. Try searching on the various parameters and see what happens.

Create the Perl Search Results Script

Like the other Perl scripts, start by including the necessary libraries and creating a CGI object.

```
#!/usr/bin/perl

use DBI;
use CGI;
require "stringutils.pl";

$error = "";
$query = new CGI;
```

Declare variables to hold the number of search matches and the number of rows returned by your database query.

```
$matchCount = 0;
$rows = 0;
```

Output the HTTP header.

```
print $query->header();
```

Get the parameters submitted to this script.

```
$description = $query->param('description');
$environment = $query->param('environment');
$category = $query->param('category');
```

If any of the parameters were provided, perform the database search.

```
if($description
    ||$category||$environment)
{
```

Connect to the database.

```
$dbh = DBI->connect("dbi:mysql:bugs", "stephen", "");
```

Create an SQL statement that selects bugs from the database that match the information submitted by the client. SQL queries use the where clause to limit the results. In this case, use the where clause with the LIKE operator to test if the parameters provided by the user match some part of the values in the database. For the description, match either the short or full description field in the database. Use || to indicate or and && to indicate and when creating the compound where clause. Use the $matchCount variable to indicate if a || operator is needed.

```
$sql = "select * from BUGS where ";

if($description)
{
    $matchCount++;
    $sql .= "(description like \'%$description%\')";
    $sql .= " || (shortdesc like \'%$description%\')";
}

if($environment)
{
    if($matchCount > 0)
    {
        $sql .= " && ";
    }

    $matchCount++;
    $sql .= "(environment like \'%$environment%\')";
}

if($category)
{
    if($matchCount > 0)
    {
        $sql .= " && ";
    }

    $matchCount++;
    $sql .= "(category like \'%$category%\')";
}
```

Execute the SQL and get the results.

```
$sth = $dbh->prepare($sql);
$rows = $sth->execute();
}
```

Reset $matchCount to zero.

```
$matchCount = 0;
```

Begin to output the page. This will need two HTML sections separated by the
Perl loop that outputs the HTML for the search results.

```
print << 'EOD';

<html>
<head>
<title> Bug Tracker - Search Results</title>
</head>
<body bgcolor="#ffffff" link="#006699" vlink="#006699">

<center>
<table border=0 cellpadding=0 cellspacing=0 width=600><tr><td>

<center>
<font face="Verdana,Arial,Helvetica" size=+1>
<a href="/cgi-bin/addbug.pl">Submit a Bug</a> <a href="/cgi-
bin/searchbug.pl">Search Bug Database</a>
</font>
</center>

<font face="Verdana,Arial,Helvetica" size=+3>
<b>
Search Results
</b>
</font>

<blockquote>
<font face="Verdana,Arial,Helvetica" size=+1>
EOD
```

Conclude the first half of the HTML, and don't forget to put a blank line after
the EOD. Use a for loop to display the search results. Keep track of the number
of results in $matchCount. For each bug found, display its short description as
a link to the bug details page for that bug.

```
for($i=0;$i<$rows;$i++)
{
    $matchCount++;

    ($id,$shortdesc,$descirption,$workaround,$date,$category,$environment)
     = $sth->fetchrow_array();

    print "<a href=\"/cgi-bin/bugdetails.pl?id=$id\">$shortdesc</a><br>"
}
```

If no bugs were found, let the user know with a simple message.

```
if($matchCount == 0)
{
    print "No results found."
}
```

Finally, output the remainder of the HTML document.

```
print << 'EOD';

</font>
</blockquote>
</td></tr></table>

</center>


</body>
</html>

EOD
```

Be sure to include a blank line after the EOD tag. Now install this final script and test the entire project.

Step 7: Test the Bug Tracking System

Regardless of the version you chose to use, Perl or Java, testing the tracking system should be about the same.

First, make sure that all the files are installed and that your database install script worked. Then access the index.html page for this project.

Try to submit a bug. If you can't even access the add bug page, then that page has a problem. The Java version should send compile errors to you, while the Perl version will just fail. In the Perl case, try running it from the command line. The CGI module should request input from you if the program is working. If not, then you will get an error message. Fix errors before proceeding.

If the script doesn't produce an error, but it can't get the ID or the insertion fails, this indicates a database connectivity problem. Check your database permissions and the user name/password you used in your JHTML or Perl files.

Once you can submit bugs, you should be redirected to the details page. Again, if an error occurs use the error message to debug that script.

Add a few bugs with different descriptions, environments, and categories. Then try to search for these bugs. Again, if the results page fails, use the error messages it generates to fix it. For the Perl version, try running it on the command line to fix it.

Throughout your test, you will be making sure that the links point to the appropriate URLs. If a link has a problem, check your installation and links.

Wrap Up

Once you complete this project you should see the ease with which Java and a relational database can be combined to create a powerful Web application. Leveraging the scripting engine from Project 2 allows you to create dynamic Web pages quickly, while still providing the full power of Java. Perl, on the other hand, is another portable and popular solution for Web programming. Both allow you to create programs quickly. Using scripts that combine form handling and dynamic HTML creation is a great way to organize code, centralize possible bugs, and reduce maintenance costs.

To test your understanding of the concepts presented in this project, you can add some new features to the project. Try to allow the user to suggest workarounds when he or she votes. Another feature would be managing any weird characters in the strings submitted by the user. For simplicity, this project was programmed to pass these characters through and may cause the SQL code to fail. Finally, you could customize the tracker to meet the specific needs of your projects, including project-by-project tracking, custom categories for bugs, and a report mechanism for printing all bugs with a specific severity.

CORBA-based Course Registration Framework and Server

Project Objectives

In this project, you will learn how to:

- Create a defining interface for CORBA
- Access objects using CORBA
- Interoperate between Java and C++ with distributed objects

 ## YOU WILL NEED

- ✔ The JDK 1.2, also called Java 2 (includes the CORBA packages; you can use 1.1 but you will need to include the packages manually)
- ✔ A Web server (I used Apache)
- ✔ Java programming experience; C++ experience is helpful
- ✔ Experience with Web programming, like CGI, is helpful
- ✔ Experience with SQL is helpful
- ✔ The MySQL database
- ✔ A JDBC driver to connect to the database
- ✔ The MICO and JacORB ORBs (discussed in detail later)

Although this project is implemented using MySQL, you could port it to other databases available on Linux, including Postgres, mSQL, and others. Also, the two ORBs used are representative of the freely available Linux ORBs. You can use these or a commercial ORB in actual products. Installation of the two ORBs used here is discussed in the Appendix. Keep in mind that each ORB, as discussed in this chapter, may provide different interfaces; you may need to change the code discussed here to match your implementation.

Memo

To: Stephen
From: Training

Stephen, we want to put our course registration system online.
Can you create a prototype for managing courses? We need to
track the scheduled classes for each course and the students in
each class. Also, we are going to want to use a variety of tools
with this system, so we want to make the information available
on the network.

Training

Memo

To: Training
From: Stephen

Training, I have attached a prototype course registration
framework. The framework stores data in a relational database
and makes the information available as objects using CORBA. I
have included a sample client of the framework that displays
the available courses using C++. Let me know what else I can
do to help.

Stephen

About This Project

The Common Object Request Broker Architecture (CORBA) is a powerful tool for network communication in programs, especially due to its language-independent nature. In this project you create both Java and C++ programs that access the registration server. One warning before you get started: The project is focused on the CORBA interactions and doesn't create a lot of tools for users to manage courses. Only a report generator is provided with the project. You will need to create other tools, like a registration application, if you want to use the framework in a production environment.

This project creates a simple course registration framework. The framework provides several objects that model the course registration process. Once implemented, the framework can be used to build a server that makes objects available via a CORBA ORB. The actual registration data is stored in a database by the CORBA objects to make them persistent.

Basic Concepts and Design

The Common Object Request Broker Architecture, CORBA, defines a powerful language- and platform-neutral technology for distributed objects. Distributed objects are objects that reside in one program and can send messages to objects in another program. The real power of CORBA over other technologies discussed in other chapters, such as RMI, is that CORBA supports multiple implementation languages. Therefore, a C++ program can send messages to objects in a Java program. This project demonstrates Java-to-C++ interoperability. The CORBA architecture defines a number of components used to implement the communication between objects. These components include the following:

- ORBs to manage communication
- IIOP for communication between ORBs
- Interfaces to define the messages that can be sent
- Skeletons and stubs for implementing the interprocess communication
- Services for accsessing and extending ORB functionality

At the center of the CORBA specification is the idea of an *Object Request Broker (ORB)*. The ORB mediates messages between objects. The ORB implements all of the code to hide the work of interprocess communication from the program so that the programmer can think about sending messages to objects and not about network connectivity issues or marshalling and decoding data.

ORBs can be implemented in a number of ways. At the highest level, the ORB can be implemented as a set of functions/objects included in the CORBA application. One level down from the applications that use CORBA, an ORB can be implemented as a service process. In this case, a client library allows the programs to interact with the ORB, but the actual message delivery is managed at the server process level. Finally, ORBs can be implemented as services embedded in the operating system. By making it part of the OS, the ORB can optimize message delivery. It is also possible for the ORB to leverage kernel-level security information to make message passing more secure.

In all cases, the programmer using an ORB expects the ORB vendor to provide a library that can be used to interact with the ORB and therefore with other objects. The ORB vendor is also expected to provide the external tools necessary to develop an application with that ORB. One of these tools in particular, the IDL compiler, is discussed in more detail later in this chapter.

In order to get a feeling for what the CORBA architecture looks like in action, let's look at a couple of examples. Figure 4.1 shows two messaging examples. The first shows a message coming from an object in Program1 sending a message, via CORBA, to another object in Program1. Notice that the ORB's client library is described by two boxes, the *stub* and *skeleton*. The stub and skeleton represent the library code used to encode and decode the messages sent through the ORB. In the case of a local message, the ORB will do its best to optimize away the interprocess communication and make this work like a straight message call.

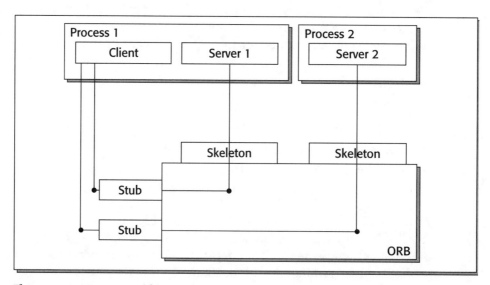

Figure 4.1   Messages within an ORB.

The second example in Figure 4.1 is a message from Process1 to Process2, where both use the same ORB. This might mean that they use the same ORB library or that the messages pass through a server process. In either case, the same stub and skeleton architecture from the first example is used to control communication with the ORB.

The third example of how CORBA can be used is shown in Figure 4.2. In this example, the objects are not only in separate processes, they use different ORBs to handle their interprocess communication. Now the ORBs need a way to communication with each other. The solution for this communication is a protocol called the *General Inter-ORB Protocol (GIOP)*. This protocol defines a standard way for ORBs to communicate. An implementation of GIOP called the *Internet Inter-ORB Protocol* (IIOP) is used when the ORBs are networked via TCP/IP. Most new ORB implementations support IIOP.

NOTE

As of this writing, Sun has released early-access versions of an RMI over IIOP technology that will allow RMI programs to interact via IIOP with CORBA programs. Check java.sun.com for the latest news on this technology.

A component called the Object Adaptor handles the communication with the ORB. The stub and skeleton from Figure 4.2 are designed to work with the

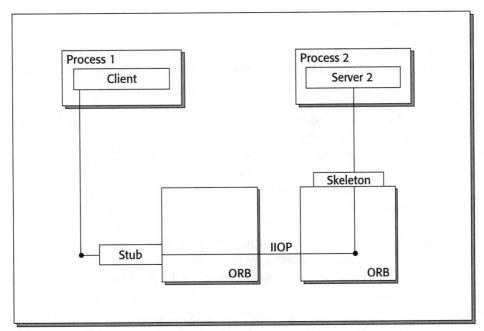

Figure 4.2   Messages between ORBs.

Object Adaptor to get their work done. In this project, you will see two references to the Object Adaptor. First, the string BOA refers to the basic object adaptor. This is the standard adaptor used for messaging within the ORB. Second, the string POA refers to the portable object adaptor. This adaptor makes sure that the objects registered with it will be available to other ORBs via IIOP. MICO, the C++ ORB used in this project, relies mainly on the BOA, while JacORB, the Java ORB used in this project, has adopted the POA convention.

In order for two objects to communicate, they must agree on an interface for defining the messages that can be sent, their arguments, and the return values. In Java, these interfaces would be defined as Java interfaces, or simply as the methods defined in a class. In C, an interface would be defined in a header file, as a collection of types and functions. In ObjectiveC they are defined as a protocol. Because CORBA has always been designed to be language neutral, it was not possible to create a language-dependent interface definition. Instead, the creators of the CORBA standard, a group called the *Object Management Group (OMG)*, defined a new language called the *Interface Definition Language (IDL)*.

IDL can be used to define an interface, the methods the interface contains, and the specification for those methods. Interfaces can also define some datatypes and even relationships between interfaces. Although a complete introduction to IDL is not possible here, this project does define a number of constructs in IDL and provides you with a basic understanding of what it does and how.

 NOTE

For more information on CORBA and IDL, take a look at *Instant CORBA* by Robert Orfali, Dan Harkey, and Jeri Edwards (Wiley, 1997), and *Java Programming with CORBA, Third Edition* by Andreas Vogel (Wiley, 2000).

Developers use IDL to define the interface between their programs. But the programs aren't written in IDL; they are written in Java, C++, or another language that has ORBs to support it. That's a very telling phrase, "support it." One of the jobs of an ORB is to provide the tools to map IDL onto a programming language and, in the process, create any template code necessary to communicate with the ORB via the Object Adaptor. JacORB, for example, provides tools only for converting IDL to Java. JacORB, in its current state, can be used only by Java programmers. Other ORBs support different languages, and some support multiple languages. MICO, the other ORB used in this project, supports C++, but a Perl mapping is also available for MICO from a persistent Perl programmer.

To give you an idea of how the IDL gets mapped into a language, let's take a quick look at the IDL-to-Java mapping.

- IDL modules map to Java packages.
- Interfaces map to a Java interface, as well as the stubs and skeletons.
- Standard data types map directly (strings to Strings, sequences to Arrays).
- Enumerations map to classes.
- Operations map to methods.

The people who defined the mapping tried to provide the user of that map with familiar constructs for generic definitions.

That brings us to the point where we need to write code. There are two participants in the CORBA relationship: *senders* and *receivers*. The message senders use interfaces. The message receivers implement interfaces. In most cases, the sender is called the *client* and the receiver is called the *server*. Keep in mind that this use of server and client doesn't say anything about the computer itself. For example, the server could well be a Palm Pilot program while the client is the desktop machine.

Let's look at the interface implementors first. The implementors' job is to compile the IDL to their implementation language and make sure that all of the interfaces are implemented correctly. To implement an interface you need to know what your ORB wants you to do. Often, an implementor subclasses a generated class and implements the interface methods as defined in the generated code. Specifically, using JacORB, you subclass a generated class and implement methods from a Java interface that corresponds to the IDL interface. Once the interface is implemented, the server programmer also has to write a program that creates objects and makes them available to clients via the ORB.

Clients that use an interface rely on stubs or dynamic invocation to send messages to the ORB. The client has to know how to use the ORB's libraries to connect to the server object. Once connected, the server object acts as the interface that defined it so the client just uses regular messaging to interact with it. Keep in mind that although the networking underlying CORBA is transparent, it is still there. When you use CORBA or any other interprocess communication there is the possibility of exceptions that don't exist in a single-program environment. For example, a mad axe man could chop the cable connecting the two machines, resulting in a loss of connection.

Newer CORBA standards, 2.0 and above, and the related ORBs support the idea of dynamic interfaces and a dynamic messaging model. Dynamic invocation, as it is called, is a standard set of IDL interfaces that the ORB vendor implements. Using these interfaces, the client can discover information about the server and send messages to the server without the intermediate IDL. Dynamic invocation does add some startup cost to a program, but it can be optimized by the ORB to provide reasonable ongoing performance.

That leaves just one key component in the client/server relationship to discuss. How does the client find the server object? In most cases, a service called the naming service is used to perform this rendezvous. The server registers with the name service, associating an object with a name, much like the service implemented in Project 1. The client uses the name to locate the server object. Some ORBs also provide a trading service that works like naming, only instead of a name a role is used to identify an object. For example, with names you might look for regserver; with trading you might look for a printmanager.

In order for the naming to work, the ORB associates a unique internal reference with each object. This reference is loaded into the naming server. It is also possible to write these references to disk or make them available on a Web server. The server writes the reference to disk and the client reads the reference and uses it to connect to the server. You will use this technique to create the IIOP connection between your ORBs in this project. Because two ORBs are used, they don't share the name server and require this intermediate step.

And that's CORBA. You'll find that ORBs can provide other standard services such as transaction management and object persistence. But, although standard, these services are not required, and many ORBs implement only a few of the available services. While you are studying the project, keep in mind the following definitions:

CORBA. An architecture for networking objects.

ORB. A server or library that allows objects to communicate between programs.

IDL. A language for defining interfaces between objects.

POA and BOA. Adaptors for talking to your ORB's client library.

MICO. The C++-based ORB used in this project.

JacORB. The Java-based ORB used in this project.

For this project, you will create a number of programs. First, the RegServer provides an object interface to a course registration framework. The framework defines objects that model the information in a registration database. Clients can access the server and through it obtain information about available courses, as well as register for courses. At the heart of the registration framework, pictured in Figure 4.3 is the Registrar. The Registrar maintains a list of available courses and can be used to add courses to the system. Each course keeps a list of *Gigs*. A Gig is a single scheduled class for that course. The Gigs keep track of the students registered for that class. Each student can provide his or her name and e-mail address.

Once the server is implemented, you create a client to test it and one to generate a report. All of the code in this project is Java, except the report generator, which is written in C++ to demonstrate the interoperability of CORBA.

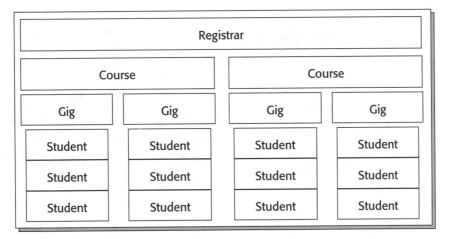

Figure 4.3 Course registration framework.

Step 1: Create the Database

The database for this project requires three tables. The first, COURSES, stores the name and number of the classes for which students can register. The second, GIGS, stores information about the date and location for the scheduled occurrences of a course. The third and final table, REG, stores information about the students registered for a particular Gig. The columns for each table are listed in Tables 4.1 through 4.3.

Table 4.1   COURSES Table

COLUMN NAME	DESCRIPTION
course_num	An ID number for the course
name	The name used to describe the course to students

Table 4.2   GIGS Table

COLUMN NAME	DESCRIPTION
id	A unique ID for this Gig, created by the database
scheduled_date	The date for which the class is scheduled
location	Where this class will occur
cancelled	A flag indicating if the class is cancelled: 1 if cancelled, 0 otherwise
course_num	The course associated with this class

Table 4.3 REG Table

COLUMN NAME	DESCRIPTION
`student_name`	The student's name
`student_email`	The student's e-mail address
`registration`	The date that the student registered
`cancelled`	The date that the student cancelled, or empty if the student is still registered
`gig_id`	The ID for the class for which the student registered

For my implementation of this project, I have used MySQL for the database and the JDBC driver used in previous projects to connect to it. The database itself is called courses and was created using the command:

```
mysqladmin create courses
```

Depending on your installation, you may need to include user name and password information for this step.

Once the database is created, add the tables using the Java program shown next. This program connects to the database, removes existing tables, adds the new tables, and disconnects. The connection information is stored in a separate properties file so that it is easy to update without editing and recompiling the CoursesDBBuilder class. This file looks something like this:

```
jdbc.driver=org.gjt.mm.mysql.Driver
jdbc.url=jdbc:mysql://127.0.0.1:3306/courses
jdbc.user=stephen
jdbc.password=
```

When the program is run, it expects the name of this file to be db.properties and for the file to be in the CLASSPATH.

Start the program off by importing the appropriate packages and declaring a class called CourseDBBuilder with a main method.

```
import java.sql.*;
import java.util.*;
import java.io.*;

public class CoursesDBBuilder
{
    public static void main(String[] args)
    {
        System.out.println("CoursesDBBuilder starting");
```

Surround the entire main method in a try-catch block to handle any exceptions.

```
try
{
```

Declare a variable to hold the resource bundle and an input stream to read it.

```
ResourceBundle resources;            InputStream in = null;
```

Read in the Properties file.

```
in =
ClassLoader.getSystemResourceAsStream("db.properties");

resources = new PropertyResourceBundle(in);

in.close();
```

Load the JDBC driver class, and connect to the database.

```
Class.forName(resources.getString("jdbc.driver"));
System.out.println("Loaded the JDBC driver");

Connection conn = DriverManager.getConnection(
                    resources.getString("jdbc.url")
        ,resources.getString("jdbc.user")
        ,resources.getString("jdbc.password"));

System.out.println("Connected to DB");
```

Turn off auto commit so that all of the database operations happen in the same transaction.

```
conn.setAutoCommit(false);
```

Create a statement that can be used to issue commands across the connection.

```
Statement s = conn.createStatement();
```

Create the COURSES table by first dropping it to get rid of existing data and then creating it.

```
try
{
    s.executeUpdate("drop table COURSES");
}
catch(SQLException exp)
{
    System.out.println("Already dropped COURSES");
}

s.execute("CREATE TABLE COURSES(course_num varchar(64)"
                +", name varchar(255))");
System.out.println("Created table COURSES");
```

Create the GIGs table, again, dropping it first to remove existing data.

```
try
```

```
        {
            s.executeUpdate("drop table GIGS");
        }
        catch(SQLException exp)
        {
            System.out.println("Already dropped GIGS");
        }

        s.execute("CREATE TABLE GIGS("
                        +"id int AUTO_INCREMENT PRIMARY KEY"
                        +", scheduled_date varchar(255)"
                        +", location varchar(255)"
                        +", course_num varchar(64)"
                        +", cancelled int)");
        System.out.println("Created table GIGS");
```

Create the REG table.

```
        try
        {
            s.executeUpdate("drop table REG");
        }
        catch(SQLException exp)
        {
            System.out.println("Already dropped REG");
        }

        s.execute("CREATE TABLE REG(student_name varchar(255)""
                        +"",student_email varchar(255)"
                        +", gig_id int"
                        +",registration varchar(64) ""
                        +"",cancelled varchar(64))");
        System.out.println("Created table REG");
```

Close the statement, commit the current transaction, and close the connection.

```
        s.close();
        System.out.println("Closed statement");

        conn.commit();
        conn.close();
        System.out.println("Committed and closed connection");

    }
```

Clean up the try-catch block.

```
    catch(Throwable e)
    {
        System.out.println("exception thrown:");

        if (e instanceof SQLException)
            printSQLError((SQLException)e);
        else
            e.printStackTrace();
```

```
        }
        System.out.println("DBBuilder finished");
    }
    static void printSQLError(SQLException e)
    {
        while (e != null) {
            System.out.println(e.toString());
            e = e.getNextException();
        }
    }
}
```

Before you run the server, you will need to compile and run this program to build the database.

Step 2: Define the IDL Interfaces

You need four IDL interfaces for this project, one for each component in the registration framework. To group these, create an IDL module called course_registration. This module maps to a Java package and a C++ namespace. This file is available on the CD-ROM under the name course_registration.idl.

```
module course_registration
{
```

The Student interface provides accessor methods, methods that return the value of a property, for student information. You might want to add other accessors to this interface to support address, phone number, and other information.

```
interface Student
{
    string getName();
    string getEmail();
    boolean isCancelled();
};
```

The Gig interface returns a list of students. To make this list more accessible, define a sequence type that stores students. This is an IDL construct that maps onto a Java array (Student[]) and in C++ generates a template-based collection class that acts like an array.

```
    typedef sequence <Student> students;
```

The Gig interface provides accessors and methods for getting all of the students. Notice that the interface uses the student's data type defined previously. Also, the Gig provides methods to register and unregister a student. Registration causes data to be inserted in the database. Unregistering a student will just as-sign a date to the cancelled field in the REG table, but it doesn't remove the reg-istration entry in the database. This ensures that the administrator can tell if a student was ever registered and when the registration was cancelled.

```
interface Gig
{
    boolean isCancelled();
    void cancel();

    long getId();
    string getDate();
    string getLocation();

    students getStudents();
    void register(in string name,in string email);
    void unregister(in string email);
};
```

Declare a sequence type, using the sequence key word and <> operator, to hold Gig objects. Name the sequence Gigs.

```
    typedef sequence <Gig> gigs;
```

The Course interface uses this new type to return a list of the Gigs for a course. There are also accessors for getting the name and number for a course, as well as methods for adding Gigs and removing them.

```
interface Course
{
    gigs getGigs();
    Gig addGig(in string date,in string location);
    void removeGig(in long id);

    string getName();
    string getNumber();
};
```

The final interface, Registrar, also requires a sequence type definition to pro-vide access to all of the available courses. The Registrar also provides methods for getting a course by number and adding courses to the system.

```
    typedef sequence <Course> courses;

interface Registrar
{
    courses getCourses();
    Course getCourse(in string number);
    Course addCourse(in string number,in string name);
};

};
```

This framework should provide a basic structure for creating a course registration system. A production system will require more functionality and data. For example, student phone numbers should be maintained, and a way to remove courses from the system, or at least a way to mark them as deprecated, could be necessary.

Once defined, these interfaces need to be compiled into Java and C++. Install MICO and JacORB as described in the Appendix. Then run the IDL compiler for each on the course_registration.idl file. To run JacORB I used:

```
> /stephen/JacORB/bin/idl course_registration.idl
```

This creates a directory called course_registration that corresponds to the course_registration package. All of the files that the ORB needs are generated in this director including the Java interface that corresponds to the Registrar, Student, Gig, and Course IDL interfaces.

For MICO I ran:

```
> source /usr/local/lib/mico-setup.sh
> /usr/local/bin/idl course_regisration.idl
```

Notice that MICO requires some setup for the environment before you run programs. If you decide to use MICO extensively, you may want to make this step automatic for your login. Running the MICO IDL compiler generates two files: course_registration.h and course_registration.cc. These files contain all of the C++ definitions required by MICO to implement the IDL interfaces.

Step 3: Implement the Registration Framework

Next you need to implement the IDL interfaces. For consistency, I used Java to implement these interfaces, although you could also implement them in C++ to use the MICO ORB. In either case, you will need to include the generated code and subclass generated classes that represent the basis for each IDL interface.

Implement Student

In the case of JacORB, a class called POA_Student was created for the Student interface. Each of the other interfaces generated a similar class. To implement Student, subclass POA_Student. For convention, name the new class StudentImp, for Student implementation.

```
package course_registration;

import course_registration.*;
public class StudentImp extends POA_Student
{
```

The student objects cache data from the database about a student. Use local variables to store the name, e-mail, and cancellation date.

```
protected String name;
protected String email;
protected String cancelled;
```

Next, provide a constructor for StudentImp that takes the three data items, name, e-mail, and cancelled, as arguments.

```
public StudentImp(String n,String e,String c)
{
    name = n;
    email = e;
    cancelled = c;
}
```

To help with debugging, implement toString to print out the instance variables.

```
public String toString()
{
    return name+" "+email+" "+isCancelled();
}
```

Provide accessors for each of the instance variables like the ones below.

```
public String getName()
{
    return name;
}

public String getEmail()
{
    return email;
}

public void setCancelled(String s)
{
    cancelled = s;
}

public boolean isCancelled()
{
    boolean retVal = false;

    if((cancelled != null)&&(cancelled.length()>0)) retVal = true;

    return retVal;
}
}
```

Student is the easiest implementation because it doesn't return any objects and it doesn't need to communicate with the database.

Implement Gig

The implementation for Gig, described next, is perhaps the largest in this chapter. Unlike Student, Gig does include returning objects and communicating with the database, so it will add a couple of new concepts to this discussion. Start the GigImp class by declaring that it is a member of the course_registration package. Import the other classes in the framework as well as the java.util and java.sql packages.

```
package course_registration;

import course_registration.*;
import java.util.*;
import java.sql.*;
```

Like StudentImp, GigImp extends a class generated by the JacORB IDL to Java compiler. In this case the class is called POA_Gig.

```
public class GigImp extends POA_Gig
{
```

Gigs keep track of their course, date, location, ID, cancelled flag, and students. For convenience, students are tracked in a hashtable with the e-mail as key and StudentImp objects as the values.

```
    protected CourseImp course;
    protected String date;
    protected String location;
    protected int id;
    protected boolean cancelled;
    protected Hashtable students;
```

Next, provide a constructor for each Gig that accepts values for all of the instance variables except the list of students. The Gig will retrieve this list from the database.

```
    public GigImp(int id,String date,String location,CourseImp
course,boolean cancelled)
    {
        this.id = id;
        this.date = date;
        this.location = location;
        this.course = course;
        this.cancelled = cancelled;
    }
```

The accessors for the Gigs cancelled attribute are short and long. Getting the cancelled value just returns a boolean flag. Cancelling a Gig, as shown below, requires that you connect to the database and update the Gig table to show that the Gig is cancelled. The instance variable cancelled should also be set to true so that it is not necessary to go to the database to check if the Gig is cancelled. This caching does have the side effect that the courses database shouldn't be changed to another program while the registration framework is in use because the caches will become invalid.

To improve performance, all of the registration objects share a database connection. This connection is held by the registrar object. So the line:

```
course.getRegistrar().getConnection()
```

shown in the code that follows returns a shared database connection. The registrar also keeps track of a connection to the ORB used in later methods.

```
public boolean isCancelled()
{
    return cancelled;
}

public void cancel()
{
    Connection conn;
    Statement s=null;

    cancelled = true;

    try
    {
        conn = course.getRegistrar().getConnection();

        s = conn.createStatement();

        s.execute("update GIGS set cancelled=1 where id="+id);
    }
    catch(Exception e)
    {

    }
    finally
    {
        try
        {
            if(s!=null) s.close();
        }
        catch(Exception ignore)
        {
        }
    }
}
```

To get the ID, date, and location for this Gig, provide accessor methods.

```
public int getId()
{
    return id;
```

```
    }

    public String getDate()
    {
        return date;
    }

    public String getLocation()
    {
        return location;
    }
```

The JacORB IDL compiler maps the sequences you defined into Java arrays. The getStudents method returns an array of students. The first time this method is called, the student information is loaded from the database and cached as StudentImp objects in the hashtable called students. Unfortunately, that doesn't mean that you can create an array with the StudentImp objects and return them. This method introduces one of the complexities of implementing CORBA programs. When you want to refer to a server object, in a way that will support CORBA messaging, you must acquire your reference to that object from the ORB. In other words, although the Gig tracks StudentImp objects that it loads from the database, it must get the references from these objects from the ORB before returning them to the client. To make sure that you perform this conversion, the StudentImp object doesn't even implement the Student interface so the compiler will not allow a StudentImp object in the Student[] array.

```
    public Student[] getStudents()
    {
        Student[] retVal = null;
        Enumeration elements;
        Vector holder = new Vector();
        int i,max;
```

In order to perform the StudentImp to Student conversion, you need to use the JacORBs portable object adaptor, POA, and an object called a *tie* that relates implementation and reference objects. Declare a variable called POA to store your reference to the POA. Also declare a variable called pct to represent a tie between the StudentImp and Student classes. This tie was generated for you by the IDL compiler.

```
        org.omg.PortableServer.POA poa=null;
        POA_Student_tie pct;
```

The POA is available by name from the ORB. Get the ORB from the registrar object and ask it to find a reference for the RootPOA object. The syntax for this step involves a couple of important concepts. First, the ORB is responsible for resolving object references. Second, the references that the ORB returns are generically typed, so helper classes are used to narrow the reference to a specific type. In this case the POAHelper class narrows the generic reference to the

POA type. These helpers are either provided by the ORB or generated when the IDL is compiled. For example, a StudentHelper class was generated to narrow arbitrary references to Student objects. In Java, narrowing is basically type casting with some exception handling thrown in. The narrow process will also perform any necessary setup for the generated classes. All of these helpers are available on the CD-ROM. Take a look at them if you are interested in how narrowing works, as well as the other methods provided.

```
try
{
    poa =org.omg.PortableServer.POAHelper.narrow(
        course.getRegistrar()
                .getOrb().resolve_initial_references("RootPOA"));
}
catch(Exception exp)
{
    poa = null;
}
```

Next, use the shared database connection to get all of the students and add them to the hashtable as StudentImp objects.

```
if(students == null)
{
    Connection conn;
    Statement s=null;
    ResultSet rs;

    try
    {
        conn = course.getRegistrar().getConnection();

        s = conn.createStatement();

        rs = s.executeQuery("select * from REG where"
                +" gig_id="+id);

        students = new Hashtable();

        while(rs.next())
        {
            students.put(rs.getString("student_email")
                ,new StudentImp(
                    rs.getString("student_name")
                ,rs.getString("student_email")
                ,rs.getString("cancelled")));
        }
```

Iterate over the hashtable and add the StudentImp objects to a vector for further processing.

```
        elements = students.elements();
```

```
while(elements.hasMoreElements())
     holder.addElement(elements.nextElement());

max = holder.size();
```

Using the vector as measure, create an array to hold the students, and return them.

```
retVal = new Student[max];
```

For each StudentImp object in the holder vector, create a POA_Student_tie and set the tie's ORB. This tie generates a reference to the StudentImp as seen by the ORB. Narrow the reference, and put it in the array. This way the array stores references to the StudentImp that can be passed to the client and used to message the server.

```
for(i=0;i<max;i++)
{
    pct =
     new POA_Student_tie((StudentImp)holder.elementAt(i));
    pct._orb(course.getRegistrar().getOrb());

    retVal[i] =
StudentHelper.narrow(poa.servant_to_reference(pct));
    }
}
catch(Exception exp)
{
    students = null;
    retVal = null;
}
```

Close the database statement when you're done.

```
finally
{
    try
    {
        if(s!=null) s.close();
    }
    catch(Exception ignore)
    {
    }
}
}
```

If the students hashtable is already built, you create the array of students using the ties to convert implementation objects to references.

```
else
{
    elements = students.elements();

    while(elements.hasMoreElements())
```

```
                        holder.addElement(elements.nextElement());

            max = holder.size();

            retVal = new Student[max];

            for(i=0;i<max;i++)
            {
                try
                {
                    pct =
                     new POA_Student_tie((StudentImp)holder.elementAt(i));
                    pct._orb(course.getRegistrar().getOrb());

                    retVal[i] =
                        StudentHelper.narrow(poa.servant_to_reference(pct));
                }
                catch(Exception exp)
                {
                    break;
                }
            }
        }
```

Finally, return the array of Student reference to the caller.

```
            return retVal;
    }
```

Implement the register method, shown next, to add a student to the students table and to insert the student's information into the REG table of the database. Use the getStudents method to initialize the students cache if the table has not been loaded yet.

```
    public void register(String name,String email)
    {
        Connection conn;
        Statement s=null;
        StringBuffer sql = new StringBuffer();

        if(students == null) getStudents();

        try
        {
            conn = course.getRegistrar().getConnection();

            s = conn.createStatement();

            sql.append("insert into REG ");
        sql.append("(student_name,student_email,gig_id");
        sql.append(",registration,cancelled)");
        sql.append(" values ('");
            sql.append(name);
            sql.append("','");
            sql.append(email);
```

```
        sql.append("',");
        sql.append(id);
        sql.append(",'");
        sql.append(new java.util.Date());
        sql.append("','')");

        s.execute(sql.toString());

        students.put(email,new StudentImp(name,email,""));
    }
    catch(Exception e)
    {
    }
    finally
    {
        try
        {
            if(s!=null) s.close();
        }
        catch(Exception ignore)
        {
        }
    }
}
```

To unregister a student, first make sure that the students table is initialized. Then update the StudentImp object and update the database by adding a value for cancelDate to the appropriate row in the REG table.

```
public void unregister(String email)
{
    Connection conn;
    Statement s=null;
    StudentImp student;
    String cancelDate;

    if(students == null) getStudents();

    try
    {
        conn = course.getRegistrar().getConnection();

        student = (StudentImp) students.get(email);

        if(student != null)
        {
            cancelDate = (new java.util.Date()).toString();

            student.setCancelled(cancelDate);
            s = conn.createStatement();

            s.execute("update REG set cancelled='"+cancelDate
                +"' where student_email='"+email+"' and gig_id="+id);
        }
```

```
        }
        catch(Exception e)
        {

        }
        finally
        {
            try
            {
                if(s!=null) s.close();
            }
            catch(Exception ignore)
            {
            }
        }
    }
}
```

That concludes the implementation of GigImp. This class is a good example of
how enterprise-level programming often involves combining several technologies, in this case CORBA and database access.

Implement Course

The implementation for Course, shown next, is similar to the implementation
of Gig. The same techniques are used to keep a cached list of the Course's Gigs
and to convert the cached GigImp objects to Gig references for returning to
the client. In this case, the CourseImp class is implemented as a subclass of
POA_Course.

```java
package course_registration;

import course_registration.*;
import java.util.*;
import java.sql.*;

public class CourseImp extends POA_Course
{
    protected RegistrarImp registrar;
    protected Vector gigs;
    protected String name;
    protected String number;

    public CourseImp(String number,String name,RegistrarImp reg)
    {
        this.name = name;
        this.number = number;
        this.registrar = reg;
    }
```

The getGigs method uses the database to get a list of the Gigs for this course. Then these Gigs are converted to GigImp objects. Finally, these implementation objects are converted to references for use by the client and returned.

```
public Gig[] getGigs()
{
    Gig[] retVal = null;
    Enumeration elements;
    Vector holder = new Vector();
    int i,max;
    org.omg.PortableServer.POA poa=null;
    POA_Gig_tie pct;

    try
    {
        poa =org.omg.PortableServer.POAHelper.narrow(
                        getRegistrar().getOrb()
                        .resolve_initial_references("RootPOA"));
    }
    catch(Exception exp)
    {
        poa = null;
    }

    if(gigs == null)
    {
        Connection conn;
        Statement s=null;
        ResultSet rs;
        GigImp newGig;

        try
        {
            conn = getRegistrar().getConnection();

            s = conn.createStatement();

            rs = s.executeQuery("select * from GIGS where "
                        + "course_num='"+number+"'");

            gigs = new Vector();

            while(rs.next())
            {
                newGig = new GigImp(rs.getInt("id")
                 ,rs.getString("scheduled_date")
                 ,rs.getString("location")
                 ,this
                 ,(rs.getInt("cancelled")==0)?false:true);

                gigs.add(newGig);
            }

            elements = gigs.elements();
```

```
            while(elements.hasMoreElements())
              holder.addElement(elements.nextElement());

            max = holder.size();

            retVal = new Gig[max];

            for(i=0;i<max;i++)
            {
                pct = new POA_Gig_tie((GigImp)holder.elementAt(i));
                pct._orb(getRegistrar().getOrb());

                retVal[i] =
                  GigHelper.narrow(poa.servant_to_reference(pct));
            }
        }
        catch(Exception exp)
        {
            gigs = null;
            retVal = null;
        }
        finally
        {
            try
            {
                if(s!=null) s.close();
            }
            catch(Exception ignore)
            {
            }
        }
    }
    else
    {
        elements = gigs.elements();

        while(elements.hasMoreElements())
          holder.addElement(elements.nextElement());

        max = holder.size();

        retVal = new Gig[max];

        for(i=0;i<max;i++)
        {
            try
            {
                pct = new POA_Gig_tie((GigImp)holder.elementAt(i));
                pct._orb(getRegistrar().getOrb());

                retVal[i] =
                  GigHelper.narrow(poa.servant_to_reference(pct));
            }
            catch(Exception exp)
            {
```

```
                            break;
                    }
            }
    }

    return retVal;
}
```

To add a Gig, the addGig method inserts the date and location for the new Gig into the database. Then a GigImp object is created for the new Gig. This GigImp is converted to a reference for use by the client and returned.

```
public Gig addGig(String date,String location)
{
    Connection conn;
    Statement s=null;
    StringBuffer sql = new StringBuffer();
    int id=0;
    GigImp retVal = null;
    Gig realRetVal = null;
    org.omg.PortableServer.POA poa=null;
    POA_Gig_tie pct;

    try
    {
        poa =org.omg.PortableServer.POAHelper.narrow(
        getRegistrar().getOrb().resolve_initial_references("RootPOA"));
    }
    catch(Exception exp)
    {
        poa = null;
    }

    if(gigs == null) getGigs();

    try
    {
        conn = getRegistrar().getConnection();

        s = conn.createStatement();

        sql.append("insert into GIGS ")
        sql.append("(id,scheduled_date,location")
        sql.append(",course_num,cancelled) values (null,'");
        sql.append(date);
        sql.append("','");
        sql.append(location);
        sql.append("','");
        sql.append(number);
        sql.append("',0)");

        if(s.executeUpdate(sql.toString()) != 0)
        {
            if(s instanceof org.gjt.mm.mysql.Statement)
```

```
                        {
                            id = (int)
                              ((org.gjt.mm.mysql.Statement)s).getLastInsertID();
                        }
                        else
                        {
                            throw new Exception("Couldn't get id.");
                        }
                    }
                    retVal = new GigImp(id
                        ,date
                        ,location
                        ,this
                        ,false);

                    gigs.addElement(retVal);
                }
                catch(Exception e)
                {
                    retVal = null;
                }
                finally
                {
                    try
                    {
                    if(s!=null) s.close();
                    }
                    catch(Exception ignore)
                    {
                    }
                }

                try
                {
                    pct = new POA_Gig_tie(retVal);
                    pct._orb(getRegistrar().getOrb());

                    realRetVal = GigHelper.narrow(poa.servant_to_reference(pct));
                }
                catch(Exception exp)
                {
                    realRetVal = null;
                }

                return realRetVal;
        }
```

When a Gig is removed from the course it is deleted from the database and
from the vector stored in the Gigs instance variable.

```
public void removeGig(int id)
    {
```

```java
Connection conn;
Statement s=null;
int i,max=0;
Gig cur;

try
{
    conn = getRegistrar().getConnection();

    s = conn.createStatement();

    s.execute("delete from GIGS where id="+id);
}
catch(Exception e)
{

}
finally
{
    try
    {
        if(s!=null) s.close();
    }
    catch(Exception ignore)
    {
    }
}

if(gigs != null) max = gigs.size();

for(i=0;i<max;i++)
{
    cur = (Gig) gigs.elementAt(i);

    if(cur.getId() == id)
    {
        gigs.removeElementAt(i);
        break;
    }
}
}
```

Like the other objects in this framework, the CourseImp implements accessors for its public attributes.

```java
public String getName()
{
    return name;
}

public String getNumber()
{
    return number;
}
```

```
    public RegistrarImp getRegistrar()
    {
        return registrar;
    }
}
```

The CourseImp class uses the same techniques as the Gig class to implement its methods. You may have noticed one indirection when adding a Gig—the GigImp is cached, but its reference is returned to the caller.

Implement Registrar

The last interface to implement is the first one that clients encounter—that is, the Registrar interface. A Registrar will be registered for access by clients. Once clients connect to the Registrar, they can access the courses, Gigs, and students. As a result, the design for this framework uses the RegistrarImp as a central repository for the shared database connection and access to the ORB.

```
package course_registration;

import course_registration.*;
import java.util.*;
import java.sql.*;
import java.io.*;

public class RegistrarImp extends POA_Registrar
{
    protected Connection connection;
    protected Hashtable courses;
    protected org.omg.CORBA.ORB orb;
```

When created, the RegistrarImp object must be provided with the name of the properties file to use for initializing the database connection. Within its constructor, the RegistrarImp class needs to make the database connection and initialize a reference to the ORB. If either of these fails, an exception is thrown, and the program trying to instantiate the registration framework should handle this exception itself.

```
    public RegistrarImp(String propertiesFile) throws Exception
    {
        ResourceBundle resources;
        InputStream in=null;

        in = ClassLoader.getSystemResourceAsStream(propertiesFile);

        resources = new PropertyResourceBundle(in);

        in.close();

        Class.forName(resources.getString("jdbc.driver"));

        connection = DriverManager.getConnection(
```

```
                        resources.getString("jdbc.url")
             ,resources.getString("jdbc.user")
             ,resources.getString("jdbc.password"));

     orb = org.omg.CORBA.ORB.init();
}
```

Implement accessor methods for the CourseImp and GigImp class to use in order to access the database connection and ORB.

```
public Connection getConnection()
{
    return connection;
}

public org.omg.CORBA.ORB getOrb()
{
    return orb;
}
```

Next, implement getCourse to make sure that the courses hashtable is initialized, and get the course from that hashtable before converting it to a reference and returning the reference to the caller.

```
public Course getCourse(String number)
{
    Course retVal = null;
    org.omg.PortableServer.POA poa=null;
    POA_Course_tie pct;

    if(courses == null) getCourses();

    try
    {
        poa =org.omg.PortableServer.POAHelper.narrow(
                getOrb().resolve_initial_references("RootPOA"));

        pct = new POA_Course_tie((CourseImp) courses.get(number));
        pct._orb(getOrb());

        retVal = CourseHelper.narrow(poa.servant_to_reference(pct));
    }
    catch(Exception exp)
    {
        retVal = null;
    }

    return retVal;
}
```

The getCourses method is like getGigs in Course or getStudents in Gig. It builds the list of courses from the database, then creates an array from the courses instance variable that contains the references to each CourseImp.

```
public Course[] getCourses()
```

```
{
    Course[] retVal = null;
    Enumeration elements;
    Vector holder = new Vector();
    int i,max;
    org.omg.PortableServer.POA poa=null;
    POA_Course_tie pct;

    try
    {
        poa =org.omg.PortableServer.POAHelper.narrow(
            getOrb().resolve_initial_references("RootPOA"));
    }
    catch(Exception exp)
    {
        poa = null;
    }

    if(courses == null)
    {
        Connection conn;
        Statement s=null;
        ResultSet rs;

        try
        {
            conn = getConnection();

            s = conn.createStatement();

            rs = s.executeQuery("select * from COURSES");
            courses = new Hashtable();

            while(rs.next())
            {
                courses.put(rs.getString("course_num")
                  ,new CourseImp(rs.getString("course_num")
                        ,rs.getString("name"),this));
            }

            elements = courses.elements();

            while(elements.hasMoreElements()
              holder.addElement(elements.nextElement());

            max = holder.size();

            retVal = new Course[max];

            for(i=0;i<max;i++)
            {
                pct =
                  new POA_Course_tie((CourseImp) holder.elementAt(i));
                pct._orb(getOrb());
```

```
                    retVal[i] =
                       CourseHelper.narrow(poa.servant_to_reference(pct));
                }

            }
            catch(Exception exp)
            {
                courses = null;
                retVal = null;
            }
            finally
            {
                try
                {
                    if(s!=null) s.close();
                }
                catch(Exception ignore)
                {
                }
            }
        }
        else
        {
            elements = courses.elements();

            while(elements.hasMoreElements())
               holder.addElement(elements.nextElement());

            max = holder.size();

            retVal = new Course[max];

            for(i=0;i<max;i++)
            {
                try
                {
                    pct =
                     new POA_Course_tie((CourseImp) holder.elementAt(i));
                    pct._orb(getOrb());

                    retVal[i] =
                       CourseHelper.narrow(poa.servant_to_reference(pct));
                }
                catch(Exception exp)
                {
                    break;
                }
            }
        }

        return retVal;
}
```

To add a course, make sure that the courses hashtable is initialized. Then insert the data in the database, cache the new course as a CourseImp in the courses hashtable, convert the CourseImp to a reference, and return the reference to the caller.

```java
public Course addCourse(String number,String name)
{
    Connection conn;
    Statement s=null;
    StringBuffer sql = new StringBuffer();
    int id;
    CourseImp retVal = null;
    Course realRetVal = null;
    org.omg.PortableServer.POA poa=null;
    POA_Course_tie pct;

    try
    {
        poa =org.omg.PortableServer.POAHelper.narrow(
            getOrb().resolve_initial_references("RootPOA"));
    }
    catch(Exception exp)
    {
        poa = null;
    }

    if(courses == null) getCourses();

    try
    {
        conn = getConnection();

        s = conn.createStatement();

        sql.append("insert into COURSES (course_num,name) values ('");
        sql.append(number);
        sql.append("','");
        sql.append(name);
        sql.append("')");

        s.execute(sql.toString());

        retVal = new CourseImp(number,name,this);
        courses.put(number,retVal);
    }
    catch(Exception e)
    {
        retVal = null;
    }
    finally
    {
        try
        {
```

```
                if(s!=null) s.close();
            }
            catch(Exception ignore)
            {
            }
        }

        try
        {
            pct = new POA_Course_tie(retVal);
            pct._orb(getOrb());

            realRetVal =
                CourseHelper.narrow(poa.servant_to_reference(pct));
        }
        catch(Exception exp)
        {
            realRetVal = null;
        }

        return realRetVal;
    }
}
```

That completes the Registration framework implementation. You should be able to compile the entire course_registration package now. This will compile the generated files as well as the ones you just completed. Next you will use the framework to create a Registration server.

Step 4: Implement the Server

Implementing a server that makes the Registration framework available to clients is actually pretty simple. All the server has to do is instantiate a Registrar object and make that object accessible to clients. The server implemented here makes the Registrar available via two separate mechanisms. First the JacORB name server is used to register the object for access by other JacORB applications. Then a string version of the Registrar object's reference is written to disk for use by IIOP applications.

```
import java.io.*;
import course_registration.*;

public class RegServer
{
```

This entire server is implemented in the class RegServer as a single main method.

```
    public static void main( String[] args )
    {
```

When creating the server, you should initialize the ORB with the command-line arguments. This convention allows the ORB vendor to request that the caller use particular arguments to indicate ORB-specific configuration parameters.

```
org.omg.CORBA.ORB orb = org.omg.CORBA.ORB.init(args, null);

try
{
    org.omg.PortableServer.POA poa =
    org.omg.PortableServer.POAHelper.narrow(
        orb.resolve_initial_references("RootPOA"));
```

Create the RegistrarImp with the name of the database properties file, and store the reference for registering with the name server, and save it to disk.

```
org.omg.CORBA.Object o =
    poa.servant_to_reference(new RegistrarImp("db.properties"));
```

Register the RegisterImp reference under the name RegistrarServer using the JacORB name server.

```
jacorb.naming.NameServer.registerService( o
                                        , "RegistrarServer" );
```

Ask the ORB to convert the reference object into a string that other ORBs can use to find the RegistrarImp. Write this string to a file. In the solution I used a file that is accessible via the Web server. This would allow programs on other computers to access the registration server by first loading the file via HTTP and then using that reference to access the server.

```
try
{
    BufferedWriter out= new BufferedWriter(
        new FileWriter("/home/httpd/html/RegServer.ref" ) );

    out.write(orb.object_to_string(o));
    out.newLine();
    out.close();
}
catch(IOException ex )
{
    System.out.println( "Could not open file" );
    System.exit( -1 );
}
}
catch(Exception e)
{
    e.printStackTrace();
}
```

Finally, use the ORB object's run method to start the server listening for client requests. This method will not return, and it continues listening for requests until the program is terminated.

```
            orb.run();
    }
}
```

At this point you can compile and run the RegServer program. To run the program you will need to do two things. First, run the JacORB name server. On my installation I do this by typing:

```
> /stephen/jacorb/bin/ns /home/httpd/html/NS_Ref
```

where the name of the program is *ns* and the command line argument is the path to a file used by the name server to store object references.

Once the name server is running you can run the RegServer. To ensure that the environment is correct, however, you don't want to run the Java interpreter directly. Instead use the jaco script provided with the JacORB. For my installation, I type:

```
>/stephen/jacorb/bin/jaco RegServer
```

You should type something similar depending on your JacORB installation. Notice that although the server was designed to support ORB configuration flags on the command line, I haven't used any for this project.

Step 5: Test the Server

Two test programs are provided on the CD-ROM. The first, shown below, is written in Java and inserts some data into the Course Registration system. The second, written in C++, uses the techniques discussed in the next step of this project but is not included here.

To test the server, the following program connects using the name server, adds a course, adds a Gig for that course, and registers several students in the Gig. One student is unregistered before the Gig is cancelled. Finally the students for the Gig are printed to the console to see if their information is correct. This program needs to import the course_registration package to gain access to the interfaces defined there.

```java
import java.util.*;
import course_registration.*;

public class RegistrarTest
{
    public static void main(String args[])
    {
        try
        {
            Course course;
```

```
Gig gig;
Student[] students;
int i,max;
```

To access the Registrar, use the RegistrarHelper to narrow a reference located by name from the name server. This returns an object that implements the Registrar interface, as defined in the code generated from the course_registration.idl file.

```
Registrar reg
= RegistrarHelper.narrow(
    jacorb.naming.NameServer.locate("RegistrarServer"));
```

Once connected, you use the CORBA objects like normal Java objects. This is the real power of technologies like CORBA and RMI. They make distributed object messaging transparent. The only warning is to remember that unlike messages to local objects, these messages can throw networking exceptions that should be handled on the client.

```
course = reg.addCourse("aa101","Advertising Intro.");

gig = course.addGig("June 7, 1999","Detroit");
gig.register("Sam Waters","sam@water.com");
gig.register("Cam Riefsnieder","cam@water.com");
gig.register("Tre Ramsneed","ram@water.com");

gig.unregister("ram@water.com");
gig.cancel();

students = gig.getStudents();

max = students.length;

for(i=0;i<max;i++)
{
    System.out.println(students[i].getName()
        +" "+students[i].getEmail()
        +" "+students[i].isCancelled());
}
}
catch(Exception exp)
{
    exp.printStackTrace();
}
}
}
```

Try compiling and running the RegisterTest program. Make sure to use the jaco script to run the application rather than accessing Java directly.

```
>/stephen/jacorb/bin/jaco RegServer
```

By running this test script you have inserted some information into the registration database. Try adding more data to the test program so that you have several courses in the database. In the next section, you will use C++ to create a CGI script that will display the current contents of the Registration Server.

Step 6: Implement a Report Generator

To demonstrate how CORBA can support communication between programs written in different languages, the next step in this project implements a CGI script in C++ that displays the current registration information. This CGI script is implemented in two parts. First, there is a C++ program that connects to the RegServer program written in Java. Second, there is a shell script that calls the C++ program with the necessary CORBA configuration information. In particular, the script passes the string object reference saved to file by the server to the client. Using this reference, the client can connect to the CORBA server.

Like the server, the client needs to access an ORB. Because JacORB supports only Java, I chose another popular free ORB called MICO. MICO is written in and supports C++. More important, MICO supports IIOP so that it can communicate with the JacORB associated with the RegServer.

Start the client by including the .h file created when you compiled the IDL file:

```
#include "course_registration.h"
```

Next, implement the entire CGI script in a single main function.

```
int main( int argc, char *argv[] )
{
```

Create a reference to the MICO ORB. Use this ORB object to create a reference to the basic object adaptor.

```
CORBA::ORB_var orb = CORBA::ORB_init( argc, argv, "mico-local-orb" );
CORBA::BOA_var boa = orb->BOA_init (argc, argv, "mico-local-boa");
```

This script is run with two command-line arguments. The first argument includes CORBA configuration information; the second is the object reference. Make sure that both arguments are provided and turn the object reference from a string into the actual object.

```
assert(argc == 2);
CORBA::Object_var obj = orb->string_to_object(argv[1]);
```

This gives you a generic object reference. Narrow the reference to a Registrar_var, a reference to the Registrar object.

```
course_registration::Registrar_var registrar =
        course_registration::Registrar::_narrow(obj);
```

Declare variables to store references to the objects you will need. These include the various sequences, which will be implemented as templatized collection classes. You also need a reference to individual objects and iterator variables to walk through the various collections required to make the report.

```
course_registration::courses_var courses;
course_registration::Course_var course;
course_registration::gigs_var gigs;
course_registration::Gig_var gig;
course_registration::students_var students;
course_registration::Student_var student;
int i,maxCourses;
int j,maxGigs;
int k,maxStudents;
```

Next, get the courses sequence from the registrar object. This will be a templatized implementation that is accessed by the [] operator.

```
courses = registrar->getCourses();
```

Retrieve the length of the sequence.

```
maxCourses = courses->length();
```

Write out the header for and start of your HTML report.

```
cout << "Content-Type: text/html" << endl << endl;
cout <<"<html><head><title>Course Registration Report</title></head>";
cout << endl;
cout << "<body>" << endl;
```

Loop over the courses collection, getting each course and storing it in the course variable.

```
for(i=0;i<maxCourses;i++)
{
    course = courses[i];
```

Print out the current course information.

```
    cout << "<h1>" << course->getNumber() << ": ";
    cout << course->getName() << "<h1>" << endl;
```

Use a list to indent the Gig information for each course.

```
    cout << "<ul>" << endl;
```

Get the Gigs sequence from the current course. Iterate over the sequence, and print out information about each Gig. Use the isCancelled method to print out an optional string indicating that the Gig is cancelled.

```
    gigs = course->getGigs();

    maxGigs = gigs->length();
    for(j=0;j<maxGigs;j++)
```

```
    {
        gig = gigs[j];

        cout << "<h3>" << gig->getLocation() <<": "<< gig->getDate();

        if(gig->isCancelled())
        {
            cout << " <font color=red>"
            cout << "<i>cancelled</i></font>"<<"<h3>"<<endl;
        }
        else cout   << "<h3>"<< endl;
```

For each Gig, print out the students registered for that Gig. Again, use the isCancelled flag to separate cancelled students from regular students.

```
        students = gig->getStudents();

        maxStudents = students->length();

        cout << "<ul>" << endl;

        for(k=0;k<maxStudents;k++)
        {
            student = students[k];
            cout <<"<li>"<<student->getName();
            cout <<" - "<<student->getEmail();

            if(student->isCancelled())
                cout <<" <font color=red><i>cancelled</i></font>"<<endl;
            else cout << endl;
        }

        cout << "</ul>" << endl;
    }

    cout << "</ul>" << endl;
    }

    cout << "</body></html>" << endl;

    return 0;
}
```

Compile the C++ program. You will need to include the MICO libraries as part of the compilation process. You may also need to include the dynamic linking library. On my machine I used the command line:

```
>c++ -L/usr/local/lib -lmico2.2.7 -ldl -o course_report
course_registration.cc
```

Create the shell script to call the course_report program. You will need to include the mico-setup.sh script in your initialization. Initialize the MICO ORB to not use code sets because these are not supported by JacORB. As a short cut, use cat to pass the contents of the string reference to the client program. Update the script that follows to the appropriate paths for your installation.

```
#!/bin/sh

source /usr/local/lib/mico-setup.sh

/home/httpd/cgi-bin/course_report -ORBNoCodeSets `cat
/home/httpd/html/RegServer.ref`
```

Copy both files to your CGI directory, and try accessing them using a Web browser.

Wrap Up

CORBA is a powerful technology for linking applications. As you research CORBA further, you will discover that there are also a number of useful services that the Object Management Group has built into or included with the CORBA standard. In situations where you are linking programs written in different languages, especially legacy applications, CORBA can form the foundation for your communication libraries. Mixed with a messaging technology like the one discussed in Project 7, CORBA can create a powerful network of applications.

A JNDI Service Provider

Project Objectives

In this project, you will learn how to:

- Program a JNDI service provider
- Use RMI in distributed programs
- Partition a program into client and server

 YOU WILL NEED

✔ JDK 1.1 or 1.2

✔ Java programming experience

✔ JNDI libraries1.2

✔ Experience with RMI is helpful

The Appendix provides a discussion on how to acquire and install the JDK and JDNI libraries.

Memo

To: Stephen
From: Project Manager

Stephen, we are creating a number of programs that need to access and communicate with the same objects. Can you create a server that will store objects with a name so that our programs can use that server as a rendezvous point?

Project Manager

Memo

To: Project Manager
From: Stephen

ProjMan, I have attached the server you described. The interface for this server uses JNDI so that we can upgrade it to LDAP or another commercial server once the initial development is complete.

Stephen

About This Project

Internet and intranet applications rely heavily on naming and directory services for accessing network resources. These services provide network-wide sharing of information related to users, machines, other network services, and remote applications. The Java Naming and Directory Interface (JNDI) is an API that describes a standard Java library for accessing naming and directory services such as DNS (Domain Naming Service), LDAP (Lightweight Directory Access Protocol), RMI (Remote Method Invocation), or even the file system on your computer. JNDI is powerful because it allows different services to be linked through a single API, enabling Java applications using JNDI to navigate seamlessly across files systems, databases, servers, and so on. For example, you could look up a specific RMI registry by requesting the information from an LDAP server, then use the same JNDI API to request a specific object from the registry and save a reference to the object in your file system using the JNDI API, yet again.

In this project you create a simple network naming provider that Java programs can access using the Java Naming and Directory Interface (JNDI). This isn't a huge project. Rather, it provides you with a nice introduction to Java programming on Linux, including network applications. The results of this project are used in Project 7, a Messaging Server, while the skills that you acquire can be used throughout the book.

Basic Concepts and Design

The design for your naming service is pictured in Figure 5.1. Clients of the service use the JNDI interfaces to access the server. The server allows the clients to access objects on the network by a unique name.

In order to understand when and how to use JNDI you must be familiar with certain terms such as *directory* and *naming service*. A naming service provides a method for mapping unique identifiers, or names with a specific value, range of values, or object that is referenced by the name service. For example, the Domain Name System (DNS) is an Internet naming service that maps the Internet address of computer systems, such as 192.42.172.21, with simple names, such as pri.com. These names allow users direct access to remote computer systems through recognizable names. In the case of DNS, the name and IP are registered with InterNIC, which maintains the map. Other services allow programs to register names and objects.

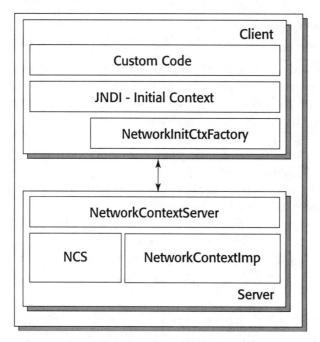

Figure 5.1 Naming server architecture.

The mapping between a name and a unique object is referred to as a name *binding*. One of the most obvious computer naming services is the file system on your computer. Each file and each directory have a name that identifies it. When you create a file you give it a name. This is the name binding for your data so it can be retrieved by name later. When you rename a file you are actually rebinding the file to a new name.

You can have a file with the same name, in the same directory as someone else has on their computer, yet the files can contain completely different data. This is possible because the file system manager handles only the files on your computer. This limited scope of control of a naming service is called its *namespace*. By having multiple namespaces, names can be reused appropriately without conflicts.

A compound name is a sequence of names that conform to the naming convention of a namespace. In a file system you can have a compound name such as /usr/tmp/myfile.txt. /, usr, tmp, myfile.txt are each names of objects in the file system. The names /, usr, and tmp map to directories, and myfile.txt maps to a file. Together they create compound names that are, for example, different from /usr/local/myfile.txt. This concept is similar to compound keys in a relational database.

Composite names span multiple namespaces. A common place where you see composite names is on the World Wide Web. A URL, for instance, usually consists of at least three parts. For example, the URL http://www.wiley.com/ index.html consists of the name of the protocol used, http:, the name of the server where the resource is located, //www.wiley.com, and the name of the resource, index.html.

Directory services are types of naming services that provide a structure to the underlying values. Typically this structure is hierarchical. For example, most computer file systems are hierarchical. They usually start with a root directory and have a series of subdirectories, each containing files. While this directory structure is common, other attributes of the resources within a directory service namespace can vary greatly. For example, one directory service could be capable of setting information such as the file access permissions or the modified date; other directory services such as LDAP allow the definition of arbitrary attributes on a resource.

Each node of a directory structure can be referred to as a *context*. Directory services allow you to read and modify attributes attached to contexts and have the ability to search a context using those attributes as a filter. For example, you could search an LDAP directory service for all people working in the marketing department named "Joe."

Lightweight Directory Access Protocol (LDAP) directory service provides a lightweight version of the X.500 directory service that could run on the TCP/IP protocol stack. This protocol has become popular and can be found as a common service integrated in other products such as Netscape's Enterprise server. It allows networked users access to information and resources in a consistent fashion. The attributes associated with a context are variable, a trait that provides flexibility but does require extra discipline by administrators to adhere to consistent naming structures. In Project 6 you create several programs that access an LDAP server.

Figure 5.2 illustrates the JNDI architecture. The JNDI API is a Java Extension API and is contained in the packages javax.naming, javax.naming.directory, and javax.naming.spi. All of these are contained in a single JAR file called jndi.jar. The package javax.naming is the basic API used typically to look up objects and values in a naming service such as an RMI object registry. The package javax.naming.directory contains a slightly more sophisticated API used for filtered searching of and modifying hierarchical values in directory and naming services such as LDAP. Although JNDI provides a common, unified API for name services, each name service requires a service provider that maps JNDI into the specific operations supported by the name service. Areas in which name services differ are description of names, organization of the namespace,

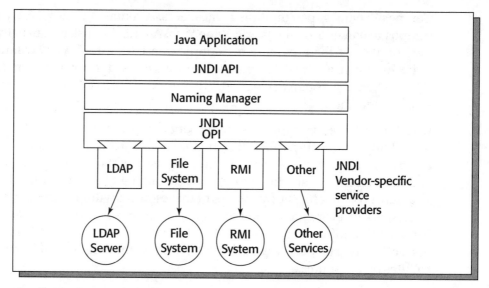

Figure 5.2 JNDI architecture.

schema description (if any), and the list of operations supported such as inserting and searching for objects and values in the service. Clients of a service provider should be familiar with the JNDI interface. Clients interested in writing a service object class should be familiar with SPI. These service providers create libraries using the javax.naming.spi package, which contains classes, and interfaces that define the behavior of a JNDI service provider. In this project you perform the steps to implement a service provider based on the interfaces in javax.naming.spi.

A great feature of JNDI is that it enables all of the various resources in an enterprise, including files, printers, servers, security services, databases, and business processes, to work together. Most directory services have the ability to manage a set of resources. JNDI allows you to leverage the strengths of many services.

This project requires some form of networking library to create the connection between a client of the naming service and the naming server. The easiest choice for distributed programming with Java is RMI, the Remote Method Invocation library.

Java Remote Method Invocation became a core part of the JDK in version 1.1 and continues to supply the main distributed object interface for Java programmers. RMI is a mechanism that enables an object on one Java virtual machine to invoke methods on an object in another Java virtual machine. RMI is the Java version of what is generally known as a remote procedure call (RPC), but with the ability to pass one or more objects along with the request and with the concept of a procedure replaced by a message between objects. The relationship between the two objects is defined by an interface that extends the Remote interface. On the client machine, a proxy called a *stub* is used to send messages from the local machine to the remote object. The stub implements all the methods of the remote interface of the remote object. The stub's implementation forwards the messages including parameters to the remote object.

NOTE

The message sender in these discussions is called the client, while the receiver is called the server. These terms should not be confused with client/server computing because in RMI it is possible for the same object or program to act as both a client and a server.

The process of packaging up the message and parameters is called *marshalling*. When the messages arrive at the remote server, the message and parameters are "unmarshalled" and the real object method is invoked. The result of the method is returned through a similar mechanism. The effect of all this is that issuing remote calls is nearly transparent to the developer of the client application. Figure 5.3 illustrates the typical use of RMI.

RMI consists of five packages and three utilities. Table 5.1 lists the purpose of each.

It may seem that RMI is large, but for most cases you need to use only a few methods and interfaces from each package to successfully implement a distributed object solution with RMI. In fact, fewer than 25 lines of code are used to define the RMI relationships in this project.

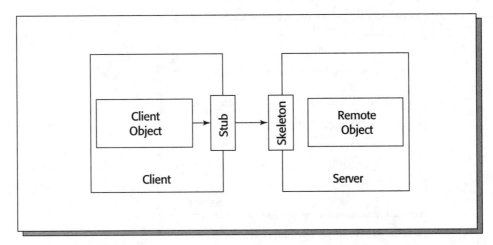

Figure 5.3 RMI architecture.

Table 5.1 RMI Components

COMPONENT	PURPOSE
java.rmi	Organizes client-side RMI classes, interfaces, and exceptions
java.rmi.server	Organizes server-side RMI classes, interfaces, and exceptions
java.rmi.registry	Organizes classes for managing the RMI naming services
java.rmi.dgc	Organizes classes used to manage distributed garbage collection
java.rmi.activation	Organizes the classes used to implement activate-on-demand RMI services
rmic	A compiler that generates the stubs and skeletons used by RMI to implement distributed communication
rmiregistry	A utility server that provides a naming service for RMI; associates names with objects
rmid	A utility server that supports the RMI activation framework (Java 2 only)

In order to complete this project, you define seven classes. These classes and their relationships to each other are pictured in Figure 5.4. All of the code for this project, except the test program, is contained in a package called networkctx for organizational and encapsulation purposes.

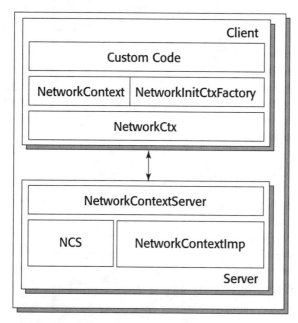

Figure 5.4 Naming context design.

Clients access a NetworkCtx that implements the javax.naming.Context interface. This context creates an RMI connection to the server and uses that connection to bind objects to names or to find objects by name. The server uses a NetworkContext to represent each connection from the client. These server contexts rely on a global hashtable to map objects and names.

Step 1: A Test Program

Before diving into the naming context, let's look at a program that uses the naming context. This small example should give you an idea of how programs interact with JNDI service providers. In particular, notice that this test program is not required to import the network context packages, and it refers to them only once, by name, as a string. This makes it possible for JNDI-based programs to change providers with minimal work.

The test program is called TestNetwork, and it is really just a main method with a helper method. No TestNetwork objects are created to run the program.

```
import java.util.*;
import javax.naming.*;

class TestNetwork
{
```

The TestNetwork main method starts by creating a hashtable. This hashtable, called env, represents the environment that is passed to the JNDI service provider and libraries. The values of a JNDI context's environment determine the provider used, as well as the configuration parameters passed to that provider.

In this case, the first environmental parameter, stored in the JNDI constant Context.INITIAL_CONTEXT_FACTORY, tells the JNDI libraries what class to use to create the context object. In this project, this is networkctx.NetworkInitCtxFactory. Again, this value is passed in as a string, so that the program can be reconfigured easily to use another context.

```
    public static void main(String[] args)
    {
        // Set up to use factory
        Hashtable env = new Hashtable();

        env.put(Context.INITIAL_CONTEXT_FACTORY,
            "networkctx.NetworkInitCtxFactory");
```

The second environmental parameter is called Context.PROVIDER_URL. This value is passed to the service provider code. In this project, the service provider uses this URL to access the server and should provide the correct IP address for the server. For the purposes of this test program, the IP address is provided on the command line and accessed here as args[0].

```
env.put(Context.PROVIDER_URL,
    "rmi://"+args[0]+":4798"+"/networkctx.NetworkContext");
```

Once the environment is created, the JNDI library class InitialContext is used to create a proxy for the actual network context. This new object is of type Context and is stored here in the initctx variable.

```
try
{
    Context initctx = new InitialContext(env);
```

After creating the initial context, the test program binds several objects into the context. This binding associates objects with a name. For example, the string "binding_a" is bound to the name "a".

```
initctx.bind("a", "binding_a");
initctx.bind("b", "binding_b");
initctx.bind("c", "binding_c");
initctx.bind("l",new Integer(4));
```

Using a method defined here, the test prints out all of the bindings for the current context. These bindings are accesses using the listBindings method that takes an argument indicating parameters related to the list function. For example, you could constrain the list to a particular string or directory. In the case of your simple naming service, this argument is ignored.

```
printBindings("original", initctx.listBindings(""));
```

Bindings can be removed, using unbind, or altered using rename and rebind. The code that follows performs several changes to the network context and prints the new bindings to the console. Comparing the two printouts allows the test to make sure that the network context is running.

```
    initctx.unbind("b");
    initctx.rename("a", "aa");
    initctx.bind("d", "binding_d");
    initctx.rebind("c", "new_binding");

    printBindings("after changes", initctx.listBindings(""));
}
catch (NamingException e)
{
    e.printStackTrace();
}
}
```

The printBindings method takes an enumeration called a NamingEnumeration and prints the values in this enumeration. Each value is a Binding object that maps a name to an object value.

```
static void printBindings(String msg, NamingEnumeration bl)
{
    System.out.println(msg);

    if (bl == null)
        System.out.println("No items in list");
    else
    {
        try
        {
            while (bl.hasMore())
            {
                Binding b = (Binding)bl.next();
                System.out.println(b.getName()
                                    + ":" + b.getObject());
            }
        }
        catch (NamingException e)
        {
            e.printStackTrace();
        }
    }
}
```

This test program should give you some idea about how the client interacts with the network context. In the next step, you define the interface between the client code for your service provider and the server.

Step 2: Defining the Interface between the Client and Server

The initial relationship between the client and the server is managed by an interface called NetworkCtxServer. This interface defines the name under which the server is registered using RMI and the port on which the server accepts connection. Also, this interface defines the createContext method used to create a context object for the client. Keep in mind that the clients don't see this interface; rather, the client code uses this interface to interact with the server.

```
package networkctx;

import java.util.*;
import java.rmi.*;
import networkctx.*;

public interface NetworkCtxServer extends Remote
{
    public static final String REG_NAME
                        ="networkctx.NetworkContext";
```

```
public static final int PORT = 4798;

public NetworkContext createContext(Hashtable env)
    throws RemoteException;
}
```

The NetworkContext object returned by the context server implements the interface that follows. This interface is essentially the javax.naming.Context interface with the appropriate exceptions defined for RMI. In particular, all of the methods can throw RemoteExceptions. This is a requirement for RMI programs because the program can never know when an exception could occur in a network application.

```
package networkctx;

import java.util.*;
import java.rmi.*;
import javax.naming.*;
import networkctx.*;

public interface NetworkContext extends Remote
{
```

When a client wants to find an object it uses the lookup method passing in a name.

```
public Object lookup(String name)
  throws NamingException, RemoteException;
```

To add an object to a context, the client calls bind with the object and name.

```
public void bind(String name, Object obj)
  throws NamingException, RemoteException;
```

To replace an existing object, the client calls rebind with the name and the new object to associate with that name.

```
public void rebind(String name, Object obj)
  throws NamingException, RemoteException;
```

To remove objects from the context, the client calls unbind and passes in the name of the object to remove.

```
public void unbind(String name)
  throws NamingException, RemoteException;
```

Clients can change the name of an object by calling rename and passing in the old and new names.

```
public void rename(String oldname, String newname)
  throws NamingException, RemoteException;
```

A context can return a list of its contents two ways. First, the list method will return an enumeration of names. Second, the listBindings will return an enumeration of Binding objects that relate the names and values. Both methods use a special type of enumeran called NamingEnumeration.

```
public NamingEnumeration list(String name)
  throws NamingException, RemoteException;

public NamingEnumeration listBindings(String name)
  throws NamingException, RemoteException;
```

Some JNDI naming contexts can maintain an environment that affects the data that they hold or the way it is accessed. This environment is managed with the addToEnvironment, removeFromEnvironment, and getEnvironment methods. These methods are included in this interface, but they are not really used by the Naming server defined in this project.

```
public Object addToEnvironment(String propName, Object propVal)
  throws NamingException, RemoteException;

public Object removeFromEnvironment(String propName)
  throws NamingException, RemoteException;

public Hashtable getEnvironment()
  throws NamingException, RemoteException;
```

When a context is no longer required, it can be closed to clean up resources.

```
public void close()
  throws NamingException, RemoteException;
}
```

The client code for your service provider uses these two interfaces to communicate with the server. The server code implements the interfaces.

Step 3: Defining the Client

The client code for your JNDI service provider is divided into three classes. The context factory is defined in the class NetworkInitCtxFactory. This class's job is to create new factories from the environment provided by the user. The extent of this class's implementation is a single method called getInitialContext that instantiates a NetworkCtx object. This method is called by the JNDI libraries as necessary.

```
package networkctx;

import java.util.*;
import java.rmi.*;
import javax.naming.*;
import javax.naming.spi.*;
import networkctx.*;

public class NetworkInitCtxFactory
```

```
    implements InitialContextFactory
{
    public Context getInitialContext(Hashtable env)
    {
        return new NetworkCtx(env);
    }
}
```

NetworkNameParser

The second class in the client side of your implementation is the Network-NameParser. This class implements the NameParser interface as defined by the JNDI libraries. Its job is to parse string names into Name objects. This implementation is very simple and uses the CompoundName class provided with JNDI to create a Name that represents a flat, case-sensitive name.

```
package networkctx;

import javax.naming.*;
import java.util.*;
import java.io.*;
import networkctx.*;

class NetworkNameParser
 implements NameParser, Serializable
{
    protected static Properties syntax = new Properties();

    static
    {
        syntax.put("jndi.syntax.direction", "flat");
        syntax.put("jndi.syntax.ignorecase", "false");
    }

    public Name parse(String name)
      throws NamingException
    {
        return new CompoundName(name, syntax);
    }
}
```

NetworkCtx

The final client class is the most complex. NetworkCtx implements the Context interface defined in JNDI. The implementation for this interface is one of straight message forwarding. When the NetworkCtx receives a message it forwards that message to a NetworkContext object on the server and returns the server's response. All RMI exceptions are handled by the NetworkCtx and translated into more JNDI-appropriate equivalents. For example, the bind method throws NamingExceptions when network problems occur.

```
package networkctx;

import java.util.*;
import java.rmi.*;
import java.rmi.server.*;
import javax.naming.*;
import javax.naming.spi.*;
import networkctx.*;

class NetworkCtx
 implements Context
{
```

In order to do its work, the NetworkCtx uses a NetworkNameParser to create Names and a reference to the NetworkContext object on the server. This object, called remote, is created in the constructor.

```
static NameParser myParser = new NetworkNameParser();

protected NetworkContext remote;
```

When constructing a NetworkCtx, it is necessary to provide an environment containing the provider URL. This URL is used to connect to the server using the Naming class in java.rmi. This class provides a loop-up method that returns an object reference from a URL. Once a connection to the server is made, the server is asked to create a context from the client's environment.

Note that in order for RMI to work correctly, you must set the System's SecurityManager to an RMISecurityManager.

```
NetworkCtx(Hashtable environment)
{
    try
    {
        String url =
          (String) environment.get(Context.PROVIDER_URL);

        NetworkCtxServer server=null;

        if(System.getSecurityManager()==null)
            System.setSecurityManager(new RMISecurityManager());

        if(url != null)
        {
            server = (NetworkCtxServer) Naming.lookup(url);

            if(server != null)
            {
                remote = server.createContext(environment);
            }
        }
    }
    catch(Exception exp)
    {
```

```
            System.out.println(exp);
            remote = null;
        }
    }
```

The remainder of the NetworkCtxt class definition is shown next. The methods you need to define are all proxies for the server equivalents. Many of these methods support two versions, one taking a String name and the other a Name object. In these cases, the Name version uses the String version.

```
//lookup will find the object for a name and return it
public Object lookup(String name)
 throws NamingException
{
    Object retVal = null;

    try
    {
        retVal = remote.lookup(name);
    }
    catch(NamingException exp)
    {
        throw exp;
    }
    catch(Exception exp)
    {
        throw new NamingException(exp.toString());
    }

    return retVal;
}

//lookup will find the object for a Name, as a string, and return it
public Object lookup(Name name) throws NamingException
{
    return lookup(name.toString());
}

//bind associates an object with a name
public void bind(String name, Object obj) throws NamingException
{
    try
    {
        remote.bind(name,obj);
    }
    catch(NamingException exp)
    {
        throw exp;
    }
    catch(Exception exp)
    {
        throw new NamingException(exp.toString());
    }
```

```java
}

public void bind(Name name, Object obj) throws NamingException
{
    bind(name.toString(), obj);
}

//rebind reassociates an object with a string
public void rebind(String name, Object obj) throws NamingException
{
    try
    {
        remote.rebind(name,obj);
    }
    catch(NamingException exp)
    {
        throw exp;
    }
    catch(Exception exp)
    {
        throw new NamingException(exp.toString());
    }
}

public void rebind(Name name, Object obj) throws NamingException
{
    rebind(name.toString(), obj);
}

//unbind removes an existing binding
public void unbind(String name) throws NamingException
{
    try
    {
        remote.unbind(name);
    }
    catch(NamingException exp)
    {
        throw exp;
    }
    catch(Exception exp)
    {
        throw new NamingException(exp.toString());
    }
}

public void unbind(Name name) throws NamingException
{
    unbind(name.toString());
}

//rename changes the existing name of a binding
public void rename(String oldname, String newname)
```

```
            throws NamingException
{
    try
    {
        remote.rename(oldname,newname);
    }
    catch(NamingException exp)
    {
        throw exp;
    }
    catch(Exception exp)
    {
        throw new NamingException(exp.toString());
    }
}

public void rename(Name oldname, Name newname)
        throws NamingException
{
    rename(oldname.toString(), newname.toString());
}

//list returns all of the objects matching a name
public NamingEnumeration list(String name)
 throws NamingException
{
    NamingEnumeration retVal = null;

    try
    {
        retVal = remote.list(name);
    }
    catch(NamingException exp)
    {
        throw exp;
    }
    catch(Exception exp)
    {
        throw new NamingException(exp.toString());
    }

    return retVal;
}

public NamingEnumeration list(Name name)
        throws NamingException
{
    return list(name.toString());
}

//listBindings returns all of the bindings matching a name
public NamingEnumeration listBindings(String name)
        throws NamingException
```

```
{
    NamingEnumeration retVal = null;

    try
    {
        retVal = remote.listBindings(name);
    }
    catch(NamingException exp)
    {
        throw exp;
    }
    catch(Exception exp)
    {
        throw new NamingException(exp.toString());
    }

    return retVal;
}
public NamingEnumeration listBindings(Name name)
        throws NamingException
{
    return listBindings(name.toString());
}

//methods to control the subcontext are not supported
// Since there isn't one
public void destroySubcontext(String name) throws NamingException
{
    throw new OperationNotSupportedException(
            "NetworkCtx does not support subcontexts");
}

public void destroySubcontext(Name name) throws NamingException
{
    destroySubcontext(name.toString());
}

//methods to control the subcontext are not supported
// Since there isn't one
public Context createSubcontext(String name)
        throws NamingException
{
    throw new OperationNotSupportedException(
            "NetworkCtx does not support subcontexts");
}

public Context createSubcontext(Name name) throws NamingException
{
    return createSubcontext(name.toString());
}

//Performs a lookup
public Object lookupLink(String name) throws NamingException
```

```
{
    return lookup(name);
}

public Object lookupLink(Name name) throws NamingException
{
    return lookupLink(name.toString());
}

//Gets the name parser this provider uses
public NameParser getNameParser(String name)
        throws NamingException
{
    return myParser;
}

public NameParser getNameParser(Name name) throws NamingException
{
    return getNameParser(name.toString());
}

//Creates a compound name from two pieces
public String composeName(String name, String prefix)
        throws NamingException
{
    Name result = composeName(new CompositeName(name),
                            new CompositeName(prefix));

    return result.toString();
}

public Name composeName(Name name, Name prefix)
        throws NamingException
{
    Name result = (Name)(prefix.clone());
    result.addAll(name);

    return result;
}

//Adds values to the provider's environment
public Object addToEnvironment(String propName, Object propVal)
        throws NamingException
{
    Object retVal = null;

    try
    {
        retVal = remote.addToEnvironment(propName,propVal);
    }
    catch(NamingException exp)
    {
        throw exp;
    }
    catch(Exception exp)
```

```
    {
        throw new NamingException(exp.toString());
    }

    return retVal;
}

//Removes values from the provider's environment
public Object removeFromEnvironment(String propName)
        throws NamingException
{
    Object retVal = null;

    try
    {
        retVal = remote.removeFromEnvironment(propName);
    }
    catch(NamingException exp)
    {
        throw exp;
    }
    catch(Exception exp)
    {
        throw new NamingException(exp.toString());
    }

    return retVal;
}

//Gets the provider's environment
public Hashtable getEnvironment() throws NamingException
{
    Hashtable retVal = null;

    try
    {
        retVal = remote.getEnvironment();
    }
    catch(NamingException exp)
    {
        throw exp;
    }
    catch(Exception exp)
    {
        throw new NamingException(exp.toString());
    }

    return retVal;
}

//Closes the client's connection to the server
public void close() throws NamingException
{
    try
```

```
        {
            remote.close();
        }
        catch(NamingException exp)
        {
            throw exp;
        }
        catch(Exception exp)
        {
            throw new NamingException(exp.toString());
        }
    }
}
```

For the most part this class is easy to implement, relying more on patience than skill. Almost all of the methods are identical, in that they forward a call to the server and handle remote exceptions that occur. The next step defines the server that receives these messages.

Step 4: Defining the Server

The server for your network naming provider is defined in four classes. Two of these classes implement the name and binding enumerations that you encountered in Step 1. One class implements the NetworkContext interface and the final class acts as the server program, implementing the main method.

NetworkContextImp

First, let's look at the NetworkContextImp class that implements the NetworkContext interface. One of these objects is created for each client.

```
package networkctx;

import java.util.*;
import java.io.*;
import java.rmi.*;
import java.rmi.server.*;
import javax.naming.*;
import javax.naming.spi.*;
import networkctx.*;
```

RMI requires that classes implementing objects that will be network accessible must extend java.rmi.server.RemoteObject. In general, the easiest way to do this is to extend UnicastRemoteObject and inherit the network behaviors defined there.

```
class NetworkContextImp extends UnicastRemoteObject
  implements NetworkContext
{
```

As with the NetworkCtx object, the NetworkContextImp uses a Network-NameParser to manage names.

```
static NameParser myParser = new NetworkNameParser();
```

Each context manages its own environment. In a more feature-rich service provider this environment could determine the configuration for each context. Here it is mainly implemented for completeness and otherwise ignored.

```
protected Hashtable myEnv;
```

To make the naming service global, all of the contexts have to share the name-object bindings. Store them in a static hashtable in the NetworkContextImp class with the name bindings.

```
protected static Hashtable bindings;
```

To access the global table, provide methods to get, put, get the list of names from, and remove bindings. All of these methods should be synchronized to prevent thread conflicts.

```
protected static synchronized Object get(String name)
{
    Object retVal = null;

    if(bindings != null) retVal = bindings.get(name);

    return retVal;
}

protected static synchronized void put(String name, Object o)
{
    if(bindings == null) bindings = new Hashtable();

    bindings.put(name,o);
}

protected static synchronized Object remove(String name)
{
    Object retVal = null;

    if(bindings != null) retVal = bindings.remove(name);

    return retVal;
}

protected static synchronized Enumeration keys()
{
    Enumeration retVal = null;

    if(bindings != null) retVal = bindings.keys();

    return retVal;
}
```

When created, a NetworkContextImp calls its parent's constructor for inherited initialization and makes a copy of its environment to ensure autonomy.

```
NetworkContextImp(Hashtable environment)
    throws RemoteException
{
    super();

    if(environment != null)
        myEnv = (Hashtable)environment.clone();
}
```

The following four methods show how the network context implements the core context methods, including lookup and bind. Each method checks the validity of the name provided before adding, removing, or updating the global bindings hashtable appropriately. In the case of a lookup, the null and empty strings are treated as special and will return a new network context with the same environment as this one.

```
public Object lookup(String name)
  throws NamingException, RemoteException
{
    if ((name == null) || name.equals(""))
    {
        return (new NetworkContextImp(myEnv));
    }

    Object answer = get(name);

    if (answer == null)
    {
        throw new NameNotFoundException(name + " not found");
    }

    return answer;
}

public void bind(String name, Object obj)
  throws NamingException, RemoteException
{
    if ((name == null) || name.equals(""))
    {
        throw new InvalidNameException("Cannot bind empty name");
    }

    if (get(name) != null)
    {
        throw new NameAlreadyBoundException(
                        "Use rebind to override");
    }

    put(name, obj);
}
```

```
public void rebind(String name, Object obj)
 throws NamingException, RemoteException
{
    if ((name == null) || name.equals(""))
    {
        throw new InvalidNameException("Cannot bind empty name");
    }

    put(name, obj);
}

public void unbind(String name)
 throws NamingException, RemoteException
{
    if ((name == null) || name.equals(""))
    {
        throw new InvalidNameException("Cannot unbind empty name");
    }

    remove(name);
}

public void rename(String oldname, String newname)
 throws NamingException, RemoteException
{
    if ((oldname == null) || (newname == null)
            ||oldname.equals("") || newname.equals(""))
    {
        throw new InvalidNameException("Cannot rename empty name");
    }

    if(get(newname) != null)
    {
        throw new NameAlreadyBoundException(newname +
                                            " is already bound");
    }

    Object oldBinding = remove(oldname);

    if (oldBinding == null)
    {
        throw new NameNotFoundException(oldname + " not bound");
    }

    put(newname, oldBinding);
}
```

Listing the bindings for a network context relies on the two enumeration classes, NetworkNames and NetworkBindings, defined next. These methods also support context chaining, so that if a context name is provided to the list commands that context will be listed, rather than the original context.

```
public NamingEnumeration list(String name)
 throws NamingException, RemoteException
```

```
{
    if((name == null) || name.equals(""))
    {
        return new NetworkNames(keys(),this);
    }

    Object target = lookup(name);

    if (target instanceof Context)
    {
        return ((Context)target).list("");
    }

    throw new NotContextException(name + " cannot be listed");
}

public NamingEnumeration listBindings(String name)
 throws NamingException, RemoteException
{
    if((name == null) || name.equals(""))
    {
        return new NetworkBindings(keys(),this);
    }

    Object target = lookup(name);

    if (target instanceof Context)
    {
        return ((Context)target).listBindings("");
    }

    throw new NotContextException(name + " cannot be listed");
}
```

The JNDI Context interface requires that a context can manage its environment.
The following three methods implement this interface with minimal code.

```
public Object addToEnvironment(String propName, Object propVal)
 throws NamingException, RemoteException
{
    if (myEnv == null)
        myEnv = new Hashtable();

    return myEnv.put(propName, propVal);
}

public Object removeFromEnvironment(String propName)
 throws NamingException, RemoteException
{
    if(myEnv == null) return null;

    return myEnv.remove(propName);
}

public Hashtable getEnvironment()
 throws NamingException, RemoteException
```

```
{
    if (myEnv == null)
        myEnv = new Hashtable();

    return myEnv;
}
```

When the client library closes the network connection it resets its environment for completeness.

```
public void close()
 throws NamingException, RemoteException
{
    myEnv = null;
}
}
```

NetworkNames

As mentioned previously, the methods that list the context of a NetworkContext return custom enumerations. It is necessary to create special enumerations because they must implement the NamingEnumeration interface as well as the Enumeration interface. The two classes, NetworkNames and NetworkBindings, shown here implement the NamingEnumeration interface using an Enumeration provided by the network context.

```
class NetworkNames
 implements NamingEnumeration, Serializable
{
    Vector names;
    int curIndex;
    NetworkContext ctx;
```

A NetworkNames object is created with a NetworkContext and an enumeration for the context's bindings. In its constructor, a new NetworkNames object should copy these bindings so that they can be accessed by other methods. By copying the data, the NetworkNames object becomes valid even if the context changes.

```
    NetworkNames(Enumeration cursor, NetworkContext nc)
    {
        names = new Vector();
        curIndex = 0;
        ctx = nc;

        while(cursor.hasMoreElements())
        {
            names.addElement(cursor.nextElement());
        }
    }
```

As with all enumerations, the NetworkNames object has methods to see if it has more elements. The hasMoreElements method checks to see if there are more elements based on the current index. The hasMore method adds a twist to this process by throwing an exception if there are no more elements.

```
public boolean hasMoreElements()
{
    return (curIndex < names.size());
}

public boolean hasMore()
 throws NamingException
{
    boolean retVal = false;

    retVal = hasMoreElements();

    if(!retVal)
        throw new NamingException("No more names.");

    return retVal;
}
```

The nextElement method is used to get the next item in the NetworkNames enumeration. This method creates a NameClassPair for the next item and returns it. The current item's index is stored in the curIndex instance variable.

```
public Object nextElement()
{
    Object retVal = null;
    String name;
    String className;

    if(curIndex < names.size())
    {
        try
        {
            name = (String) names.elementAt(curIndex);
            className = ctx.lookup(name).getClass().getName();
            retVal = new NameClassPair(name, className);
        }
        catch(Exception exp)
        {
            retVal = null;
        }

        curIndex++;
    }

    return retVal;
}
```

The next method is added by JNDI to act like nextElement with the twist that it throws an exception if there are no more elements.

```
        public Object next() throws NamingException
        {
            Object retVal = null;

            retVal = nextElement();

            if(retVal == null)
                throw new NamingException("No more pairs.");

            return retVal;
        }
    }
}
```

NetworkBindings

In the same way that NetworkNames provides an enumeration over the names
in a NetworkContext, NetworkBindings provides the same methods over the
bindings in a NetworkContext.

```
class NetworkBindings
 implements NamingEnumeration, Serializable
{
    Vector names;
    int curIndex;
    NetworkContext ctx;

    NetworkBindings(Enumeration cursor, NetworkContext nc)
    {
        names = new Vector();
        curIndex = 0;
        ctx = nc;

        while(cursor.hasMoreElements())
        {
            names.addElement(cursor.nextElement());
        }
    }

    public boolean hasMoreElements()
    {
        return (curIndex < names.size());
    }

    public boolean hasMore()
     throws NamingException
    {
        boolean retVal = false;

        retVal = hasMoreElements();

        if(!retVal)
            throw new NamingException("No more names.");

        return retVal;
    }
```

```
    public Object nextElement()
    {
        Object retVal = null;
        String name;
        String className;

        if(curIndex < names.size())
        {
            try
            {
                name = (String) names.elementAt(curIndex);
                retVal = new Binding(name, ctx.lookup(name));
            }
            catch(Exception exp)
            {
                retVal = null;
            }

            curIndex++;
        }

        return retVal;
    }

    public Object next() throws NamingException
    {
        Object retVal = null;

        retVal = nextElement();

        if(retVal == null)
            throw new NamingException("No more pairs.");

        return retVal;
    }
}
```

NCS

The final class in this project defines the server program. This class is called
NCS, for NetworkContextServer, and performs two functions. First, it implements the main method for the application. Second, it implements the NetworkCtxServer interface and registers an NCS object using RMI technology for
access from the clients.

```
package networkctx;

import java.io.*;
import java.util.*;
import java.security.*;
import java.rmi.*;
import java.rmi.server.*;
```

```
import networkctx.*;

public class NCS extends UnicastRemoteObject
implements NetworkCtxServer
{
    public NCS() throws RemoteException
    {
    }
```

Each time the NCS object is asked to create a context for a client it creates a new NetworkContextImp and returns it.

```
    public NetworkContext createContext(Hashtable env)
        throws RemoteException
    {
        NetworkContext retVal =
            new NetworkContextImp(env);

        return retVal;
    }
```

The main method for NCS performs five tasks. First, it sets up the security manager to support RMI. Second, it loads the configuration properties from a properties file. Third, it creates an NCS object. Fourth, it creates an RMI registry used to make the NCS object accessible by name from the client. Finally, it binds the NCS object to the registry.

Each of these tasks is shown below, as well as the print statements used to update the user on the server's status as it launches.

```
    public static void main(String args[])
    {
        // Create and install a security manager
        SecurityManager mng;
        NCS ncs;
        InputStream propsIn;
        Properties sysProps;
        Properties properties;
        String codebase;
        String server;

        try
        {
            System.out.println("Setting Security Manager.");
            mng = new RMISecurityManager();
            System.setSecurityManager(mng);
            System.out.println("Set Security Manager.");

            //Load the properties file
            propsIn
                = ClassLoader.getSystemResourceAsStream(
                                "networkctx/networkctx.properties");
```

```
                    properties = new Properties();
                    properties.load(propsIn);

                    //Update the system props for class loading
                    //fails for an applet but that's okay
                    try
                    {
                        sysProps = System.getProperties();

                        codebase = (String)
                            properties.get("java.rmi.server.codebase");

                        if(codebase == null)
                        {
                            codebase = "file:/"
                                    + sysProps.getProperty("user.dir")
                                    +"/";
                        }

                        sysProps.put("java.rmi.server.codebase"
                                        ,codebase);

                        System.setProperties(sysProps);
                    }
                    catch(Exception ignore)
                    {
                    }

                    System.out.println("Creating server.");
                    ncs = new NCS();
                    System.out.println("Created server.");

                    System.out.println("Starting to bind server.");

                    java.rmi.registry.Registry privateReg =
           java.rmi.registry.LocateRegistry.createRegistry(NetworkCtxServer.PORT);

                    privateReg.rebind(NetworkCtxServer.REG_NAME,ncs);

                    System.out.println("NCS bound in registry");
                }
            catch (Exception e)
            {
                System.out.println("Network Context Server: "
                                    + e.getMessage());
                e.printStackTrace();
                System.exit(0);
            }
        }
    }
}
```

That completes the server code. The next step is to compile the code, run the
server, and run the test program.

Step 5: Running the Server

To compile the server execute the following commands:

```
javac networkctx/*.java
rmic -d . networkctx.NetworkContextImp
rmic -d . networkctx.NCS
```

The two calls to rmic generate the stubs and skeletons used by RMI to implement remote messaging. Once the commands are compiled, you should make sure that the networkctx/networkctx.properties file is correct. Then run the server by typing:

```
java networkctx.NCS &
```

on the command line. Compile and run the test program to make sure that the server is working properly.

Wrap Up

This project should have given you a basic understanding of JNDI and how it can be used to access network or local service in a standard way. In the next project you use this knowledge to access an LDAP server. LDAP provides a directory context for information rather than the flat naming context implemented here.

We also used RMI in this project to create a network application. Other projects will use RMI for the same purposes. In particular, Project 7 will use RMI to create a messaging server that sends multiple object types across the network.

6

Accessing an LDAP Server

Project Objectives

In this project, you will learn how to:

- Create an LDAP search program in Java
- Create an LDAP search program in Perl
- Create an LDAP search program in C

 ## YOU WILL NEED

✔ OpenLDAP or another LDAP server (www.openldap.org)

✔ JDK, JNDI libraries, and Java programming experience

✔ Perl programming experience and the Perl LDAP modules

✔ C programming experience

Memo

To: Stephen
From: Programmer

Stephen, I am supposed to update our application from using a flat file to using the LDAP server. What is LDAP anyway, and can you send me some examples of how to access an LDAP database?

Programmer

Memo

To: Programmer
From: Stephen

Programmer, here is an example that connects to an LDAP database to perform search. I am sending three versions, one each in Java, Perl, and C, so that you can see how the various libraries work.

Stephen

About This Project

As networking has become prevalent, both inside and outside the corporate headquarters, many companies have discovered the need for a centralized location to store user information such as login names and contact lists.

The solution to this need can come in a number of forms. The first solution is a file shared by multiple users. Another solution is a relational database. These databases store data in tables with columns to separate attributes for each entry and rows to indicate an entry.

A third solution that has gained in use over the last few years is the *directory server*. A directory server is a special kind of database that stores data in a hierarchical structure.

In this project you connect to one of the more popular directory services called *LDAP*, the Lightweight Directory Access Protocol. The application you create searches the database for values based on a filter, perhaps the most common operation on a directory server. Because LDAP is a protocol and not a language-specific mechanism, you can access it from a number of programming languages. This project creates the same search program in three languages— Java, Perl, and C—to show how flexible LDAP can be and how easy it is to install and use on Linux.

Basic Concepts and Design

A directory server is a type of database. It manages a hierarchical structure of name-value pairs. By limiting the structure of the data and optimizing for read operations, a directory server can provide high performance in suitable applications, such as e-mail programs, single sign-on, and other applications that relate a few name-value pairs with a particular entity.

LDAP originally was designed to simplify access to a feature-rich directory server based on the X.500 protocol. Developers realized that a standalone LDAP server could be created and optimized to manage only data provided for in the LDAP protocol. This data, and the protocol itself, are designed to follow four basic models:

- An information model that defines what type of data is stored
- A naming model that defines how the data is stored and how a client can access it
- A functional model that defines what you can do with the data
- A security model that can be used to protect the data

Information in an LDAP server is organized into *entries*. An entry contains a collection of named attributes. Each attribute has a type and a collection of values, as pictured in Figure 6.1. An attribute's type indicates the type of data the values will be. The type also can control how the data is searched. A number of predefined types are provided in the LDAP standard. For example, one type of attribute would be a string that is not case sensitive. The values for this attribute would have to be strings of characters, and their case would be ignored during the search.

LDAP entries are arranged in a tree structure that uses organizations or location to organize entries. This organization is not necessary or tied to the LDAP standard itself, but it is a standard way of setting up corporate LDAP servers because most of the current applications use LDAP to store information about people and other resources. By building the database off location and organization it is easy to search for resources using these two constraints.

LDAP naming is similar to naming in a file system. An entry is known by its complete, or distinguished, name that represents its hierarchical path. The steps along the path are separated by commas, with each step indicated by a name-value pair. Each pair is called a *relative distinguished name* (RDN). For example, an entry might have the name:

```
cn=Barbara Jensen, o=University of Michigan, c=US
```

In this case, the organization information (o=University of Michigan) is an RDN. Notice that unlike a file system path the distinguished name starts with the most specific and works toward the generic.

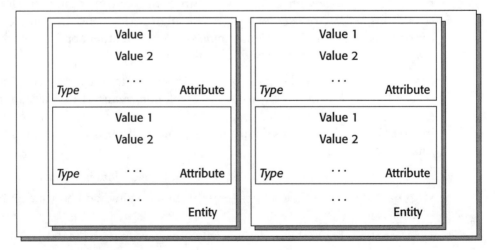

Figure 6.1 LDAP information model.

Functionally, an LDAP server is designed to perform the following operations:

- Search for an entry
- Compare entries
- Add, modify, or delete entries
- Modify a single attribute of the entry
- Bind and unbind with the client
- Cancel or abandon an operation in progress

This project focuses on the search capability of an LDAP server. When searching, you will provide a *base* and a *filter*. The base is used as the root of the search. The filter is the search string used to find entries under the specified base. A search filter contains a set of RDNs that can contain wildcards and other control characters.

Security for an LDAP server is generally based on access control lists. Depending on the API, a client program binds to the server with a user name and password. Based on this identification, the server can limit the operations that that client program can perform.

Typically, a program that accesses an LDAP server will perform four steps:

1. Initialize the library and bind the client to the server
2. Perform an operation
3. Process any results
4. Close the LDAP connection and clean up

The program created in this project performs a search operation based on two command-line arguments, a base and a filter. The results of the search are printed to standard out.

NOTE

I used the OpenLDAP server and test database for this project; see the Appendix for installation instructions. You should be able to use the Java and Perl programs on other servers without modification. You may need to modify the C version, as discussed later.

Creating an LDAP Search Program in Java

The first program in this project is written in Java and uses the JNDI packages discussed in Project 5 to connect to the LDAP server. The LDAP driver for JNDI is provided by Sun in the com.sun.jndi.ldap package. For commonality, and to keep the code for this project minimal, the search program is implemented in a single class called Search, in the main method. This allows the program to be run on the command line, and it minimizes your work. Import the necessary packages for this project.

```
import java.util.*;
import javax.naming.*;
import javax.naming.directory.*;

public class Search
{
    public static void main(String args[])
    {
```

Step 1: Check the Command-Line Arguments

Like the other versions of this project, the Java search program expects the user to supply a base and a filter. If these are not provided, the program fails. Use an if statement to test that the string array passed into main has a length of at least two. If not, print out a message that tells the user how to use the program, then exit the program.

```
if(args.length<2)
{
    System.out.println("usage: java Search base filter");
    System.exit(0);
}
```

Step 2: Connect to the LDAP Server

In order to create a JNDI context you need to tell the JNDI packages what factory and server to use. In this case, you use the LDAP context factory to create a JNDI context for your LDAP server and provide the URL for the LDAP server you want to use to test this project. Create a hashtable to hold the environment information used by the LDAP libraries to create our initial context. Specify the LDAP context and a URL that connects to your LDAP server.

```
Hashtable env = new Hashtable();

env.put(Context.INITIAL_CONTEXT_FACTORY
    ,"com.sun.jndi.ldap.LdapCtxFactory");
env.put(Context.PROVIDER_URL,"ldap://brisco:9009");
```

As with all network programming, accessing an LDAP server can result in an exception, so the entire search functionality should be placed inside a try-catch block. In a more commercial context, you can use multiple try-catch blocks to handle specific errors at each step of the process. The start of my try-catch block is shown here for code completeness.

```
try
{
```

In Project 5, you created a naming server for JNDI. LDAP relies on the JNDI directory interfaces to provide access to its complete functionality. As a result, you need to create a directory context, DirContext, rather than a plan Naming Context. Declare a variable of type DirContext and set it equal to a new InitialDirContext created with the environment defined previously. This should give you a directory context for your LDAP server.

```
DirContext ctx = new InitialDirContext(env);
```

Step 3: Perform the Search

Searches on a directory are controlled by a set of constraints or controls. The primary control that you rely on defines the scope of the search. In this case, you want to search everything under the base that the user provided on the command line. Other options are to limit the search to a particular entry in the database or to a single level of the database. A SearchControls object is used to define these constraints. The SearchControls can also be used to limit the number of entries returned or the attributes returned. Create a new SearchControls object and store it in a variable called constraints. Tell constraints to use SUB-TREE_SCOPE for search.

```
SearchControls constraints = new SearchControls();

constraints.setSearchScope(SearchControls.SUBTREE_SCOPE);
```

Perform the search with the context's search method and capture the resulting enumeration called results. Use results to access each of the matching entries. Notice that you call the search method with the base, filter, and constraints:

```
NamingEnumeration results
 = ctx.search(args[0], args[1], constraints);
```

Step 4: Process the Results

Use a while loop to access each entry in the enumeration. For each entry returned by the search, you are going to print its distinguished name and attributes. The values in the enumeration are an instance of SearchResult, a subclass Binding mentioned in Project 5.

```
while (results != null && results.hasMore())
{
        SearchResult si = (SearchResult)results.next();
```

The name of the search result will be its full distinguished name. Print out the results of calling getName on the search result object.

```
System.out.println(si.getName());
```

Attributes are provided via a special Attributes object that can return an enumeration for accessing the individual attributes. An Attributes object is basically a collection of attributes, like a hashtable. Enumerations can be provided for the attribute IDs or for attribute objects. You also can use an Attributes object to create a collection of attributes. Declare a variable called attrs and initialize it to the current search result's attributes. Then declare a NamingEnumeration called cursor and initialize it to attrs's attributes using the getAll method. Finally, loop over the attributes using cursor and a while loop, as shown here.

```
Attributes attrs = si.getAttributes();
NamingEnumeration cursor = attrs.getAll();

while(cursor.hasMoreElements())
    {
```

For each attribute, get its ID and a list of its values. Define a local variable called attr to hold the next element in the cursor enumeration. Define another variable called attrId and initialize it to the current attributes ID using the getID method. Finally, define an Enumeration variable called vals and initialize it to all of the attribute's values using the getAll method.

```
Attribute attr = (Attribute) cursor.next();
String attrId = attr.getID();
Enumeration vals = attr.getAll();
```

For each value, print a string indicating the ID and value of that portion of the entry. Use a while loop to iterate through the collection of attribute values. For each value, print the attribute's ID and a string representation of the next value.

```
while(vals.hasMoreElements())
        System.out.println("\t"+attrId
              +" = "+vals.nextElement());
```

Once all of the values are printed, the program is done. Close up the various loops and the try-catch block.

```
        }
    }
}
catch (Exception exp)
{
    System.err.println("Search example failed.");
```

```
                    exp.printStackTrace();
            }
        }
}
```

Step 5: Test Your Program

If you install OpenLDAP and run the test programs, there will be a few entries in test database. Run the server on the test database and try a couple of searches. On my installation I can run the LDAP server in standalone mode, slapd, using the following command lines:

```
>cd openldap/tests
>../servers/slapd/slapd -f ./data/slapd-master.conf -p 9009 -d 5
```

This will run the server using the test database on port 9009. Now run the search program, like this:

```
>java Search "o=University of Michigan, c=US" "sn=Jensen"
```

Using this base and filter you should access two entries in the test database.

Creating an LDAP Search Program in Perl

The Perl version of the search program is very similar to the Java version. In this case, you use the Net::LDAP module to access the LDAP server. You will also need to use the BER module that defines the encoding-decoding routines used by the LDAP client library so declare these modules at the top of your program, as shown here:

```
#!/usr/bin/perl

use Convert::BER;
use Net::LDAP;
```

Step 1: Check the Command-Line Arguments

Make sure that the user called the program correctly. Use @ARGV to check that two command-line arguments were provided. If not, exit the program using die, and print a message that tells the user how to invoke this script.

```
die "usage: perl search.pl base filter\n" if (@ARGV != 2);
```

Step 2: Connect to the LDAP Server

In Perl, the connection to the LDAP database is managed by an LDAP object. Create one of these objects with the appropriate server name and port. Declare a local variable called $ldap. Initialize $ldap to a new Net::LDAP object. The method used to create the connection expects a host name, port, and debug level. If the connection process fails, exit the program and print out the error message stored in $@.

```
my $ldap;

$ldap = Net::LDAP->new('brisco',port => 9009,debug => 0,) || die $@;
```

Once it is created, you bind the LDAP object to the server using the bind method shown here. This binding forms the actual connection.

```
$ldap->bind();
```

Step 3: Perform the Search

Next, use the LDAP object's search method, shown next, to perform the search with the command-line arguments as the base and filter. You can also pass parameters to the search method that control the number of items returned (sizelimit), the time limit for the search (timelimit), and the scope of the search (scope). In this case, just set the search base to $ARGV[0] and the search filter to $ARGV[1]. If the search fails, exit the program and print $@ to the command line. If it succeeds, capture the results in a variable called $results.

```
$results = $ldap->search(
        base   => $ARGV[0],
        filter => $ARGV[1]) || die $@;
```

Step 4: Process the Results

The results of the search are returned in a special results object. This object provides access to the LDAP entries as an array of Entry objects. Use the $results' entries property to get the list of entries. Iterate over the entries using a foreach loop. Capture each entry in a variable called $entry, and use it to print out information to the user.

```
@entries = $results->entries;

foreach $entry (@entries)
{
```

Print the distinguished name first. The distinguished name is available via the entries' dn property, as shown here.

```
    print $entry->dn,"\n";
```

For each attribute in the entry, print all of the values that attribute contains. Use the entries' attributes property to get an array of attribute names. Then create a foreach loop that captures the attributes in a variable called $attr. Remember that each attribute has a set of values, so put another foreach loop inside the first one to iterate over the values for each attribute and capture them in a variable called $val. Finally, print the name of the attribute as stored in $attr.

```
foreach $attr ($entry->attributes)
{
    foreach $val ($entry->get($attr))
    {
        print "\t$attr";
```

If this is not a text attribute, print the string "binary" instead of the value of the attribute, as shown here.

```
        if (!$istext{lc($attr)})
        {
            print " = $val\n";
        }
        else
        {
            print " (binary)\n";
        }
    }
}
}
```

Complete the program by disconnecting, or unbinding, from the LDAP server using the $ldap object's unbind method. If this fails, indicate the problem to the user by exiting and printing the value of $@ to the console.

```
$ldap->unbind() || die($@);
```

Step 5: Test Your Program

If you install OpenLDAP and run the test programs, there will be a few entries in the test database. Run the server on the test database and try a couple of searches. On my installation I can run the LDAP server in standalone mode, slapd, using the following command lines:

```
>cd openldap/tests
>../servers/slapd/slapd îf ./data/slapd-master.conf îp 9009 îd 5
```

This will run the server using the test database on port 9009. Now run the search program, like this:

```
>./perl search.pl "o=University of Michigan, c=US" "sn=Jensen"
```

Using this base and filter you should access two entries in the test database.

Creating an LDAP Search Program in C

The last version of the search program is the C version. The solution to this project on the CD-ROM and shown in the text that follows was written and tested on the OpenLDAP server's C API. If you use another LDAP API you may need to alter the code slightly. In particular, different libraries expect differing levels of memory management from the client program.

The LDAP API used in the search program is declared in the lber.h and ldap.h files. Include these at the top of your program.

```
#include <stdio.h>
#include <stdlib.h>
#include <string.h>
#include <lber.h>
#include <ldap.h>
```

You can implement this entire program in one main function.

```
int main(int argc,char **argv )
{
```

You will need several variables to complete this project. The most obvious one is a pointer to an LDAP structure that represents the connection to the server. Next is a pointer to an LDAPMessage. This will be used to store the results sent by the server to this client. Finally, you will want temporary holders for the filter and base strings provided by the user.

```
    char *filter, *base;
    LDAP *ld;
    LDAPMessage *result;
```

Step 1: Check the Command-Line Arguments

First make sure that the program was executed correctly. The argc variable should be at least 3. Note that C, unlike Perl, expects the first command-line argument to be the name of the program, so we need three arguments instead of two. If there are not enough arguments, print a message to the user telling him or her how to invoke this program and exit.

```
    if(argc < 3)
    {
        printf("usage: search base filter\n");
        exit(0);
    }
```

Next, copy the command-line arguments into your strings for use when calling the LDAP api functions.

```
base = strdup(argv[1]);
filter = strdup(argv[2]);
```

Step 2: Connect to the LDAP Server

Initialize the client software using the ldap_init function. This will return a pointer to an LDAP structure. Call ldap_init with the name of your server and its port. Capture the result in the variable called ld.

```
ld = ldap_init("brisco",9009);
```

Test if the return value of ldap_init stored in ld is NULL. If ld is NULL, then the client initialization failed and the search program should fail. Print out an error message and exit. If ld is not NULL, you can bind to the ldap server.

```
if(ld==NULL)
{
    printf("Error connecting to server\n");
    exit(1);
}
```

Bind the LDAP client structure to the server using the ldap_bind_s function. This will authenticate the client, or in this case, start up the connection. Shown next, ldap_bind_s is called with four arguments: the LDAP pointer stored in ld, the name and password, and an authentication method. In this example, we are not providing a name or password so NULL is used for both. The result of the ldap_bind_s function is one of the flags defined in the LDAP header files. In this case, if it is not LDAP_SUCCESS, the binding failed and you should print a message to the user and exit.

```
if(ldap_bind_s(ld, NULL, NULL, LDAP_AUTH_SIMPLE) != LDAP_SUCCESS )
{
    printf("Error binding to server.\n");
    exit( 1 );
}
```

Step 3: Perform the Search

Perform the search using the ldap_search_s function. This is one of a few search functions that your LDAP API can provide. ldap_search_s accepts a pointer to an LDAPMessage as an argument and uses that pointer to return the search results. A flag is returned to indicate success or failure. Other arguments include the LDAP pointer, the base and filter strings, the scope of the search, and the attributes to return. Pass in NULL for the array of attribute names and 0 as a flag indicating that all attributes should be returned, whether or not they are in that array.

```
if(ldap_search_s(ld, base, LDAP_SCOPE_SUBTREE, filter
                , NULL, 0, &result)
        == LDAP_SUCCESS)
{
```

Step 4: Process the Results

The search results are returned in an LDAPMessage structure. This structure can contain several entries, each of which will be represented as another LDAPMessage. Declare a variable called entry that represents a pointer to an LDAPMessage structure; you will use these variables to hold the entries as you process them.

```
LDAPMessage *entry;
```

Declare char pointers to store the names of each attribute and the distinguished name as shown here:

```
char *a, *dn;
```

LDAP uses a standard encoding for the data in each entry. Declare a BerElement variable to reference the list of values in an entry and an array of bervals to point to the list of values for a particular attribute.

```
BerElement *ber;
struct berval **bvals;
```

Using a for loop, get the first entry in the result set, print its information, and loop over the remaining entries printing their information as well.

```
for(entry = ldap_first_entry(ld, result)
    ; entry != NULL
    ; entry = ldap_next_entry(ld, entry))
{
```

For each entry get its distinguished name and print it. Free the memory for the distinguished name using either free or ldap_memfree, depending on the API you are using.

```
dn = ldap_get_dn(ld, entry);
printf("%s\n", dn);
free(dn);
```

After printing the distinguished name, loop over the attributes in the entry. Use the same BerElement reference for all attributes. This ensures that the data for the entry is decoded appropriately.

```
for(a = ldap_first_attribute( ld, entry, &ber)
    ; a != NULL ; a = ldap_next_attribute( ld, entry, ber))
{
```

When you access an attribute, you will get its name as a return value from the ldap_first_attribute or ldap_next_attribute function. The values for the attribute can be accessed a number of ways. In this example, I accessed the values as an array of bervals and printed the string associated with the first value.

```
            bvals = ldap_get_values_len( ld, entry, a);

            if(bvals != NULL)
            {
                printf("\t%s = %s\n",a,bvals[0]->bv_val);
```

Various methods are provided to free the different elements of the LDAP API. Use ber_bvecfree to release the memory used by the values array.

```
                ber_bvecfree(bvals);
            }
        }
```

With the OpenLDAP API the BerElement should not be freed. At least, this resulted in a segmentation fault on my installation. Check the documentation on your server to determine what elements to free.

```
            /*if(ber != NULL) ber_free(ber,0);*/
        }
    }
    else
    {
        printf("No elements found.\n");
    }
}
```

Finally, unbind the LDAP client library from the server and free the string copies that contain the filter and base.

```
    ldap_unbind( ld );
    free(filter);
    free(base);

    exit(0);
}
```

Step 5: Test Your Program

Compile your C program linking in the ldap and lber libraries.

If you install OpenLDAP and run the test programs, there will be a few entries in test database. Run the server on the test database, and try a couple of searches. On my installation I can run the LDAP server in standalone mode, slapd, using the following command lines:

```
>cd openldap/tests
>../servers/slapd/slapd -f ./data/slapd-master.conf -p 9009 -d 5
```

This will run the server using the test database on port 9009. Now run the search program, like this:

```
>search "o=University of Michigan, c=US" "sn=Jensen"
```

Using this base and filter you should access two entries in the test database.

Wrap Up

Accessing an LDAP server is relatively simple. The real challenge for an enterprise is to design an LDAP database that fulfills the needs and provides optimal access. To tackle this challenge I suggest starting at the OpenLDAP site and possibly getting a book that discusses LDAP exclusively.

Now that you have completed studying this project, you should be more than ready to dive into the LDAP-specific documentation and begin programming with this new, powerful standard. I hope that you also see how Linux can be used to run LDAP servers and clients, making it an even more powerful addition to the enterprise developer's tool kit.

A Messaging Server

Project Objectives

In this project, you will learn how to:

- Use RMI to implement distributed object communication
- Use JNDI to register and find objects
- Access MySQL using JDBC, including BlOB data
- Implement a persistent queue-based messaging service
- Create peer-to-peer and publish-subscribe messaging client libraries

 YOU WILL NEED

✔ The JDK 1.1 or 1.2

✔ Java programming experience

✔ The standard JMS and JNDI libraries from Sun

✔ Experience with SQL and messaging is helpful

✔ The MySQL database

✔ A JDBC driver to connect to the database

✔ The Network Naming Context from Project 5

Although this project is implemented using MySQL you could port it to other databases available on Linux, including Postgres and mSQL.

Memo

To: Stephen
From: Manager

Stephen, we need to tie our various data sources together. For example, we want to link the HR applications with the Oracle financial database. Can you suggest a mechanism for performing this integration?

Manager

Memo

To: Manager
From: Stephen

Manager, a lot of companies are starting to use messaging services to perform this type of integration. The messaging provides a standard way for programs to communicate. Create teams that write adaptors for the various resources, like HR and Oracle, then use a reliable messaging scheme to create notifications between the various system adaptors. I have included a basic messaging service that we can use during development. The API for this service is provided via the Java Messaging Service, JMS, so we can switch to a commercial JMS provider for deployment.

Stephen

About This Project

For the last few years, the concept of a messaging system has become a popular method for integrating computer systems. In this context, messaging is a distributed programming technique in which each communication between two programs is a well-defined package or message. Often the message is forwarded through a server, but the implementation is really vendor dependent. In an attempt to provide a standard method for accessing these messaging services in Java, Sun and its partners defined the *Java Messaging Service (JMS)*. JMS is a collection of Java packages for accessing a messaging service. The JMS packages define interfaces that a messaging vendor implements.

This project describes a program and library called MiniJMS. MiniJMS is a JMS service provider that can be used to create messaging applications with Sun's Java Messaging Service (JMS) Application Programmers Interface (API). This service provider is by no means a complete, commercial messaging solution, but it does provide an example of a multitier enterprise application. MiniJMS works well on Linux, making it a usable messaging solution in your Linux environment.

 CAUTION

This is an advanced project that requires Java programming experience.

This project contains about 5000 lines of code in 35 classes, making it rather large to include the entire example in the text. I've included and described only the key code for this project. The complete code is available on the CD-ROM. MiniJMS relies on several enterprise APIs. First and foremost, it implements part of the JMS. This implementation relies on the Java Naming and Directory Interface (JNDI) for finding resources, the Remote Message Interface (RMI) for network connections, and the Java Database Connectivity library (JDBC) for message persistence.

 NOTE

You should familiarize yourself with the JMS and JNDI APIs before diving into this project. JNDI is used in Projects 5 and 6, while JDBC is used in Projects 3, 4, and 8. Also check out java.sun.com and www.javaworld.com.

MiniJMS implements the majority of the JMS API, but it is not intended for commercial use. This implementation doesn't support the message selectors; it is not designed to plug into an application server, and it doesn't support distributed transactions.

Despite these limitations, MiniJMS does provide a basic messaging framework and JMS provider that uses server-based message management. It provides persistent messaging, saving messages to a Java Database Connectivity (JDBC) compliant database. Also, MiniJMS provides an easy testing ground for understanding and testing JMS applications. On top of this, MiniJMS implements both of the messaging models defined by JMS, even though this is not required by the specification.

Basic Concepts and Design

Messaging is the mechanism programs use to communicate with each other. In this sense messaging is like RMI, or even sockets. Messaging, though, is based on a fundamental entity called a *message*. The message represents the content of a single communication between two or more programs. Programs that use messaging send and receive *atomic messages*, meaning that each message exists on its own, separate from other messages that the client receives. In this respect, messaging is more like using TCP/IP packets or even UDP datagrams than it is like sockets because TCP/IP and UDP deal in small packets of data rather than a continuously open connection. In effect, messaging is the process of communicating between programs by creating, sending, and receiving messages.

Normally, messaging support is provided via a library, a server, or some other middleware. The term *message-oriented-middleware (MOM)*, often refers to an infrastructure that supports messaging. MOM defines what a message looks like to the program, how a program sends a message, and how a program receives a message. The Java Messaging Service (JMS) provides a standard Java-based interface to the messaging services of a MOM or some other provider.

There are two basic designs for a messaging provider. The first design, pictured in Figure 7.1, uses messages to communicate directly between applications.

The second design, shown in Figure 7.2, uses a server to support messaging. In this case, clients connect to a server that distributes messages for them. Clients that want to receive messages register with the server for notification. This design is more like that of the post office, where a central entity manages message delivery.

The advantage of the server approach is that services such as load balancing, message persistence, and security can be administered and upgraded in a single location. This brings up an important point: Messaging providers can include a variety of services on top of the basic ability to send and receive messages. When looking at a provider you might ask the following questions:

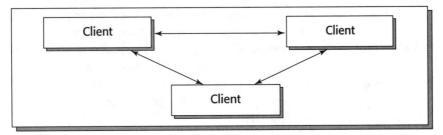

Figure 7.1   Client-based messaging.

What happens to a message if the intended receiver is not available? Many providers either will store messages for later delivery or, if specified, will ignore these messages.

What happens when the server goes down? Obviously, messages won't go anywhere, but how does the client figure this out?

Do all clients receive all messages? Providers normally will define the concept of a message destination. Clients that want to receive messages indicate the destination to which they are listening.

Can any client send messages to any other client? Providers can provide mechanisms for limiting which clients can send to which destinations, or they can at least require clients to choose a destination to limit the receivers for a message.

What can a message include? On top of the basic design for a messaging system, there is the definition of the messages themselves. Depending on a provider's goals, they might support binary messages, text messages, messages that have key-value pairs, or even messages that support objects as the message body. The limitations on message content are often driven by the systems that a provider supports and the performance constraints that the

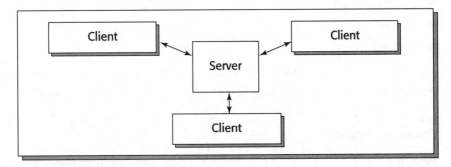

Figure 7.2   Server-based messaging.

provider places on its products. For example, sending arbitrary objects can be a performance nightmare because it involves an arbitrary format and size. On the other hand, limiting all messages to 10-character strings allows the provider to optimize its software for these messages. In general, the actual choices available to a messaging programmer lie somewhere toward the arbitrary side of these two extremes, with a performance cost associated with message size and complexity.

I hope that these questions will help you to determine the requirements you have and find the provider that fulfills them.

At this point, you may be asking yourself, so what? What do I get for using these messages? The answer is, "It depends." It really does. For some applications RMI, HTTP, or sockets are the right solution. For example, if you just want to talk to your Oracle database you probably don't need to add the messaging abstraction in the middle of that relationship. Messaging is useful where you want to separate the destination or networking from the client's code. For example, a messaging service might ensure that the insert statements that you want to make for that database arrive. If the database is unavailable now because you are using a laptop on an airplane, the service will deliver the insert messages later. The messaging service decouples the sender and receiver, which allows them to work together without being designed to specifically and exclusively work with each other. In a moment you'll see how this decoupling has advantages in a number of areas. First, a few core concepts in the messaging world need to be addressed.

Messaging Domains

The concept of messaging can be further specialized into several domains. These domains are used to define which client receives a message. The most common domains are these:

- Point-to-point
- Publish-subscribe
- Request-reply

Each of these domains defines different models for the programs that are communicating. Not all MOM providers will provide all of these models.

Point-to-Point

Point-to-point messaging is designed to allow one client to send messages to another client. This may or may not be a one-way relationship. In other words, the sender may not be a receiver and vice-versa. There are two basic models for point-to-point messaging. The simplest is to have a client send a message directly to another client, similar to the way RMI sends messages between objects in a program. A messaging interface, however, could hide some of the mechanics of the messaging process, especially by handling the exceptions that occur.

The more common point-to-point model is based on the concept of a *queue*, pictured in Figure 7.3. Senders put messages into a queue. The receiver takes messages out of the queue. Often this queue is stored on the messaging server, and it even can be stored in a relational database for reliable persistence. The Java Messaging Service uses the queue approach to point-to-point messaging, although it doesn't prohibit the implementation from using direct messaging.

The defining factor in point-to-point messaging is that there is a single receiver for the messages. For example, an HR system could send a particular message directly to the financials system, and to no other.

Publish-Subscribe

Publish-subscribe messaging is designed for situations in which multiple programs should receive the same messages. JMS defines publish-subscribe around the concept of a *topic*. Publishers send messages to a topic; subscribers receive all of the messages sent to a topic. This model is especially useful in situations where a group of programs want to notify each other of a particular occurrence. For example, the HR system could publish a message indicating a new hire, the financials could use the notification to update the payroll database, and the facilities system could generate a new phone number.

The defining factor in this model is that there can be multiple senders and receivers. It is not necessary that the programs act as both, only that the system supports both. An example of publish-subscribe is pictured in Figure 7.4.

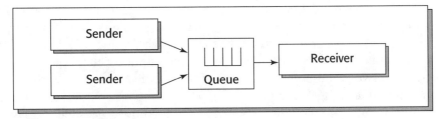

Figure 7.3   Queue-based messaging.

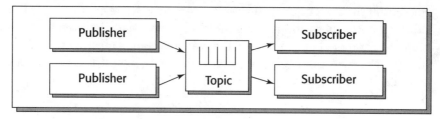

Figure 7.4 Publish-subscribe messaging.

Request-Reply

Request-reply is the standard object messaging format. A program sends a message and expects to receive a message in return. Often this messaging domain is defined as a subset of one of the other two. For example, a point-to-point system can support publish and subscribe by making both points sender and receiver.

JMS doesn't specifically support request-reply, although it does allow it, in the context of the other methods, via the use of a reply to field in a message. In JMS, you can reply to a message by checking for this field and sending a message to the queue or topic that it contains.

Applications of Messaging

Messaging has gained in popularity over the last couple years because of its flexibility and the advantages it provides in a variety of applications. Some of the applications in which it is making headway are distributed programming, business integration, and notification.

By definition, messaging is a form of *distributed programming* because it involves communication between programs. Messaging, however, adds the level of abstraction generated by the concept of a message. Unlike distributed programming systems such as RMI or CORBA, messaging encapsulates the message being sent into its own publicly defined entity. Programs can change the message type in most messaging systems, making them very flexible. This abstraction also makes it possible to use messaging to link different systems. For example, a C programmer could send and receive messages using function calls, while a Java programmer would use method calls. The messages can travel between these two programs without either client knowing the implementation language of the other. In fact, the implementation of one program could change, and the other wouldn't need to know unless the message definition changed with it.

Distributed programming often is used to implement bridges between various applications in your enterprise. This is one of the main applications of messaging. With persistent messaging, where the server stores messages for clients that are not currently available, applications are assured that their notifications are received even if the receiver currently is unavailable. For example, a company could post important messages using publish-subscribe. When a sales person returns from a trip and connects his or her computer to the network, any pending messages are downloaded and the user is notified. Although programmers could implement this persistence by hand, the messaging system can handle it for them. The work is encapsulated behind a robust, well-tested interface.

Perhaps the hottest application of messaging is business integration. All of the examples have been talking about one system talking to another system. These systems can be created with very different technologies, in which case messaging is a powerful translator. The HR system could be PeopleSoft, but the financial systems are Oracle. A programmer could create adapters that tie these systems together through messaging. If the financials change to SAP, then the adapter changes, but the other systems remain the same. The messages become the interface definition for distributed computing.

Java Messaging Service

The Java Messaging Service (JMS) is a specification, designed by a group of MOM providers and Sun, that describes how to use Java for messaging. JMS defines a set of Java interfaces. JMS providers implement these interfaces for the programmer by layering the JMS interface on top of their messaging services. JMS defines both Queues and Topics, but doesn't require the provider to implement both.

The primary goal for JMS was to provide an interface to messaging that was rich enough to make it useful, but not a conglomeration of all of the features provided by existing messaging products. Instead, it tries to maximize portability with as many features as possible. Ideally, the providers that implement JMS will do so in 100 percent pure Java to maximize portability, but this is not a requirement of the specification.

A number of companies provided Messaging Oriented Middleware, many of which have signed up to provide a JMS interface to their products. To get a list of the current JMS partners go to http://java.sun.com/products/jms. In this project, you create your own JMS service called MiniJMS.

JMS breaks messaging into two models, point-to-point and publish-subscribe. MiniJMS minimized the differences between these models as much as possible to centralize code. This centralization, though, does add a small amount of complexity to the core objects because they do double duty by supporting both models.

The design for MiniJMS is split into three layers and two packages. The first layer provides the client interfaces specified in JMS. The second layer is a set of remote interfaces for the RMI objects provided by the server. The third and final layer is the server itself. The relationship between these layers is pictured in Figure 7.5.

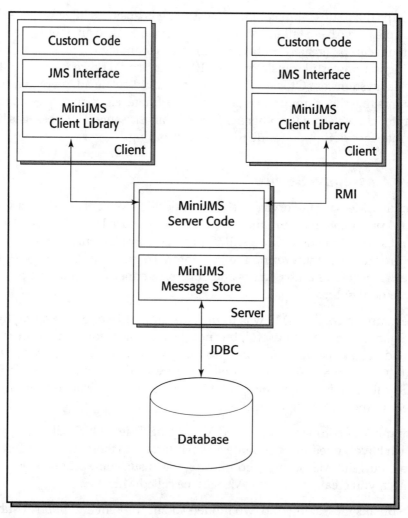

Figure 7.5 MiniJMS design.

The server code is organized into the minijmsserver package, while the remaining two layers are part of the minijms package.

Step 1: Prepare the System

Before you begin, make sure that you have MySQL installed on your system. Also install the JDBC driver for MySQL discussed in Project 3. Download the standard JMS and JNDI packages from java.sun.com/products and add these jar files to your class path. Both of these libraries provide interfaces and utility classes for accessing services provided by an external library. Create a new MySQL database called minijms. A small Java program called minijmsserver.BuildDB is provided on the CD-ROM to create the tables for this database.

Step 2: Define Client/Server Interface

MiniJMS requires three remote interfaces for communication between the client and the server. These interfaces are listed in Table 7.1.

RemoteMiniServer should be implemented by the root object that is registered with RMI for access by the client. This object does not take up real resources on the server and is accessed for use by the client to create connections. This interface is also used to define the name, "MiniJMSServer", used by the server to bind with the RMI registery.

```
public interface RemoteMiniServer extends java.rmi.Remote
{
    public final static String SERVER_NAME="MiniJMSServer";

    //Uses the client machine if ID is null
    RemoteMiniConnection openConnection(String clientId)
     throws RemoteException,JMSException;
}
```

Table 7.1 Client/Server Interfaces

INTERFACE	DESCRIPTION
RemoteMiniServer	The basic interface between the client and server used to create connections
RemoteMiniConnection	Fundamental connection interface used to create client IDs and sessions
RemoteMiniSession	The interface between a session on the client and its representation on the server

Connections to the server are represented on the server by objects that implement RemoteMiniConnection. These objects take up server resources, and thus they support the close method. Connections are used to create client identifiers for use by the system to tag each client application/computer. The default is the client's IP address. This causes all of the applications on that machine to share some of the resources and messages in the server. In other words, if two applications on the same computer use the same ID, they will share the messages for a particular destination. Clients can change this behavior by specifying a user name when creating the connection. DurableTopicSubscribers also bypass this default by using their name to register for messages.

```
public interface RemoteMiniConnection extends java.rmi.Remote
{
    public String getClientId()
      throws RemoteException;

    public RemoteMiniConnection close()
      throws RemoteException, JMSException;//should return null

    //tracks sessions, and closes on close
    public RemoteMiniSession createSession()
      throws RemoteException, JMSException;
}
```

The connection's main job is to create sessions. Notice that the connection interface doesn't include all of the methods in javax.jms.Connection. Many of these methods are handled on the client. Only the minimal necessary information travels to the server. Because sessions represent message processors, I have broken them into the client and server portions for better code management.

RemoteMiniSession defines a number of methods. These methods are listed in Table 7.2. Many represent the associated methods in the javax.jms.Session interface and are used by the client's session object to notify the server of a requested function.

The methods in this interface are the key protocol between the client and the server. The concepts of registering for a destination, sending, and receiving are used extensively in the client library.

Step 3: Create the Client Library

All of the code that a JMS client needs is provided in the minijms package. This includes all of the classes that the client interacts with, as detailed by the JMS specification. The mapping between the specification and MiniJMS is described in Table 7.3. This table hints at one of the design techniques used in MiniJMS to simplify the code. In several cases, more than one of the JMS types are im-

Table 7.2 RemoteMiniSession Methods

METHOD	DESCRIPTION
`public void setTransacted(boolean tf)` `Throws RemoteException, JMSException;`	Tells the remote session if it is transacted.
`public RemoteMiniSession close()` `Throws RemoteException, JMSException;`	Closes the remote session freeing resources.
`public Queue createQueue(String queueName)` `Throws RemoteException, JMSException;`	Creates a new Queue with the provided name, or throws an exception if the queue exists.
`public Topic createTopic(String topicName)` `Throws RemoteException, JMSException;`	Creates a new Topic with the provided name, or throws an exception if the topic exists.
`public void deleteDestination(String name)` `Throws RemoteException, JMSException;`	Deletes a destination from the system, ultimately deleting all of the messages associated with the destination.
`public void send(Message message)` `Throws RemoteException, JMSException;`	Sends a message to the MiniJMS server.
`public Message receive()` `Throws RemoteException, JMSException;`	Receives the next message for this session from the server.
`public void commit()` `Throws RemoteException, JMSException;`	Commits the received and sent messages, indicating that they have been received.
`public void rollback()` `Throws RemoteException, JMSException;`	Rolls back the sessions transaction.
`public void recover()` `Throws RemoteException, JMSException;`	Recovers the sessions transaction.

`public void acknowledge(Destination d`
`                        ,String name)`
`throws RemoteException, JMSException;`
	Acknowledges the messages for a specific destination, and name. This name can be the user name that was passed in to create the connection.

`public void registerFor(Destination dest`
`                         ,boolean durable`
`                         ,String name)`
`throws RemoteException, JMSException;`
	Internal method used to tell the server that the session has created a consumer for a particular destination. The name of the consumer is provided, and a flag indicates if it is durable.

`public void unregisterFor(Destination dest`
`                           ,String name)`
`throws RemoteException, JMSException;`
	Tells the server that a consumer was closed, possibly stopping further delivery of messages to this client, if no more consumers remain.

Table 7.3 MiniJMS Client Classes

JMS INTERFACE	MINIJMS CLASS
Destination	MiniDestination
ConnectionFactory	MiniConnectionFactory
Connection	MiniConnection
Session	MiniSession
MessageConsumer	MiniConsumer
MessageProducer	MiniProducer
Message	MiniMessage
ConnectionMetaData	MiniJMSConnectionMetaData
Queue	MiniDestination
QueueConnectionFactory	MiniQueueConnectionFactory
QueueConnection	MiniQueueConnection
QueueSession	MiniQueueSession
QueueSender	MiniProducer
QueueReceiver	MiniConsumer
TemporaryQueue	MiniTempDestination
Topic	MiniDestination
TopicConnectionFactory	MiniTopicConnectionFactory
TopicConnection	MiniTopicConnection
TopicSession	MiniTopicSession
TopicPublisher	MiniProducer
TopicSubscriber	MiniConsumer
TemporaryTopic	MiniTempDestination

plemented by a single MiniJMS class. For example, MiniDestination implements Destination, Queue, and Topic.

The message types are not included in this table, and they are discussed later. MiniJMS implements each message type in its own class.

Both Destinations and Messages are entity type objects that represent data but don't perform any real operations. Let's take a look at these two objects before the remaining client libraries so that you have a foundation for the discussion.

MiniDestination

MiniDestination objects are used to represent destinations in the MiniJMS system. A MiniDestination can be a Queue or a Topic. The object keeps a flag indicating which it should be treated as. Aside from storing a name and this isQueue flag, the destination's only other method is the getReference method. This method is defined in Referenceable, and it is used to allow the destination to be bound into a JNDI context. Support for JNDI is discussed more at the end of the section on the client library.

```java
package minijms;

//import statements removed to save space
public class MiniDestination
 implements Destination, Topic, Queue, Serializable, Referenceable
{
    protected String name;
    protected boolean isQ;

    public MiniDestination(String name, boolean isQueue)
    {
        this.name = name;
        isQ = isQueue;
    }

    public int hashCode()
    {
        return name.hashCode();
    }

    public boolean equals(Object o)
    {
        boolean retVal = false;

        if(o instanceof MiniDestination)
        {
            if((name!=null) && name.equals(o.toString()))
            {
                if(((MiniDestination)o).isQueue()
                    ==isQueue()) retVal = true;
            }
        }

        return retVal;
    }

    public String toString()
    {
        return name;
    }

    public boolean isQueue()
    {
```

```
        return isQ;
    }

    public java.lang.String getTopicName()
     throws JMSException
    {
        if(!isQ)
            return name;
        else
            throw new JMSException();
    }

    public java.lang.String getQueueName()
     throws JMSException
    {
        if(isQ)
            return name;
        else
            throw new JMSException();
    }

    public Reference getReference()
                        throws NamingException
    {
        Reference retVal;

        retVal = new Reference(MiniDestination.class.getName()
                    ,new StringRefAddr("name",name)
                    ,MiniDestinationFactory.class.getName()
                    ,null);

        retVal.add(new StringRefAddr("isQueue"
                    ,(isQ?"true":"false")));

        return retVal;
    }
}
```

MiniDestination also implements Serializable so that it can be passed around in RMI messages or saved to disk.

The MiniJMSServer uses Destinations as keys in hashtables, and it searches for them in vectors. To make this searching correct, both the hashcode and equals methods are defined to ensure that two Destinations are equal if they have the same name and isQueue flag.

MiniMessage

All messages in the MiniJMS system are represented by a MiniMessage object or an instance of a subclass of MiniMessage. This class has a lot of code, but the majority of it is accessor methods for the header fields. The code for these methods is listed next. One addition made to the regular header fields is that messages keep track of their session. This connection is used to implement the acknowledge message. MiniMessages use the property JMS_MSG_NUM to test equality with other messages. MiniMessage implements Message and Serializable so that it can be passed as part of an RMI message.

```java
package minijms;

//import statements removed to save space

public class MiniMessage
 implements Message,Serializable
{
    protected String messageId;
    protected long timeStamp;
    protected String corrId;
    protected Destination replyTo;
    protected Destination destination;
    protected String type;
    protected int deliveryMode;
    protected long expiration;
    protected int priority;
    protected boolean redelivered;
    protected Hashtable properties;
    transient protected MiniSession session;

    public MiniMessage()
    {
        deliveryMode = Message.DEFAULT_DELIVERY_MODE;
        priority = Message.DEFAULT_PRIORITY;
        expiration = Message.DEFAULT_TIME_TO_LIVE;
        type="Message";

        properties = new Hashtable();
    }

    public boolean equals(Object o)
    {
        boolean retVal = false;
        String numKey;

        try
        {
            if(o instanceof Message)
            {
                Message msg = (Message) o;

                numKey = MiniJMSMessageStore.MSG_NUM;

                if(msg.propertyExists(numKey)
                    && propertyExists(numKey))
                {
                    if(getLongProperty(numKey)
                        == msg.getLongProperty(numKey))
                    {
```

```
                            retVal = true;
                    }
                }
            }
        }
        catch(Exception exp)
        {
            retVal = false;
        }

        return retVal;
    }

    public void setMiniSession(MiniSession s)
    {
        session = s;
    }

    public MiniSession getMiniSession()
    {
        return session;
    }

    public void acknowledge() throws JMSException
    {
        if((session != null)
            && (session.getAckMode()
                ==Session.CLIENT_ACKNOWLEDGE))
        {
            session.acknowledge(destination);
        }
        else
        {
            throw new JMSException();
        }
    }

    public void clearBody() throws JMSException
    {
        //do nothing in generic case;
    }

    public String getJMSMessageID() throws JMSException
    {
        return messageId;
    }

    public void setJMSMessageID(String id) throws JMSException
    {
        messageId = id;
    }

    public long getJMSTimestamp() throws JMSException
```

```
{
    return timeStamp;
}

public void setJMSTimestamp(long timestamp) throws JMSException
{
    timeStamp = timestamp;
}

public byte [] getJMSCorrelationIDAsBytes() throws JMSException
{
    byte[] retVal = null;

    if(corrId != null)
        retVal = corrId.getBytes();

    return retVal;
}

public void setJMSCorrelationIDAsBytes(byte[] correlationID)
    throws JMSException
{
    corrId = new String(correlationID);
}

public void setJMSCorrelationID(String correlationID)
  throws JMSException
{
    corrId = correlationID;
}

public String getJMSCorrelationID() throws JMSException
{
    return corrId;
}

public Destination getJMSReplyTo() throws JMSException
{
    return replyTo;
}

public void setJMSReplyTo(Destination replyTo)
  throws JMSException
{
    this.replyTo = replyTo;
}

public Destination getJMSDestination() throws JMSException
{
    return destination;
}

public void setJMSDestination(Destination destination)
  throws JMSException
```

```
{
    this.destination = destination;
}

public int getJMSDeliveryMode() throws JMSException
{
    return deliveryMode;
}

public void setJMSDeliveryMode(int deliveryMode)
  throws JMSException
{
    this.deliveryMode = deliveryMode;
}

public boolean getJMSRedelivered() throws JMSException
{
    return redelivered;
}

public void setJMSRedelivered(boolean redelivered)
  throws JMSException
{
    this.redelivered = redelivered;
}

public String getJMSType() throws JMSException
{
    return type;
}

public void setJMSType(String type) throws JMSException
{
    this.type = type;
}

public long getJMSExpiration() throws JMSException
{
    return expiration;
}

public void setJMSExpiration(long expiration)
  throws JMSException
{
    this.expiration = expiration;
}

public int getJMSPriority() throws JMSException
{
    return priority;
}

public void setJMSPriority(int priority) throws JMSException
{
```

```
            this.priority = priority;
    }
```

The remaining code in MiniMessage is used to manage the priorities. All of the priorities are stored in a hashtable called properties. A set of convenience methods is provided to convert the objects in the hashtable to the appropriate types. For example, the method floatFor takes an object, and if the object is a String or Float, it returns a float value. Otherwise, an exception is thrown. These methods are used by the MiniMessage subclasses such as MiniMapMessage to implement all of the data type conversions specified in the JMS documentation. The clearProperties, getPropertyNames, and propertyExists methods forward the request to the properties hashtable. Only a sample of the properties methods is shown here; the remainder are available on the CD-ROM. The entire class has about 570 lines, too many to include here.

```
    public void clearProperties() throws JMSException
    {
        properties.clear();
    }

    public boolean propertyExists(String name) throws JMSException
    {
        return properties.containsKey(name);
    }

    public Enumeration getPropertyNames() throws JMSException
    {
        return properties.keys();
    }

    public boolean getBooleanProperty(String name)
      throws JMSException
    {
        return booleanFor(properties.get(name));
    }

    public byte getByteProperty(String name) throws JMSException
    {
        return byteFor(properties.get(name));
    }

    ... Code removed to save space ...

    public String getStringProperty(String name) throws JMSException
    {
        return stringFor(properties.get(name));
    }

    public Object getObjectProperty(String name) throws JMSException
    {
        return objectFor(properties.get(name));
```

```
    }

    public void setBooleanProperty(String name, boolean value)
            throws MessageNotWriteableException, JMSException
    {
        properties.put(name,new Boolean(value));
    }

    public void setByteProperty(String name, byte value)
            throws MessageNotWriteableException, JMSException
    {
        properties.put(name,new Byte(value));
    }


    ... Code removed to save space ...
    public void setStringProperty(String name, String value)
            throws MessageNotWriteableException, JMSException
    {
        properties.put(name,value);
    }

    public void setObjectProperty(String name, Object value)
            throws MessageNotWriteableException, JMSException
    {
        properties.put(name,value);
    }

    public boolean booleanFor(Object o) throws JMSException
    {
        if(o == null) throw new NullPointerException("No value.");

        if(o instanceof Boolean)
        {
            return ((Boolean)o).booleanValue();
        }
        else if(o instanceof String)
        {
            return Boolean.valueOf((String)o).booleanValue();
        }
        else
        {
            throw new JMSException("Bad Type");
        }
    }
    ... Code removed to save space ...

    public int intFor(Object o) throws JMSException
    {
        if(o == null) throw new NullPointerException("No value.");

        if(o instanceof Integer)
        {
```

```
                    return ((Integer)o).intValue();
                }
                else if(o instanceof Short)
                {
                    return ((Short)o).intValue();
                }
                else if(o instanceof Byte)
                {
                    return ((Byte)o).intValue();
                }
                else if(o instanceof String)
                {
                    return Integer.valueOf((String)o).intValue();
                }
                else
                {
                    throw new JMSException("Bad Type");
                }
        }

        public String stringFor(Object o) throws JMSException
        {
            if(o == null) throw new NullPointerException("No value.");

            return o.toString();
        }

        public Object objectFor(Object o) throws JMSException
        {
            if(o == null) throw new NullPointerException("No value.");

            return o;
        }

        public byte[] bytesFor(Object o) throws JMSException
        {
            if(o == null) throw new NullPointerException("No value.");

            if(!(o instanceof byte[]))
             throw new JMSException("Bad Type");

            return ((byte[])o);
        }
}
```

Notice that the methods for converting values all accept Strings as possible input. The stringFor method converts any object to a String.

MiniJMS provides implementations of the Message subtypes. These implementations are called MiniTextMessage, MiniMapMessage, MiniObjectMessage, MiniStreamMessage, and MiniBytesMessage. The stream and bytes messages in no way are optimized and do not support reading arbitrary bytes from the message. They should, however, be sufficient for testing.

MiniConnectionFactory

The first real working class in MiniJMS is the MiniConnectionFactory. This class acts as the super class for the MiniQueueConnectionFactory and the Mini-TopicConnectionFactory. A factory keeps track of the URL to the server.

```java
package minijms;

//import statements removed to save space

public class MiniConnectionFactory
 implements Serializable
{
    protected String url;

    public MiniConnectionFactory(String serverURL)
    {
        url = serverURL;
    }

    public String getURL()
    {
        return url;
    }
}
```

The subclasses for MiniConnectionFactory will implement Referenceable so that they can be bound to a JNDI context. MiniConnectionFactory implements only Serializable, making it and its subclasses available for RMI messaging.

MiniConnection

The connections in MiniJMS extend the MiniConnection class. This class provides the core functionality for a connection to the MiniJMS server. In particular, the connection keeps track of user name, password, client ID, and ExceptionListener for connections. MiniConnection also implements the code that creates a connection to the RMI server and stores a list of the connections sessions.

```java
package minijms;

//import statements removed to save space

public class MiniConnection implements javax.jms.Connection
{
    protected RemoteMiniServer server;
    protected RemoteMiniConnection remote;
    protected String user;
    protected String password;
    protected String clientId;
    protected ExceptionListener elistener;
```

```
    protected Vector sessions;

public MiniConnection(String url,String name,String pass)
    throws JMSException
{
    user = name;
    password = pass;
    sessions = new Vector();

    try
    {
        server = (RemoteMiniServer) Naming.lookup(url);
        remote = server.openConnection(user);
        clientId = remote.getClientId();

        if(remote==null) throw new Exception(url);
    }
    catch(Exception exp)
    {
        throw
        new JMSException("Failed to connect to server: "
                            +exp.toString());
    }
}
```

The client ID defaults to the IP address of the client or the user name. This value is used to determine to whom to deliver messages. All of the connections with the same client ID are treated as equivalent by the server and share the messages sent to it. The client ID actually is assigned by the server, so changing it involves reconnecting to the server, closing the existing connection in the process.

```
public String getClientID() throws JMSException
{
    return clientId;
}

public void setClientID(String id) throws JMSException
{
    try
    {
        if(remote != null)
        {
            remote = remote.close();
        }
    }
    catch(Exception exp)
    {
    }

    clientId = id;

    try
```

```
    {
        remote = server.openConnection(clientId);
    }
    catch(Exception exp)
    {
        throw new JMSException(exp.toString());
    }
}
```

Connections are expected to implement the method getMetaData. As shown next, a MiniConnection returns a MiniJMSConnectionMetaData object when this message is called. MiniJMSConnectionMetaData implements the ConnectionMetaData interface. Because this information is mainly about the version of the provider, the code isn't included here but is available on the CD-ROM.

```
public ConnectionMetaData getMetaData() throws JMSException
{
    return new MiniJMSConnectionMetaData();
}
```

The ExceptionListener is notified when bad errors occur. Currently MiniJMS does not notify this listener anywhere, but the code is here to perform the notification.

```
public void setExceptionListener(ExceptionListener listener)
{
    elistener = listener;
}
public void notifyListener(JMSException exp)
{
    if(elistener != null)
    {
        elistener.onException(exp);
    }
}
```

When a subclass of MiniConnection creates a session it adds the session to the list of sessions managed for this connection. Sessions will remove themselves from the list when closed.

```
public void addSession(MiniSession s)
{
    synchronized(sessions)
    {
        if(!sessions.contains(s))
        {
            sessions.addElement(s);
        }
    }
}
```

```
public void removeSession(MiniSession s)
{
    synchronized(sessions)
    {
        if(!sessions.contains(s))
        {
            sessions.removeElement(s);
        }
    }
}
```

Starting a connection tells the sessions in that connection to resume. This corresponds to the session resuming a thread that requests messages from the server.

```
public void start() throws JMSException
{
    synchronized(sessions)
    {
        int i,max;
        MiniSession session;

        max = sessions.size();

        for(i=0;i<max;i++)
        {
            session = (MiniSession) sessions.elementAt(i);
            session.resume();
        }
    }
}
```

Stopping a connection tells the sessions in that connection to suspend. This corresponds to the session suspending a thread that requests messages from the server.

```
public void stop() throws JMSException
{
    synchronized(sessions)
    {
        int i,max;
        MiniSession session;

        max = sessions.size();

        for(i=0;i<max;i++)
        {
            session = (MiniSession) sessions.elementAt(i);
            session.suspend();
        }
    }
}
```

Closing a MiniConnection closes the sessions that it is managing and notifies the server that the connection should be closed. This frees up resources on the server.

```
public void close() throws JMSException
{
    try
    {
        synchronized(sessions)
        {
            int i,max;
            MiniSession session;

            max = sessions.size();

            for(i=0;i<max;i++)
            {
                session = (MiniSession) sessions.elementAt(i);
                session.close();
            }

            sessions.removeAllElements();
        }

        if(remote != null) remote = remote.close();
    }
    catch(Exception exp)
    {
        throw new JMSException(exp.toString());
    }
}
}
```

Connections have a close relationship with their sessions in this design. This relationship is transparent to the programmer using the JMS interfaces.

MiniSession

The heart of the MiniJMS client implementation is the MiniSession class. This class defines the core behaviors of sending and receiving messages. Each session uses a separate thread to poll the server for messages. The polling uses a basic wait-on-read semantic, so it shouldn't take up CPU resources. Wait-on-read means that the session will try to read data from the server; if no data exists, the program waits for data to arrive. While waiting the session is not using CPU cycles. Rather, the operating system watches the network for the session and when data arrives the session is given the CPU again and reads the data. The bottom line is that although you use polling, where the session asks for data, it is not the foot-tapping kind of polling that uses computer resources.

Each MiniSession also contains a reference to a RemoteMiniSession. This reference is used to communicate with the MiniJMS server. Messages for a session are organized into a hashtable that groups messages by destination. Message listeners registered with consumers also are tracked by the session in a hashtable that groups them by destination.

```
package minijms;

//imports removed to save space

public abstract class MiniSession
 implements Session, Runnable
{
    protected boolean transacted;
    protected int ackMode;
    protected MessageListener listener;
    protected RemoteMiniSession session;
    protected MiniConnection conn;
    protected Hashtable messagesForDest;
    protected Hashtable listenerForDest;
    protected Random rand;
    protected Thread checker;

    public MiniSession(boolean transacted,
                       int ackMode)
    {
        this.ackMode = ackMode;
        this.transacted = transacted;

        messagesForDest = new Hashtable();
        listenerForDest = new Hashtable();

        rand = new Random();
        checker = new Thread(this);
    }
```

While the MiniSessions constructor creates the basic resources, it is up to the connection that creates a MiniSession to provide it with the RemoteMiniSession reference. This reference is obtained from the RemoteMiniConnection to which a MiniConnection has a reference.

```
    public void setRemote(RemoteMiniSession r)
        throws JMSException
    {
        session = r;

        if(session == null)
            throw new JMSException("Failed to connect.");

        try
        {
            if(transacted) session.setTransacted(true);
```

```
        checker.start();
    }
    catch(Exception exp)
    {
        throw new JMSException("Failed to connect.");
    }
}

public RemoteMiniSession getRemote()
{
    return session;
}
```

MiniSessions keep track of their connection, acknowledgment mode, and whether they are transacted in instance variables. The following methods implement accessor methods for these variables.

```
public void setConnection(MiniConnection c)
{
    conn = c;
}

//used by messages to determine if ack should
//do anything
int getAckMode()
{
    return ackMode;
}

public boolean getTransacted() throws JMSException
{
    return transacted;
}
```

Sessions make their client ID available via the getClientId method, shown next for MiniSession. Normally, a session uses its connection's client ID. If for any reason this fails, a random number is used.

```
public String getClientID()
    throws JMSException
{
    if(conn != null) return conn.getClientID();
    else return String.valueOf(rand.nextInt());
}
```

Sessions are expected to create the message that a client will send. MiniSession provides access to all of the message types, as specified in the JMS specification. When a client wants to send a message, they use the session to create it.

```
public BytesMessage createBytesMessage() throws JMSException
{
```

```
        return new MiniStreamMessage();
    }

    public MapMessage createMapMessage() throws JMSException
    {
        return new MiniMapMessage();
    }

    public Message createMessage() throws JMSException
    {
        return new MiniMessage();
    }

    public ObjectMessage createObjectMessage() throws JMSException
    {
        return new MiniObjectMessage();
    }

    public ObjectMessage createObjectMessage(Serializable object)
        throws JMSException
    {
        return new MiniObjectMessage(object);
    }

    public StreamMessage createStreamMessage() throws JMSException
    {
        return new MiniStreamMessage();
    }

    public TextMessage createTextMessage() throws JMSException
    {
        return new MiniTextMessage();
    }

    public TextMessage createTextMessage(StringBuffer stringBuffer) throws
JMSException
    {
        return new MiniTextMessage(stringBuffer);
    }
```

MiniSession provides a simple interface to MessageProducers in the MiniJMS
library for sending messages. The send method forwards the message to the
RemoteMiniSession on the server, as shown here in bold.

```
    public void send(Message message)
                throws JMSException
    {
        try
        {
            session.send(message);
        }
        catch(JMSException exp)
        {
```

```
        throw exp;
    }
    catch(Exception exp)
    {
        throw new JMSException(exp.toString());
    }
}
```

Commit, recover, and rollback also are forwarded to the server for processing.

```
public void commit() throws JMSException
{
    try
    {
        session.commit();
    }
    catch(JMSException exp)
    {
        throw exp;
    }
    catch(Exception exp)
    {
        throw new JMSException("No remote connection.");
    }
}

public void rollback() throws JMSException
{
    try
    {
        session.rollback();
    }
    catch(JMSException exp)
    {
        throw exp;
    }
    catch(Exception exp)
    {
        throw new JMSException("No remote connection.");
    }
}

public void recover() throws JMSException
{
    try
    {
        session.recover();
    }
    catch(JMSException exp)
    {
        throw exp;
    }
```

```
    catch(Exception exp)
    {
        throw new JMSException("No remote connection.");
    }
}
```

When a session is closed using the close method shown here, it stops polling the server for messages, notifies the server that it will close, and removes itself from its connection.

```
public void close() throws JMSException
{
    try
    {
        if(session != null)
        {
            checker.stop();
            session = session.close();
            conn.removeSession(this);
        }
    }
    catch(JMSException exp)
    {
        throw exp;
    }
    catch(Exception exp)
    {
        throw new JMSException("No remote connection.");
    }
}
```

MiniSessions provide a number of methods for acknowledgment. Remember that a client acknowledges a destination, not a particular message. This means that all of the messages that have been received by this session for the specified destination will be acknowledged. The session actually provides a version of acknowledgment that uses a name. This name is normally the client ID, but it can be different if a durable subscriber is used with the TopicSession. Ultimately, requests to acknowledge are forwarded to the server.

```
public void acknowledge(Destination d) throws JMSException
{
    acknowledge(d,getClientID());
}

public void acknowledge(Destination d,String name) throws JMSException
{
    try
    {
        session.acknowledge(d,name);
    }
    catch(JMSException exp)
```

```
        {
            throw exp;
        }
        catch(Exception exp)
        {
            throw new JMSException("No remote connection.");
        }
    }
```

The session manages a MessageListener. If this listener is assigned it will be the only object to receive messages for this session. This is an advanced part of the API and is not intended for use by normal clients; rather, it is designed for application servers that rely on the JMS provider for their Enterprise JavaBeans to use.

```
public MessageListener getMessageListener() throws JMSException
{
    return listener;
}

public void setMessageListener(MessageListener lst) throws JMSException
{
    this.listener = lst;
}
```

The MiniSession also keeps track of all of its consumers' MessageListeners. These listeners are associated with a particular destination and, in the case of a durable topic subscriber, have a unique name. When a listener is assigned to a destination it shares all of the messages for its session and the destination, based on its name. When a consumer is assigned a listener it registers it with the consumer's session using addMessageListenerFor.

MiniSession keeps track of listeners in vectors that are stored in a hashtable. The hashtable relates destinations to listeners. The vector stores the listeners for the destination.

Due to the persistent nature of messaging with JMS, a listener could be "owed" messages that were sent before it was registered. The MiniSession tries to assign these messages immediately on registration. The messageForNoWait method is discussed next, but basically it tries to find messages that are readily available and doesn't wait for contact with the server.

Synchronization is used to protect the hashtable of listeners.

```
public void addMessageListenerFor(MessageListener lst
                        ,Destination dest
                        ,String name)
                            throws JMSException
    {
        Vector listeners;
```

```
synchronized(listenerForDest)
{
    listeners = (Vector) listenerForDest.get(dest);

    if(listeners == null)
    {
        listeners = new Vector();
        listenerForDest.put(dest,listeners);
    }

    listeners.addElement(lst);

    //update listener with outstanding messages
    Message msg;

    try
    {
        while((msg = messageForNoWait(dest,name))!=null)
        {
            lst.onMessage(msg);
        }
    }
    catch(Exception ignore)
    {
    }
}
}
```

When a message listener is removed from a message consumer or the consumer is closed, the consumer object notifies the session of this change with removeMessageListenerFor. This method removes the listener from the listenerForDest hashtable.

```
public void removeMessageListenerFor(MessageListener lst
                                     ,Destination dest)
                                        throws JMSException
{
    Vector listeners;

    if((dest == null)||(lst==null)) return;

    synchronized(listenerForDest)
    {
        listeners = (Vector) listenerForDest.get(dest);

        if(listeners != null)
        {
            listeners.removeElement(lst);
        }
    }
}
```

Consumers provide three methods for accessing messages. In MiniJMS these messages are forwarded to the session. The first method, messageFor, takes a name and destination. It tries to find a message for that name and destination in a local store without going to the server. In fact, none of the messageFor methods access the server. Instead a thread is used to poll the server. As messages arrive to the client they are stored in a hashtable. MessageFor checks these hashtables with the method getMessageFor, and if no message is available, it waits for one using normal thread waiting. The thread that is adding messages to the messagesForDest Hashtable will call notifyAll to wake up any waiting threads and give them a shot at the messages.

Synchronization is used to protect the local message store.

```java
public Message messageFor(Destination dest,String name)
    throws Exception
{
    Message msg=null;

    synchronized(messagesForDest)
    {
        while(msg == null)
        {
            try
            {
                msg = getMessageFor(dest,name);

                if(msg != null) break;

                messagesForDest.wait();
            }
            catch(Exception exp)
            {
            }
        }
    }

    return msg;
}
```

The second version of messageFor also takes a timeout and will not wait beyond the timeout for a message. The waiting is broken into several stages to ensure that any accidental notifications do not cause the method to return. This method returns only when the actual time passed exceeds the timeout or a message is available.

```java
public Message messageFor(Destination dest,long timeout,String name)
    throws Exception
{
    Message msg=null;
    long now,start;

    start = System.currentTimeMillis();
```

```
    synchronized(messagesForDest)
    {
        while(msg == null)
        {
            try
            {
                msg = getMessageFor(dest,name);

                if(msg != null) break;

                messagesForDest.wait(timeout/10);
            }
            catch(Exception exp)
            {
            }

            now = System.currentTimeMillis();
            if((now-start)>timeout) break;
        }
    }

    return msg;
}
```

The messageForNoWait method checks for a message and if none is available in the local store returns null. This is a very quick check and doesn't wait on the server in any way.

```
public Message messageForNoWait(Destination dest,String name)
    throws Exception
{
    Message msg=null;

    synchronized(messagesForDest)
    {
        msg = getMessageFor(dest,name);
    }

    return msg;
}
```

Internally, a MiniSession uses the method getMessageFor to get messages from the local store. This method assumes that the caller synchronized the MessageForDest hashtable to protect it. Messages in the local store are organized into two hashtables. The first stores hashtable values based on destinations as keys. These hashtable values in turn store vectors of messages based on name keys. In the simple case where point-to-point messaging is used there probably will be only one name registered for a destination, and so the second hashtable will store only one item. This is overkill, but it makes the code support both messaging styles, without changing.

If an appropriate message is available when getMessageFor is called, it is returned. The session also acknowledges the message if it is not in client acknowledgment mode.

```
protected Message getMessageFor(Destination dest,String name)
    throws JMSException
{
    Message msg=null;
    Vector messages=null;
    Hashtable msgsByName;

    try
    {
        if(name == null) name = getClientID();

        msgsByName = (Hashtable) messagesForDest.get(dest);

        if(msgsByName!=null)
            messages = (Vector) msgsByName.get(name);

        if((messages != null)&&(messages.size()>0))
        {
            msg = (Message) messages.elementAt(0);
            messages.removeElementAt(0);

            if(ackMode != Session.CLIENT_ACKNOWLEDGE)
            {
                acknowledge(dest,name);
            }
        }
    }
    catch(Exception exp)
    {
        throw new JMSException(exp.toString());
    }

    return msg;
}
```

At the heart of a client's MiniSession is the run method. This method is called by a thread that is owned by the MiniSession. The run method checks for messages from the remote session and assigns them using the following algorithm.

First, if the session has a MessageListener, it receives all messages. Second, if a MessageListener is available for the message, it is notified. If multiple listeners are registered for the same destination and name, one is chosen randomly according to the JMS specification.

If no listeners are available, the message is stored in the messagesForDest hashtable, making them available to clients that use the receive methods. Note that a client can't register a listener with the name "joe" on the destination "tmp" and try to retrieve messages for the same destination with the same name using a receive message in the Consumer. These two models are mutually exclusive on a name-destinations basis. When the messagesForDest table is used, it is told to notify threads waiting on it after the new message is added.

The run method synchronizes calls to message listeners, in the sense that they will receive only the onMessage call from the single polling thread. Like the getMessageFor method, run automatically acknowledges messages, unless configured not to, when they are delivered.

```java
public void run()
{
    Message msg;
    Destination dest;
    Vector messages;
    Vector listeners;
    MessageListener lst=null;
    Hashtable msgsByName;
    String name=null;

    while(session != null)
    {
        try
        {
            msg = session.receive();

            lst = null;
            name = null;
            msgsByName = null;
            listeners = null;
            dest = null;
            messages = null;

            try
            {
            name =
            msg.getStringProperty(MiniJMSMessageStore.REG_NAME);
            }
            catch(Exception e)
            {
                name = null;
            }

            dest = msg.getJMSDestination();

            if((dest != null)&&(listener==null))
            {
                synchronized(listenerForDest)
                {
                    listeners =
                        (Vector) listenerForDest.get(dest);

                    //Pick one at random.
                    if((listeners != null)
```

```
                     && (listeners.size()>0))
        {
            int i;
            int size = listeners.size();

            if(size>1)
                i = Math.abs(rand.nextInt())
                    % listeners.size();
            else
                i = 0;

            lst = (MessageListener)
                listeners.elementAt(i);
        }
    }

    if(lst != null)
    {
        lst.onMessage(msg);

        if(ackMode != Session.CLIENT_ACKNOWLEDGE)
        {
            acknowledge(dest);
        }
    }
    else
    {
        synchronized(messagesForDest)
        {
            if(name == null) name = getClientID();

            msgsByName = (Hashtable)
                            messagesForDest.get(dest);

            if(msgsByName==null)
            {
                msgsByName = new Hashtable();
                messagesForDest.put(dest
                                    ,msgsByName);
            }

            messages = (Vector)
                        msgsByName.get(name);

            if(messages == null)
            {
                messages = new Vector();
                msgsByName.put(name,messages);
            }

            messages.addElement(msg);

            messagesForDest.notifyAll();
        }
    }
```

```
        }
        else if(listener != null)
        {
            listener.onMessage(msg);

            if(ackMode != Session.CLIENT_ACKNOWLEDGE)
            {
                acknowledge(dest);
            }
        }
    }
    catch(Exception exp)
    {
    }
    }
}
```

The MiniSession provides access to the server for deleting temporary destinations. This same method is used for temporary Queues and Topics.

```
public void deleteTemporary(MiniTempDestination q)
    throws JMSException
{
    try
    {
        session.deleteDestination(q.toString());
    }
    catch(Exception exp)
    {
        throw new JMSException(exp.toString());
    }
}
```

One of the design mechanisms behind MiniJMS is the concept of a client registering for messages on a particular destination with a particular name. The server code uses this registration to begin checking for messages on that destination and passes them on to the client. Registrations can be durable or transient. Durable registrations will be remembered between times that the client is connected to the server. Transient registrations are valid only while the client is connected to the server. By default QueueReceivers use durable registrations, as will durable TopicSubscribers. Normal TopicSubscribers are transient. The main difference between durable and transient is that the server will store up messages for a durable subscriber and will not for a transient subscriber.

A number of methods are provided to the MiniJMS client classes for registering with the session; these are shown in the code that follows. All of these result in a call to the MiniRemoteSession.

```
public void registerFor(Destination dest)
    throws JMSException
{
```

```
        registerFor(dest,true,conn.getClientID());
    }

    public void registerFor(Destination dest,String name)
        throws JMSException
    {
        registerFor(dest,true,name);
    }

    public void registerFor(Destination dest,boolean durable)
        throws JMSException
    {
        registerFor(dest,durable,conn.getClientID());
    }

    public void registerFor(Destination dest
                            , boolean durable,String name)
        throws JMSException
    {
        try
        {
            session.registerFor(dest,true,name);
        }
        catch(Exception exp)
        {
            throw new JMSException(exp.toString());
        }
    }

    public void unregisterFor(Destination dest)
        throws JMSException
    {
        unregisterFor(dest,conn.getClientID());
    }

    public void unregisterFor(Destination dest,String name)
        throws JMSException
    {
        try
        {
            session.unregisterFor(dest,name);
        }
        catch(Exception exp)
        {
            throw new JMSException(exp.toString());
        }
    }
```

When a connection suspends or resumes its sessions, the sessions suspend and resume the thread they are using to poll for messages from the server.

```
    public void suspend()
    {
```

```
        if(checker != null) checker.suspend();
    }

    public void resume()
    {
        if(checker != null) checker.resume();
    }
}
```

MiniSession is the key element in the client implementation for MiniJMS. Make sure that you are comfortable with its implementation and purpose before continuing.

MiniConsumer

Rather than implement separate consumers for the two messaging models, MiniJMS implements a single consumer that supports both. MiniConsumer is a MessageConsumer, TopicSubscriber, and QueueReceiver. Because MiniDestinations are both Queues and Topics, the consumer can use a single Destination object to represent its associated destination.

A MiniConsumer tracks its session, a MessageListener, its destination, selector, and registered name. This name is the same one used to register with the session, and it defaults to the connection's ClientID. Flags are used to indicate if a consumer that represents a TopicSubscriber should allow local messages and if this is a durable consumer or if it should unregister with the session when closed.

 NOTE

MiniJMS does not support selectors or the noLocal feature.

The following code shows the initial definition of the MiniConsumer class, including the instance variable declarations.

```
package minijms;

//Imports removed to save space

public class MiniConsumer
 implements MessageConsumer
 , TopicSubscriber, QueueReceiver
{
    protected MessageListener listener;
    protected MiniSession session;
    protected MiniDestination dest;
    protected String selector;
    protected boolean noLocal;
    protected boolean unregOnClose;
```

```
protected String regName;

public MiniConsumer(MiniSession session
                            ,MiniDestination dest)
{
    this.session = session;
    this.dest = dest;
    noLocal = false;
    unregOnClose = false;
}
```

When a MiniConsumer is closed, it notifies the session in two ways. First, if this is a nondurable consumer it unregisters its destination. Second, by setting its MessageListener to null, the session is told to remove the MessageListener from its list.

```
public void close()
   throws JMSException
{
    if(unregOnClose) session.unregisterFor(dest);
    setMessageListener(null);
}
```

Accessors are provided for the message selector, registered name, and MessageListener.

```
public String getMessageSelector() throws JMSException
{
    return selector;
}

public void setMessageSelector(String s)
 throws JMSException
{
    selector = s;
}

public MessageListener getMessageListener()
 throws JMSException
{
    return listener;
}

public void setMessageListener(MessageListener lst)
    throws JMSException
{
    if(listener != null)
    {
        session.removeMessageListenerFor(listener,dest);
    }

    listener = lst;

    if(listener != null)
```

```
            session.addMessageListenerFor(listener,dest,regName);
    }

    public String getRegName()
    {
        return regName;
    }

    public void setRegName(String name)
    {
        regName = name;
    }

    protected void setNoLocal(boolean b)
    {
        noLocal = b;
    }

    public boolean getNoLocal() throws JMSException
    {
        return noLocal;
    }
```

Consumers provide three methods for receiving messages directly. These methods call the equivalent methods in the MiniSession object.

```
    public Message receive()
     throws JMSException
    {
        Message retVal = null;

        try
        {
            retVal = session.messageFor(dest,regName);
        }
        catch(JMSException exp)
        {
            throw exp;
        }
        catch(Exception exp)
        {
            throw new JMSException("No remote connection.");
        }

        return retVal;
    }

    public Message receive(long timeOut)
     throws JMSException
    {
        Message retVal = null;

        try
        {
            retVal = session.messageFor(dest,timeOut,regName);
```

```
        }
        catch(Exception exp)
        {
            throw new JMSException("No remote connection.");
        }

        return retVal;
    }
    public Message receiveNoWait()
     throws JMSException
    {
        Message retVal = null;

        try
        {
            retVal = session.messageForNoWait(dest,regName);
        }
        catch(JMSException exp)
        {
            throw exp;
        }
        catch(Exception exp)
        {
            throw new JMSException("No remote connection.");
        }

        return retVal;
    }
```

TopicSubscribers and QueueReceivers both provide type-specific access to their destination. The MiniConsumer implements both methods, and it throws an exception if the wrong one is used.

```
    public Queue getQueue() throws JMSException
    {
        if(dest.isQueue()) return dest;
        else throw new JMSException();
    }

    public Topic getTopic() throws JMSException
    {
        if(!dest.isQueue()) return dest;
        else throw new JMSException();
    }

    public void setUnregisterOnClose(boolean tf)
    {
        unregOnClose=tf;
    }
}
```

The Consumer in MiniJMS is mainly a front for the Session, providing the basic information required to specify the destination and name for requests.

MiniProducer

Like the MiniConsumer, the MiniProducer implements all three of the producer interfaces: MessageProducer, TopicPublisher, and QueueSender. The producer keeps a reference to its session for performing the actual message sending. Configuration parameters for a producer include the default delivery mode, default priority, and default timeToLive for messages. The timeToLive in this case indicates how long the message should exist before the server cleans it up. Flags are used to indicate if a message ID and time stamp are required for each message sent.

The MiniProducer is associated with a destination and keeps track of this destination in an instance variable.

Creating a MiniProducer initializes the instance variables, for which accessor methods are provided.

```
package minijms;

//Imports removed to save space
public class MiniProducer
 implements MessageProducer,TopicPublisher,QueueSender
{
    protected MiniSession session;
    protected boolean disableMsgId;
    protected boolean disableTimestamp;
    protected int mode; //default mode
    protected int priority; //default priority
    protected int time; //default timeToLive
    protected MiniDestination dest;

    public MiniProducer(MiniSession session
                        ,MiniDestination dest)
    {
        this.session = session;
        this.dest = dest;

        disableMsgId = false;
        disableTimestamp = false;

        //default mode is not a correct value
        mode = DeliveryMode.PERSISTENT;

        priority = 4;
        time = Message.DEFAULT_TIME_TO_LIVE;
    }
    public void setDisableMessageID(boolean value)
     throws JMSException
    {
        disableMsgId = value;
    }
```

```
public boolean getDisableMessageID()
 throws JMSException
{
    return disableMsgId;
}

public void setDisableMessageTimestamp(boolean value)
 throws JMSException
{
    disableTimestamp = value;
}

public boolean getDisableMessageTimestamp()
 throws JMSException
{
    return disableTimestamp;
}

public void setDeliveryMode(int deliveryMode)
 throws JMSException
{
    mode = deliveryMode;
}

public int getDeliveryMode() throws JMSException
{
    return mode;
}

public void setPriority(int p) throws JMSException
{
    priority = p;
}

public int getPriority() throws JMSException
{
    return priority;
}

public void setTimeToLive(int timeToLive) throws JMSException
{
    time = timeToLive;
}

public int getTimeToLive() throws JMSException
{
    return time;
}
```

Closing a MiniProducer doesn't do anything because it doesn't require any server resources.

```
public void close() throws JMSException
{
}
```

Like the MiniConsumer, a MiniProducer provides access to its destination as either a Queue or Topic, throwing an exception if the wrong method is used.

```
public Queue getQueue() throws JMSException
{
    if(dest.isQueue()) return dest;
    else throw new JMSException();
}

public Topic getTopic() throws JMSException
{
    if(!dest.isQueue()) return dest;
    else throw new JMSException();
}
```

QueueSender defines four methods for sending messages. MiniProducer implements all four, but it actually relies on a single method for the actual send. The first three methods listed here simply call the fourth method using default values where appropriate.

```
public void send(Message message)
 throws JMSException
{
    if(message != null)
    {
        send(getQueue(), message, mode
            , priority, time);
    }
    else
    {
        throw new JMSException("Null Message.");
    }
}

public void send(Message message,
         int deliveryMode, int pri,
          long timeToLive) throws JMSException
{
    if(message != null)
    {
        send(getQueue(),message, deliveryMode
            ,pri,timeToLive);
    }
    else
    {
        throw new JMSException("Null Message.");
    }
}

public void send(Queue queue, Message message)
 throws JMSException
{
```

```
        if((message != null)&&(queue!=null))
        {
            send(queue, message, mode
                , priority, time);
        }
        else
        {
            throw new JMSException("Null Message.");
        }
    }
```

The final send method is the most versatile. This method configures the messages header, using the flags provided that could be the default values. If the message has a timeToLive, the expiration time is set to the current time plus this value. If time stamps are enabled, one is set, and if message IDs are enabled, one is assigned. Once configured, the producers session is told to send the message.

```
public void send(Queue queue, Message message,
        int deliveryMode, int pri,
        long timeToLive) throws JMSException
{
    long now = System.currentTimeMillis();

    if((message != null)&&(queue!=null))
    {
        if(session == null)
            throw new JMSException("No Session");

        message.setJMSDestination(queue);
        message.setJMSPriority(pri);
        message.setJMSDeliveryMode(deliveryMode);

        if(timeToLive <= 0)
            message.setJMSExpiration(0);
        else
            message.setJMSExpiration(now + timeToLive);

        if(!disableTimestamp)
        {
            message.setJMSMessageID(createId());
        }

        if(!disableTimestamp)
        {
            message.setJMSTimestamp(now);
        }

        session.send(message);
    }
    else
    {
```

```
        throw new JMSException("Null Message.");
    }
}
```

TopicPublishers also provide a number of methods for sending messages to a topic. Again these are implemented in terms of the most generic form.

```
public void publish(Message message)
 throws JMSException
{
    if(message != null)
    {
        publish(getTopic(), message, mode
            , priority, time);
    }
    else
    {
        throw new JMSException("Null Message.");
    }
}

public void publish(Message message,
        int deliveryMode, int pri,
         long timeToLive) throws JMSException
{
    if(message != null)
    {
        publish(getTopic(),message, deliveryMode
            ,pri,timeToLive);
    }
    else
    {
        throw new JMSException("Null Message.");
    }
}

public void publish(Topic topic, Message message)
 throws JMSException
{
    if((message != null)&&(topic!=null))
    {
        publish(topic, message, mode
            , priority, time);
    }
    else
    {
        throw new JMSException("Null Message.");
    }
}
```

The final publish method is the most versatile. This method configures the messages header, using the flags provided, which could be the default values. If the message has a timeToLive, the expiration time is set to the current time plus this value. If time stamps are enabled, one is set, and if message IDs are enabled, one is assigned. Once configured, the producers session is told to send the message.

```
public void publish(Topic topic, Message message,
        int deliveryMode, int pri,
          long timeToLive) throws JMSException
{
    long now = System.currentTimeMillis();

    if((message != null)&&(topic!=null))
    {
        if(session == null)
            throw new JMSException("No Session");

        message.setJMSDestination(topic);
        message.setJMSPriority(pri);
        message.setJMSDeliveryMode(deliveryMode);

        if(timeToLive <= 0)
            message.setJMSExpiration(0);
        else
            message.setJMSExpiration(now + timeToLive);

        if(!disableTimestamp)
        {
            message.setJMSMessageID(createId());
        }

        if(!disableTimestamp)
        {
            message.setJMSTimestamp(now);
        }

        session.send(message);
    }
    else
    {
        throw new JMSException("Null Message.");
    }
}
```

If message IDs are enabled, they are created using the client's IP address, the current time, and the client ID. This should ensure uniqueness across all clients in the system. In the worst case, a random number is used. JMS specifies that all Message IDs start with "ID:" so I have used that convention here.

```
protected String createId()
{
    String retVal;
```

```
        try
        {
            InetAddress here = InetAddress.getLocalHost();

            retVal = "ID:"+System.currentTimeMillis()
                        +here.getHostAddress()
                        +session.getClientID();
        }
        catch(Exception exp)
        {
            retVal =  "ID:"+System.currentTimeMillis()+Math.random();
        }
        return retVal;
    }
}
```

That concludes the generic client classes for MiniJMS. Subclasses of MiniConnectionFactory, MiniConnection, and MiniSession are provided for the two
messaging models defined in JMS.

In order to support point-to-point messaging MiniJMS implements three
classes:

- MiniQueueConnectionFactory extends MiniConnectionFactory and de-
  fines a QueueConnectionFactory.
- MiniQueueConnection extends MiniConnection and implements Queue-
  Connection.
- MiniQueueSession extends MiniSession and implements QueueSession.

In order to support publish-subscribe messaging MiniJMS implements three
different classes:

- MiniTopicConnectionFactory extends MiniConnectionFactory and defines
  a TopicConnectionFactory.
- MiniTopicConnection extends MiniConnection and implements Topic-
  Connection.
- MiniTopicSession extends MiniSession and implements TopicSession.

Rather than include the code for these specific classes here, I suggest that you
refer to the CD-ROM. All of the model-specific classes are used to create other
model-specific classes. Ultimately the session classes create MessageCon-
sumers and MessageProducers configured appropriately for their messaging
model.

 NOTE
**MiniJMS does not support QueueBrowsers, so the MiniQueueSession will throw Ex-
ceptions if they are requested.**

JNDI Support

The JMS specification refers to Destinations and ConnectionFactories as administered objects. In other words, they are objects that are bound to a JNDI context for access by a client. In general, clients do not create Queues and Topics. Instead, they look them up. The same is true for ConnectionFactories. This makes the JMS client able to change JMS providers without changing code because the Connection factory acts as the root for all of the other objects created.

Both the MiniQueueConnectionFactory and MiniTopicConnectionFactory classes implement Serializable and Referenceable to allow them to be bound into a JNDI context. MiniDestination, as you have seen, also implements this interface. The implementation for all of these classes is very similar so it is necessary to show only one here, in particular MiniDestination. The other examples are provided on the CD-ROM.

First, the MiniDestination class states that it implements Referenceable. Next, it implements the getReference method. The MiniJMS implementation creates a StringRefAddr that takes the name of the destination. Another reference is used for the isQueue value of the MiniDestination object. A custom ObjectFactory called MiniDestinationFactory is provided to perform the actual creation of objects removed from the context.

```
public Reference getReference()
                    throws NamingException
    {
        Reference retVal;

        retVal = new Reference(MiniDestination.class.getName()
         ,new StringRefAddr("name",name)
         ,MiniDestinationFactory.class.getName()
         ,null);

        retVal.add(new StringRefAddr("isQueue"
                                    ,(isQ?"true":"false")));

        return retVal;
    }
```

When a MiniDestination is bound into JNDI it is asked for this reference. The JNDI provider stores the reference, including the two string addresses.

When a client looks up the destination, a MiniDestinationFactory is created and it will be asked to create the object that is being requested from the available information. The method getObjectInstance, defined in the javax.naming.spi.ObjectFactory interface, is called on the object factory to ask it to create the new object. This method is provided information about the object, such as the name it is bound under, the context, the context's environment, and an arbitrary informational object. This info object for MiniDestinationFactory contains the Reference created by the destination before it was bound.

MiniDestinationFactory uses the Reference to recreate the MiniDestination and return it.

```java
package minijms;

//imports removed to save space.

public class MiniDestinationFactory
 implements ObjectFactory
{

    public Object getObjectInstance(
                 Object info,
                 Name name,
                 Context nameCtx,
                 Hashtable environment)
                 throws Exception
    {
        MiniDestination retVal = null;

        if(info instanceof Reference)
        {
            Reference ref = (Reference) info;
            RefAddr nameA;
            RefAddr isQA;
            String destName,isQ;
            boolean isQueue;

            nameA = ref.get("name");
            isQA = ref.get("isQueue");

            if((nameA != null)&&(isQA != null))
            {
                destName = (String) nameA.getContent();
                isQ = (String) isQA.getContent();

                isQueue = Boolean.valueOf(isQ).booleanValue();
                retVal = new MiniDestination(destName,isQueue);
            }
        }

        return retVal;
    }

}
```

To consolidate the creation of the initial JNDI context in MiniJMS clients, and to make it easy to configure, the provided examples do two things. First, they use properties files to define their context information. Second, I created a class called MiniJMSUtils that will create a context from a properties file. MiniJMS also installs the RMI security manager, saving your examples that step in the code. The properties file contains two entries for the example code. These entries configure the initial factory to the NetworkContext service provider created in Project 5 and set the URL.

```
java.naming.factory.initial=networkctx.NetworkInitCtxFactory
java.naming.provider.url=rmi://127.0.0.1:4798/networkctx.NetworkContext
```

The code for MiniJMSUtils, which follows, is basically a recipe for loading a properties file, reading it, and using the properties to create an initial context for JNDI lookups. The properties file is specified by a file name. The file must be in the class path to be found.

```
package minijms;

import minijms.*;
import minijmsserver.*;
import javax.jms.*;
import javax.naming.*;
import java.io.*;
import java.rmi.*;
import java.util.*;

public class MiniJMSUtils
{
    public static Properties properties;
    public static Context context;

    public static void init(String propsFile)
        throws Exception
    {
        // Create and install a security manager
        SecurityManager mng;
        InputStream propsIn;
        Properties sysProps;

        mng = new RMISecurityManager();
        System.setSecurityManager(mng);

        //Update the system props for class loading
        //fails for an applet but that's okay
        try
        {
            sysProps = System.getProperties();
            sysProps.put("java.rmi.server.codebase"
                    ,"file:/"
                    + sysProps.getProperty("user.dir")
                    +"/");
            System.setProperties(sysProps);
        }
        catch(Exception ignore)
        {
        }
```

```
    //Load the properties file
    propsIn
      = ClassLoader.getSystemResourceAsStream(propsFile);
    properties = new Properties();
    properties.load(propsIn);

    Properties p = new Properties();

    String user=properties.getProperty("java.naming.user");
    String password=properties.getProperty("java.naming.password");

    p.put(Context.INITIAL_CONTEXT_FACTORY,
            properties.getProperty("java.naming.factory.initial"));

    p.put(Context.PROVIDER_URL
        , properties.getProperty("java.naming.provider.url"));

if (user != null)
    {
        p.put(Context.SECURITY_PRINCIPAL, user);

        if (password == null) password = "";

        p.put(Context.SECURITY_CREDENTIALS, password);
    }

    context = new InitialContext(p);
    }
}
```

The properties and context static variables are public, and they provide easy access to a program. The following examples all initialize the MiniJMSUtils class and use its variables to get to the JNDI context. Then this context is used to access destinations by name or connection factories by name. Although I included this utility in the minijms package, it doesn't rely on any minijms code, beyond the import statements, and you could use it with other JMS providers or JNDI providers.

That's it for the discussion on the MiniJMS client library. The server is discussed next, and it includes code for accessing a database with JDBC, binding JNDI objects, adding the object factories discussed here to the JNDI context, and implementing the remote interfaces discussed above.

Step 4: Create the Server

The MiniJMS server provides a number of services. First, it implements the remote interfaces, supporting persistent messaging organized into Queues and Topics. Second, it registers the necessary objects in a JNDI context for use by the client. Finally, it maintains a database of messages for durable, nonaccessible clients.

The Message Store

At the heart of the server is the MiniJMSMessageStore. This object defines the storage scheme for messages in the MiniJMS system. Messages that are marked persistent are maintained in a database using JDBC. All messages are held in memory for the destinations to which they will be delivered. If no running sessions have registered an interest in a message it is not stored in memory, meaning that nonpersistent messages in which no client is interested are ignored.

The schema for the MiniJMSMessageStore's database contains three tables. These tables and their columns are listed in Tables 7.4 through 7.6. The messages table stores information about the persistent messages that are sent, including their destination and a reference to their location on disk. This reference is relative to a root directory configured in the server's properties file. The destinations table contains the available destinations. The ack table is used to keep track of the last acknowledged message for a particular client and a particular destination. Using the last acknowledged message, the message store can determine which messages it hasn't sent to the client yet, or at least the ones that the client hasn't acknowledged. Because the messages are numbered in ascending order, any message with a msg_num greater than the last one acknowledged has not been received.

The message store has some of the same features of the MiniSession in the client code. It organizes the registered listeners and messages into hashtables for distribution. The actual distribution is handled by the session's remote counterpart discussed in a moment. As well as storing messages, the message store is responsible for initializing the JNDI context with the available destinations. These destinations are stored in the store's database.

The MiniJMSMessageStore's instance variables hold the current messages, the context and properties files used to configure the store, a connection to a database, statements for that connection, the directory name for the directory that stores the serialized messages, and a counter used to determine the unique numbers for messages. There are also static variables that define the names for two MiniJMS-defined message properties. These properties—JMS_MSG_NUM

Table 7.4   Messages Table

COLUMN	DESCRIPTION
msg_num	The message's unique number, assigned by the message store
msg_id	The message's unique identifier
destination	The name of the destination to which the message was sent
content	The bytes for the serialized message object

Table 7.5   Destinations Table

COLUMN	DESCRIPTION
name	The destination's name
isqueue	Either "true" or "false" indicating if the destination is a Queue; otherwise, it is a Topic

and JMS_REG_NAME—store the message number and registered name associated with a message. The message number is used in the database, while the registered name associates a message with a particular MiniConsumer on the client.

The message store has a statement for most interactions with the database, while a PreparedStatement is used for statements that insert binary data into the database.

```
package minijmsserver;

//imports removed to save space

public class MiniJMSMessageStore
{
    protected Hashtable destinations;
    protected Hashtable messages;
    protected Properties props;
    protected java.sql.Connection conn;
    protected java.sql.Statement statement;
    protected java.sql.PreparedStatement pstatement;
    protected Context context;
    protected String objDir;
    protected long curId;

    public final static String MSG_NUM="JMS_MSG_NUM";
    public final static String REG_NAME="JMS_REG_NAME";
```

The constructor for MiniJMSMessageStore, shown next, is a great example of how multiple technologies can be combined. Configuration information is stored in a properties file. This information is used to create a JNDI context. A JDBC database connection is created using the same properties file, and the

Table 7.6   Ack Table

COLUMN	DESCRIPTION
msg_num	The number for the last message acknowledged
destination	The destination to which this entry corresponds
name	The name with which the consumer registered

contents of the DESTINATION table from the database are used to load
MiniDestination objects into the JNDI context. The constructor even registers
the MiniDestinationFactory with the JNDI context so that the destinations can
be bound appropriately and autonomously. In just 30-so lines of code properties, JNDI and JDBC are combined to create a unified whole.

The JMS specification says that a JMS provider should provide tools for ad-
ministrating Queues and Topics. Although no specific tools are provided by
JNDI, they can be created using the RemoteMiniSession interface or by inserting destinations into the message store's database and restarting the server.

```
public MiniJMSMessageStore(String propsFile)
     throws JMSException
 {
     String url = null;
     String user=null;
     String password=null;
     String driver=null;
     java.sql.ResultSet rs;
     boolean isQ;
     String name;
     MiniDestination dest;

     curId = System.currentTimeMillis();

     destinations = new Hashtable();
     messages = new Hashtable();

     try
     {
         MiniJMSUtils.init(propsFile);
         context = MiniJMSUtils.context;
         props = MiniJMSUtils.properties;

         context.addToEnvironment(Context.OBJECT_FACTORIES,
                         "minijms.MiniDestinationFactory");

         url = props.getProperty("db_url");
         user = props.getProperty("db_user");
         password = props.getProperty("db_password");
         driver = props.getProperty("db_driver");

         if((context == null)
             ||(url == null)||(driver == null))
         {
             throw new JMSException("Unable to connect to store.");
         }

         Class.forName(driver);

         conn = DriverManager.getConnection(url,user,password);
         conn.setAutoCommit(false);
```

```
        statement = conn.createStatement();
        pstatement
= conn.prepareStatement("insert into messages"
            +" values(?,?,?,?)");
        rs = statement.executeQuery("select * from "
            +"destinations");

        while(rs.next())
        {
            name = rs.getString("name");
            isQ
              = Boolean.valueOf(
                      rs.getString("isqueue")).booleanValue();

            dest = new MiniDestination(name,isQ);

            Vector sessions = new Vector();

            destinations.put(name,sessions);
            context.rebind(name,dest);
        }

        rs.close();
    }
    catch(JMSException ex)
    {
        throw ex;
    }
    catch(Exception exp)
    {
        throw new JMSException(exp.toString());
    }
}
```

Closing the message store frees up its JNDI context and JDBC connection. To ensure that close is called, the finalize method is implemented to call it.

```
public void close()
{
    try
    {
        context.close();
        statement.close();
        conn.close();
    }
    catch(Exception exp)
    {
    }
}

public Context getJNDIContext()
{
    return context;
}
```

```
public void finalize()
{
    close();
}
```

The nextId method returns the next message number based on the order it is called and the creation time of the message store, as initialized in the constructor.

```
protected long nextId()
{
    return curId++;
}
```

The message store is ultimately responsible for creating Queues and Topics. Before a destination can be created, the store checks that it does not already exist. Trying to create a Queue or Topic that already exists produces an exception. If the destination is created successfully, its information is inserted into the database, making it persistent. Then the destinations are bound into the JNDI context for access from clients. The store also initializes a vector to store any registered sessions listening to the new destination and stores it in the destinations hashtable.

```
public Queue createQueue(String queueName)
    throws JMSException
    {
        Queue retVal=null;

        synchronized(destinations)
        {
            Object test = null;

            if(queueName!= null)
                test = destinations.get(queueName);

            if(test==null)
            {
                Vector sessions = new Vector();

                destinations.put(queueName,sessions);

                try
                {
                    statement.executeUpdate("insert into "
                                    +"destinations "
                                    +"values(\'"
                                    +queueName
                                    +"\',\'true\')");

                    retVal = new MiniDestination(queueName,true);

                    context.rebind(queueName,retVal);

                    conn.commit();
                }
```

```java
            catch(Exception exp)
            {
                try
                {
                    conn.rollback();
                }
                catch(Exception ignore)
                {
                }

                throw new JMSException(exp.toString());
            }
        }
        else
        {
            throw new JMSException(queueName+" exists.");
        }
    }

    return retVal;
}

public Topic createTopic(String topicName)
 throws JMSException
{
    Topic retVal=null;

    synchronized(destinations)
    {
        Object test = destinations.get(topicName);

        if(test==null)
        {
            Vector sessions = new Vector();

            destinations.put(topicName,sessions);

            try
            {
                statement.executeUpdate("insert into "
                            +"destinations "
                            +"values(\'"
                            +topicName
                            +"\',\'false\')");

                retVal = new MiniDestination(topicName,false);

                context.rebind(topicName,retVal);

                conn.commit();
            }
            catch(Exception exp)
            {
                try
                {
```

```
                    conn.rollback();
                }
                catch(Exception ignore)
                {
                }
                throw new JMSException(exp.toString());
            }
        }
        else
        {
            throw new JMSException(topicName+" exists.");
        }
    }

    return retVal;
}
```

Deleting a destination is trickier than creating one. First, the destination must exist. Next, all of the messages for the destination must be removed from the database; in the process all of the serialized messages referenced in the database must be removed. Then the entry in the DESTINATION table of the database is removed, and finally all of the acknowledgment records related to the destination are removed before the destination is removed from the destinations hashtable.

```
public void deleteDestination(String destName)
    throws JMSException
{
    synchronized(destinations)
    {
        Object test = destinations.get(destName);
        ResultSet rs;
        File file;
        String content;

        if(test!=null)
        {
            try
            {
                //Delete destination
                statement.executeUpdate("delete from "
                            +"destinations "
                            +"where name=\'"
                            +destName
                            +"\'");

                //Delete acknowledgements
                statement.executeUpdate("delete from "
                            +"ack "
                            +"where destination=\'"
                            +destName
                            +"\'");
```

```
                        //delete all messages
                        statement.executeUpdate("delete from "
                                    +"messages "
                                    +"where destination=\'"
                                    + destName
                                    +"\'");

                        conn.commit();
                    }
                    catch(Exception exp)
                    {
                        try
                        {
                            conn.rollback();
                        }
                        catch(Exception ignore)
                        {
                        }
                        throw new JMSException(exp.toString());
                    }

                    destinations.remove(destName);
            }
        }
    }
```

Requests for a message by a session result in a call to nextMessageFor in the message store on the server. This method checks for messages based on the ClientID or name used by the session. If a message has been cached for that ID, it is tested to see if it has expired. If there is an unexpired message, it is returned; otherwise, if there are messages but the current one has expired, null is returned. In the case where no messages are being held currently for an ID, this method calls wait, pausing the requesting thread until it is notified of a message. NextMessageFor will be called by the RemoteMiniSession in a thread that loops to check for messages. In the case of an expired message, the loop will call this method again immediately after the null return value. Only when no messages are awaiting delivery will the wait method be called, pausing the sessions polling thread.

```
public Message nextMessageFor(String id)
        throws JMSException
    {
        Vector msgs;
        Message retVal = null;
        long now,expires;

        msgs = (Vector) messages.get(id);

        if(msgs != null)
        {
            synchronized(msgs)
```

```
        {
            now = System.currentTimeMillis();

            if(msgs.size()>0)
            {
                retVal = (Message) msgs.elementAt(0);
                msgs.removeElementAt(0);

                expires = retVal.getJMSExpiration();

                if((expires > 0)&&(expires<now))
                {
                    retVal = null;
                }
            }
            else
            {
                try
                {
                    msgs.wait();
                }
                catch(Exception ignore)
                {
                }
            }
        }
    }

    return retVal;
}
```

When the store is told to send a message it does a number of things. First, the message's destination name is retrieved. Then the destination's hashtable is queried for any sessions registered for the destination. The message is assigned a message number. If the message is persistent, it is saved to the database's MESSAGES table. Finally, if any sessions are registered listeners for the message's destination a copy of the message is added to their vector of waiting messages. For durable subscriptions and queue receivers, these messages can be stored even if the client is not running.

The session registration is stored in a RegPair object that includes the client ID and the name of the registration/subscription. Messages delivered to a sessions queue are tagged with the registered name in case multiple subscriptions are using the same session.

```
public void send(Message message)
            throws JMSException
    {
        try
        {
            String qname
```

```
            = message.getJMSDestination().toString();
Vector sessions
    = (Vector) destinations.get(qname);
int i,max;
RegPair pair;
String msgId=null;
long msgNum = nextId();
byte[] content;
Message toSend;

try
{
    msgId = message.getJMSMessageID();
}
catch(Exception e)
{
    msgId = "";
}

//Update the message table first
try
{
    message.setLongProperty(MSG_NUM,msgNum);

    if(message.getJMSDeliveryMode()
        ==DeliveryMode.PERSISTENT)
    {
        content = messageToBytes(message);

        if(content == null)
            throw new JMSException("Null Content");

        pstatement.setLong(1,msgNum);
        pstatement.setString(2,msgId);
        pstatement.setString(3,qname);
        pstatement.setBytes(4,content);

        pstatement.executeUpdate();
    }
}
catch(Exception exp)
{
    throw new JMSException(exp.toString());
}

if(sessions == null)
{
    conn.commit();
    return;
}

synchronized(sessions)
{
    max = sessions.size();
```

```
                    for(i=0;i<max;i++)
                    {
                        pair = (RegPair) sessions.elementAt(i);

                        Vector msgs = (Vector) messages.get(pair.id);

                        if(msgs == null)
                        {
                            msgs = new Vector();
                            messages.put(pair.id,messages);
                        }

                        synchronized(msgs)
                        {
                            toSend = copyMessage(message);
                            toSend.setStringProperty(REG_NAME,pair.name);

                            msgs.addElement(toSend);
                            msgs.notifyAll();
                        }
                    }
                }

                conn.commit();
            }
            catch(Exception exp)
            {
                try
                {
                    conn.rollback();
                }
                catch(Exception ignore)
                {
                }
                exp.printStackTrace();

                throw new JMSException(exp.toString());
            }
        }
```

Sessions acknowledge destinations by name and ID. This acknowledgment results in an entry in the ACK table of the database. The previous entry is deleted before the new one is added.

```
public void acknowledge(Destination d,String id, long msgNum)
        throws JMSException
    {
        //Update the message table first
        try
        {
            String qname
                = d.toString();

            statement.executeUpdate("delete from "
```

```
                                            +"ack "
                                            +"where destination=\'"
                                            + qname
                                            +"\' and name=\'"
                                            + id
                                            +"\'");

            statement.executeUpdate("insert into "
                                            +"ack "
                                            +"values(\'"
                                            + msgNum
                                            +"\',\'"
                                            + qname
                                            +"\',\'"
                                            + id
                                            +"\')");
            conn.commit();
        }
        catch(Exception exp)
        {
            try
            {
                conn.rollback();
            }
            catch(Exception ignore)
            {
            }
            throw new JMSException(exp.toString());
        }
    }
}
```

Sessions rely heavily on the concept of registration to tell the message store that they are running and want to receive messages. Registration is performed by name and client ID on a destination-by-destination basis. When a session makes a registration, it is added to the list of sessions for that destination using the ID and name. A vector also is created for the client ID if one does not already exist. This vector shares all of the pending messages for a session regardless of the name used to register for them.

Registrations are stored using RegPair objects. These objects hold an ID and name. RegPair implements hashCode and equals to ensure that two pairs with the same name and ID are equal. As always, thread synchronization is used to protect the shared sessions Vector for a destination.

The registerFor method also performs another key task related to JMS messaging. If the client registering for messages is registering for messages from a persistent queue, that client is sent all of the messages from the queue after the client's last acknowledgment. The same is true for durable topic subscribers. Queue receivers that have never acknowledged messages will receive all of the previous messages, however, while a durable subscriber will not receive any messages sent before its initial registration. Once registered, both will receive messages sent while they are disconnected from the server when they reconnect and register for them.

Nondurable subscribers and new subscribers will have a new entry placed in the ack table on registration so that if a durable subscriber reconnects it will get missed messages.

```java
public void registerFor(Destination dest
                        ,String id
                        ,String name)
    throws JMSException
{

    String qname = dest.toString();
    Vector sessions
        = (Vector) destinations.get(qname);
    RegPair pair = new RegPair();

    pair.id = id;
    pair.name = name;

    if(sessions==null)
    {
        sessions = new Vector();

        destinations.put(qname,sessions);
    }

    synchronized(sessions)
    {
        if(! sessions.contains(pair))
        {
            sessions.addElement(pair);
        }
    }

    Vector msgs = (Vector) messages.get(pair.id);

    if(msgs == null)
    {
        msgs = new Vector();
        messages.put(pair.id,msgs);
    }

    try
    {
        ResultSet rs;
        long maxAck=-1;

        rs = statement.executeQuery("select * from "
                        +"ack"
                        +" where destination=\'"
```

```
                                    +qname
                                    +"\' and name=\'"
                                    +name
                                    +"\'");

if(rs.next())
{
    maxAck = rs.getLong("msg_num");
}
else
{
    if(dest instanceof MiniDestination)
    {
        if(((MiniDestination)dest).isQueue())
        {
            maxAck = 0;
        }
    }
    else if(dest instanceof Queue)
    {
        maxAck = 0;
    }
    else
    {
        maxAck = -1;
    }
}

rs.close();

//Don't back fill totally new subscribers
//Do back fill queue receivers
if(maxAck>=0)
{
    byte[] content;
    Message msg;
    int i,max;
    long msgNum;

    //and get missed messages
    rs = statement.executeQuery("select * from "
                                +"messages "
                                +"where destination=\'"
                                +qname
                                +"\' and msg_num>"
                                +maxAck
                                +" order by msg_num asc");

    while(rs.next())
    {
        content = rs.getBytes("content");
        msgNum = rs.getLong("msg_num");
```

```
                    msg = messageFromBytes(content);

                    if(msg != null)
                    {
                        if(!msg.propertyExists(MSG_NUM))
                            msg.setLongProperty(MSG_NUM,msgNum);

                        //make sure the message isn't already
                        //waiting for delivery
                        if(!msgs.contains(msg))
                            msgs.addElement(msg);
                    }
                }

                rs.close();
            }
            else
            {
                //get this client in the list
                acknowledge(dest,name,curId-1);
            }

            conn.commit();
        }
        catch(Exception exp)
        {
            exp.printStackTrace();

            try
            {
                conn.rollback();
            }
            catch(Exception e)
            {
            }
        }
    }
}
```

When a session unregisters for a destination it is saying that it doesn't plan to retrieve messages for that destination any more. This results in removing the session from the destination's list of registered sessions and removes the client's acknowledgment entry from the ack database table. If the client reregisters, it will be treated as a new registration as discussed previously.

```
public void unregisterFor(Destination dest
                        ,String id
                        ,String name)
                        throws JMSException
{
    String qname = dest.toString();
    Vector sessions
        = (Vector) destinations.get(qname);
    RegPair pair;
```

```
                    if(sessions!=null)
                    {
                        pair = new RegPair();
                        pair.id = id;
                        pair.name = name;

                        sessions.removeElement(pair);

                        try
                        {
                            statement.executeUpdate("delete from "
                                            +"ack "
                                            +"where destination=\'"
                                            + qname
                                            +"\' and name=\'"
                                            + name
                                            +"\'");
                            conn.commit();
                        }
                        catch(Exception exp)
                        {
                            try
                            {
                                conn.rollback();
                            }
                            catch(Exception ignore)
                            {
                            }
                            throw new JMSException(exp.toString());
                        }
                    }
                    else
                    {
                        throw new JMSException("Not registered.");
                    }
                }
```

The message store implements three internal methods for managing messages. The first method copies a message by serializing it in memory and then unserializing a copy. Copying is used to ensure that the messages in memory for each session, ID, and name are not shared and can have their header fields or properties manipulated as needed. The second two methods convert messages to bytes and back.

```
    protected Message copyMessage(Message m)
    {
        Message retVal = m;
        ByteArrayOutputStream byteOut;
        BufferedOutputStream bufOut;
        ObjectOutputStream objOut;
        ByteArrayInputStream byteIn;
```

```java
        BufferedInputStream bufIn;
        ObjectInputStream objIn;

        try
        {
            byteOut = new ByteArrayOutputStream();
            bufOut = new BufferedOutputStream(byteOut);
            objOut = new ObjectOutputStream(bufOut);

            objOut.writeObject(m);

            objOut.close();

            byteIn = new ByteArrayInputStream(byteOut.toByteArray());
            bufIn = new BufferedInputStream(byteIn);
            objIn = new ObjectInputStream(bufIn);

            retVal = (Message) objIn.readObject();

            objIn.close();
        }
        catch(Exception exp)
        {
            retVal = m;
        }

        return retVal;
    }

    protected Message messageFromBytes(byte[] bytes)
    {
        Message retVal = null;
        ByteArrayInputStream byteIn;
        BufferedInputStream bufIn;
        ObjectInputStream objIn;

        try
        {
            byteIn = new ByteArrayInputStream(bytes);
            bufIn = new BufferedInputStream(byteIn);
            objIn = new ObjectInputStream(bufIn);

            retVal = (Message) objIn.readObject();

            objIn.close();
        }
        catch(Exception exp)
        {
            retVal = null;
        }

        return retVal;
    }

    protected byte[] messageToBytes(Message m)
    {
```

```
        byte[] retVal = null;
        ByteArrayOutputStream byteOut;
        BufferedOutputStream bufOut;
        ObjectOutputStream objOut;

        try
        {
            byteOut = new ByteArrayOutputStream();
            bufOut = new BufferedOutputStream(byteOut);
            objOut = new ObjectOutputStream(bufOut);

            objOut.writeObject(m);

            objOut.close();

            retVal = byteOut.toByteArray();
        }
        catch(Exception exp)
        {
            retVal = null;
        }

        return retVal;
    }
}
```

The message store represents a lot of code and ties together several enterprise frameworks including JDBC, JNDI, and JMS. By changing the store implementation, MiniJMS can alter its persistence mechanism or support other JMS specifications and versions.

The Remote Server Objects

The object that the client initially connects to using RMI is an instance of Mini-JMSServerImp that implements the RemoteMiniServer interface. This object is used to create objects that implement the RemoteMiniConnection interface. These connections are implemented in the class RemoteMiniConnectionImp. Both classes extend the UnicastRemoteObject interface and are provided on the CD-ROM. The only nonobvious aspect of either object is that the remote connection keeps track of the sessions it creates and closes them when it closes, in the same way that the MiniConnection object did.

The RemoteMiniSession implementation, called RemoteMiniSessionImp, is far more complex than the server or connection and requires some in-depth discussion.

This remote session stores several vectors of information. First the vector, called toSend, stores messages that it has been told to send but hasn't sent. This vector is used when the session is running in transacted mode. The second vector, called toReceive, stores messages that the session has retrieved from the message store but hasn't sent to the client yet. As messages are sent, they are stored in vectors contained in the histories hashtable. These histories are used to implement rollback and recover.

Temporary destinations need to be cleaned up when a session closes, so they are stored in a vector called unregOnClose. The session also keeps a flag indicating if it is transacted, a reference to the message store, its client ID, and a reference to the thread that it uses to poll for new messages in the store.

The constructor for RemoteMiniSessionImp initializes all of these variables, including the thread. The thread is suspended initially because no destinations have been registered. When a destination is registered, the thread will begin polling for messages.

```
package minijmsserver;

//imports removed to save space

public class RemoteMiniSessionImp
 extends UnicastRemoteObject
 implements RemoteMiniSession, Runnable, Unreferenced
{
    protected Vector toSend;
    protected Vector toReceive;
    protected Vector unregOnClose;
    protected Hashtable histories;
    protected boolean transacted;
    protected MiniJMSMessageStore store;
    protected Thread checker;
    protected String clientId;

    public RemoteMiniSessionImp(MiniJMSMessageStore s, String id)
        throws RemoteException
    {
        store = s;
        clientId = id;
        unregOnClose = new Vector();
        toSend = new Vector();
        toReceive = new Vector();
        histories = new Hashtable();
        checker = new Thread(this);
        checker.start();
        checker.suspend();
    }
```

Internally, the remote session uses the addMessage method to add new messages received from the store to the list of messages to send to clients. This method notifies any threads waiting for messages, in particular, threads representing client access to the RMI server.

```
    public synchronized void addMessage(Message msg)
```

```
    {
        synchronized(toReceive)
        {
            toReceive.addElement(msg);
            toReceive.notifyAll();
        }
    }
}
```

The session can be transacted, or it can rely on normal acknowledgments.

```
public void setTransacted(boolean tf)
  throws RemoteException, JMSException
{
    transacted = tf;
}
```

Because the remote session uses resources, it should be closed when not in use. Normally the client will send the close message, but the session also implements unreferenced, from the Unreferenced interface. This will be called if the remote object has no more RMI clients. Unreferencing the session causes it to close.

```
public void unreferenced()
{
    try
    {
        close();
    }
    catch(Exception ignore)
    {
    }
}
```

Closing the session stops the thread used to poll the message store. Then if it is transacted, the session rolls back in case there is an uncommitted transaction. Finally all temporary subscriptions are unregistered with the store. Temporary destinations are also deleted from the store.

```
public RemoteMiniSession close()
  throws RemoteException, JMSException
{
    try
    {
        Object[] unreg;
        Destination dest;

        checker.stop();

        if(transacted)//rollback the uncommited trans
            rollback();

        int i,max;
```

```
        max = unregOnClose.size();

        for(i=0;i<max;i++)
        {
            unreg = (Object[]) unregOnClose.elementAt(i);

            dest = (Destination)unreg[0];

            unregisterFor(dest,(String)unreg[1]);

            if((dest instanceof TemporaryTopic)
                ||(dest instanceof TemporaryQueue))
            {
                store.deleteDestination(dest.toString());
            }
        }
    }
    catch(Exception ignore)
    {
    }

    return null;
}
```

The remote session provides an interface for the client to the store for creating Queues, Topics, and deleting destinations. All exceptions are simply passed through from the store to the client.

```
//Throws an exception if one exists
public Queue createQueue(String queueName)
 throws RemoteException, JMSException
{
    return store.createQueue(queueName);
}

//Throws an exception if one exists
public Topic createTopic(String queueName)
 throws RemoteException, JMSException
{
    return store.createTopic(queueName);
}

public void deleteDestination(String queueName)
 throws RemoteException, JMSException
{
    store.deleteDestination(queueName);
}
```

When a session is asked to send a message it either stores the message for sending or sends it, depending on its transacted state. Nontransacted sessions send immediately. Transacted sessions delay sending until the commit method is called.

```
public void send(Message message)
            throws RemoteException, JMSException
{
    if(transacted)
    {
        synchronized(toSend)
        {
            toSend.addElement(message);
        }
    }
    else
    {
        reallySend(message);
    }
}
```

Really sending a message involves passing it to the message store. Any exceptions are converted to JMS exceptions to comply with the JMS specification.

```
protected void reallySend(Message message)
    throws JMSException
{
    try
    {
        //send message to store
        //May use persistant store if appropriate
        store.send(message);
    }
    catch(JMSException exp)
    {
        throw exp;
    }
    catch(Exception exp)
    {
        throw new JMSException("Failed to send message.");
    }
}
```

The MiniSession on the client uses a thread to poll the server using the RemoteSession's receive method. This method checks the list of pending messages, toReceive, and returns the first element, or oldest message found. If no messages are available, the requesting thread waits until one is available. Messages sent to the client are added to the appropriate history vector for that client in case of a call to recover or rollback.

```
public Message receive()
  throws RemoteException,JMSException
{
    Message retVal = null;
```

```
            synchronized(toReceive)
            {
                while(retVal == null)
                {
                    if(toReceive.size()>0)
                    {
                        retVal = (Message) toReceive.elementAt(0);
                        toReceive.removeElementAt(0);
                        if(retVal != null) break;
                    }
                    else
                    {
                        try
                        {
                            toReceive.wait();
                        }
                        catch(Exception exp)
                        {
                        }
                    }
                }
            }

        Vector history = historyFor(retVal);

        history.addElement(retVal);//vector is synch already

        return retVal;
    }
```

Committing a transacted remote session causes it to send any messages in toSend Vector. The session also clears out the histories vectors and acknowledges the messages in them. Only the message with the highest number is acknowledged. Committing a nontransacted session has no effect.

```
    public void commit() throws JMSException
    {
        if(!transacted) return;

        int i,max;
        Message msg;
        long num=-1;

        try
        {
            synchronized(toSend)
            {
                max = toSend.size();

                for(i=0;i<max;i++)
                {
                    msg = (Message) toSend.elementAt(i);
                    reallySend(msg);
```

```
        }
        toSend.removeAllElements();
    }

    synchronized(histories)
    {
        Enumeration cursor = histories.keys();
        Vector history;
        HistoryPair pair;
        String numKey = MiniJMSMessageStore.MSG_NUM;
        while(cursor.hasMoreElements())
        {
            pair = (HistoryPair) cursor.nextElement();
            history = (Vector) histories.get(pair);

            max = history.size();

            for(i=0;i<max;i++)
            {
                msg = (Message) history.elementAt(i);

                if(msg.propertyExists(numKey))
                {
                    num = Math.max(num
                        ,msg.getLongProperty(numKey));
                }
            }

            history.removeAllElements();

            //Acknowledge as a whole when tranacted
            if(num>0)
                store.acknowledge(pair.destination
                                ,pair.name,num);
        }
    }
    }
    catch(Exception exp)
    {
        throw new JMSException(exp.toString());
    }
}
```

Rolling back a transacted session removes all of the pending sends in the toSend vector and calls the internal method reallyRecover, discussed next. Recover calls the same method with a different argument. This argument tells the session if the recovered messages should be marked redelivered.

```
public void rollback() throws JMSException
{
    if(!transacted) return;
    toSend.removeAllElements();//throw away sends
    reallyRecover(false);
```

```
    }

    public void recover() throws JMSException
    {
        if(transacted) return;
        else reallyRecover(true);
    }
```

Both rollback and recover cause the session to take the messages from the histories vectors and put them back into the toReceive vector. This will cause them to be redelivered if the client is still available.

```
    //tf == true -> mark redelivered
    protected void reallyRecover(boolean tf) throws JMSException
    {
        try
        {
            synchronized(histories)
            {
                Enumeration cursor = histories.keys();
                Vector history;
                Destination d;
                int i,max;
                Message msg;
                HistoryPair pair;
                String name;

                synchronized(toReceive)
                {
                    while(cursor.hasMoreElements())
                    {
                        pair = (HistoryPair) cursor.nextElement();
                        history = (Vector) histories.get(pair);

                        d = pair.destination;
                        name = pair.name;

                        max = history.size();

                        for(i=(max-1);i>=0;i—)
                        {
                            msg = (Message) history.elementAt(i);
                            history.removeElementAt(i);

                            if(tf) msg.setJMSRedelivered(true);

                            //Try to get them back into approx
                            // the order
                            //they were in.
                            toReceive.insertElementAt(msg,0);
                        }
                    }

                    toReceive.notifyAll();
```

```
            }
        }
    }
    catch(Exception exp)
    {
        throw new JMSException("Failed to recover completely.");
    }
}
```

Acknowledging a destination uses the histories vectors to determine the last message sent to the client and notifies the message store with the largest message number received.

```
public void acknowledge(Destination d,String name)
  throws JMSException
{
    if(transacted) return;

    Vector history = historyFor(d,name);
    Message m =null;
    long num;

    if(history.size()>0) m = (Message) history.lastElement();

    try
    {
        if((m!=null)
            && (m.propertyExists(MiniJMSMessageStore.MSG_NUM)))
        {
            num =
             m.getLongProperty(MiniJMSMessageStore.MSG_NUM);

            store.acknowledge(d,name,num);
            history.removeAllElements();
        }
    }
    catch(Exception exp)
    {
        throw new JMSException(exp.toString());
    }
}
```

The history vectors are stored by name and destination. The session implements two internal methods for getting the history based on a message or a destination and name.

```
protected Vector historyFor(Message m)
{
    Destination d=null;
    String name=null;

    try
    {
```

```
        d = m.getJMSDestination();

        name =
         m.getStringProperty(MiniJMSMessageStore.REG_NAME);
    }
    catch(Exception exp)
    {
        name = null;
    }

    if(name == null) name = clientId;

    return historyFor(d,name);
}

protected Vector historyFor(Destination d,String name)
{
    Vector retVal=null;
    HistoryPair pair;

    if((d==null)||(name==null)) return null;

    synchronized(histories)
    {
        pair = new HistoryPair();
        pair.destination = d;
        pair.name = name;

        retVal = (Vector) histories.get(pair);

        if(retVal == null)
        {
            retVal = new Vector();
            histories.put(pair,retVal);
        }
    }

    return retVal;
}
```

When a client session registers for messages to a particular destination, the remote session is told. The registerFor method takes the destination, a name with which to register, and a flag indicating if the registration is durable, and it should last beyond the close method. Temporary destinations are treated as nondurable, even if the flag is true. This method also resumes the sessions polling thread because it now has at least one destination that can receive messages in the message store.

```
public void registerFor(Destination dest,boolean durable,String name)
    throws RemoteException,JMSException
{
    try
    {
        store.registerFor(dest,clientId,name);
```

```
                //Always unregister for temporary items
                if(!durable || (dest instanceof TemporaryTopic)
                        ||(dest instanceof TemporaryQueue))
                {
                    Object[] unreg = new Object[2];

                    unreg[0] = dest;
                    unreg[1] = name;
                    unregOnClose.addElement(unreg);
                }

                checker.resume();
            }
            catch(JMSException exp)
            {
                throw exp;
            }
            catch(Exception exp)
            {
                throw new JMSException(exp.toString());
            }
        }
    }
```

Unregistering for a destination is passed directly to the store using the sessions client ID and the provided name.

```
    public void unregisterFor(Destination dest,String name)
        throws RemoteException,JMSException
    {
        try
        {
            store.unregisterFor(dest,clientId,name);
        }
        catch(JMSException exp)
        {
            throw exp;
        }
        catch(Exception exp)
        {
            throw new JMSException(exp.toString());
        }
    }
```

The run method used by the polling thread simply checks the store for messages and adds them to the toReceive vector.

```
    public void run()
    {
        while(store != null)
        {
            Message next;

            try
```

```
        {
            next = store.nextMessageFor(clientId);

            if(next != null) addMessage(next);
        }
        catch(Exception ignore)
        {
        }
    }
  }
}
```

In the same way that the MiniSession is the workhorse on the client, the Re-moteMiniSessionImp, combined with the message store, is the workhorse on the server.

The Server MiniJMS

The server itself is implemented in a small class called MiniJMS. This class contains only a main method. The server must be run with an IP address on the command line indicating the machine containing the server's rmiregistery. For example, you might run it using:

```
> java minijmsserver.MiniJMS 192.168.0.172
```

The main method creates the message store using a hard-coded properties file discussed next. The store creates the JNDI context into which the server binds a TopicConnectionFactory and a QueueConnectionFactory. The ObjectFactories for these two classes are also provided to the JNDI context.

Finally, the server creates the MiniJMSServerImp object and binds it to a private RMI registry. At this point the server is running and waiting for connections. Notice that the connection factories bound into JNDI use the same server IP as the RMI registry, which allows the server to potentially register with another computer.

The server prints the message to the console, indicating its status during each stage of initialization.

```
package minijmsserver;

import minijms.*;
import minijmsserver.*;
import javax.jms.*;
import javax.naming.*;
import java.io.*;
import java.rmi.*;
import java.util.*;

public class MiniJMS
{
```

```java
    public static final int MINIJMS_PORT=6774;

    public static void main(String args[])
    {
        MiniJMSServerImp server;
        MiniJMSMessageStore store;
        Context context;
        String serverURL=null;
        Properties props;
        java.rmi.registry.Registry privateReg;

        System.setErr(System.out);

        try
        {
            if(args.length>0)
            {
                serverURL = "rmi://"+args[0]+":"+MINIJMS_PORT+"/"
                            +MiniJMSServer.SERVER_NAME;
            }
            else
            {
                System.out.println("No Server Specified.");
                System.exit(0);
            }

            System.out.println("Creating store.");
            store = new
MiniJMSMessageStore("minijmsserver/minijmsserver.properties");
            System.out.println("Created store.");

            System.out.println("Creating server.");
            server = new MiniJMSServerImp(store);
            System.out.println("Created server.");

            System.out.println("Binding factories to context.");
            context = store.getJNDIContext();

            context.addToEnvironment(Context.OBJECT_FACTORIES,
                            "minijms.MiniTConnFactoryFactory");

            context.addToEnvironment(Context.OBJECT_FACTORIES,
                            "minijms.MiniQConnFactoryFactory");

            context.rebind("QueueConnectionFactory"
,new MiniQueueConnectionFactory(serverURL));

            context.rebind("TopicConnectionFactory"
,new MiniTopicConnectionFactory(serverURL));

            System.out.println("Bound factories to context.");

            System.out.println("Starting to bind server.");

            privateReg =
java.rmi.registry.LocateRegistry.createRegistry(MINIJMS_PORT);
```

```
        privateReg.rebind(MiniJMSServer.SERVER_NAME, server);

            System.out.println("Mini JMS bound in registry");
        }
        catch (Exception e)
        {
            System.out.println("Mini JMS: "
                                    + e.getMessage());
            e.printStackTrace();
            System.exit(0);
        }
    }
}
```

The properties file used by the server defines the database connection information, the directory that the store uses to store messages, and the JNDI connection information.

```
db_url=jdbc:mysql://127.0.0.1:3306/minijms
db_driver=org.gjt.mm.mysql.Driver
db_user=stephen

java.naming.factory.initial=networkctx.NetworkInitCtxFactory
java.naming.provider.url=rmi://127.0.0.1:4798/networkctx.NetworkContext
```

The code supports a user name and password on the database connection information, but I have not used one in this example.

Step 5: Building and Running MiniJMS

MiniJMS, in the default configuration, relies on a MySQL database called minijms. You can use the minijmsserver.BuildDB script to create the database. Simply alter the script or create a different one that generates the database schema discussed in the section on the MiniJMSMessageStore.

In order to compile and use MiniJMS, you need to install the JMS libraries on your computer. These are in a package called javax.jms. You also need the JNDI libraries. All of these libraries can be obtained from the JavaSoft Web site at www.javasoft.com. All of these libraries must appear in your class path.

Running JMS is a three-step process. First, make sure that all of the library files are in your class path, including a jar file that contains the minijms and minijmsserver packages. This jar file is available on the CD-ROM. Next, start the network context server. Finally, start the MiniJMS server. This server is called minijmsserver.MiniJMS and takes a single command-line argument containing the IP address of the local host. This address is used to find the RMI registry. For example, you might enter:

```
> java minijmsserver.MiniJMS 192.168.0.172
```

The CD-ROM contains several programs for testing the server. These are located in the Project7/tests directory and include a sender and receiver for both the queue and topic models. Run one sender and several receivers to see what happens. If you encounter a problem with the tests, check that the messages are stored in the database. Make sure that the name server is running and make sure that you are using the same names for the destinations on each end.

Wrap Up

MiniJMS is a large application that ties together several Java enterprise frameworks including JNDI, JDBC, and RMI. The main take-home points from this example are these:

- Use properties files when possible. This allows easier reconfiguration of the program.

- Use JNDI to access objects whose implementation should be hidden from the programmer. MiniJMS uses JNDI to register the destinations and connection factories, allowing the programmer to access these objects without knowing their implementation details or actual class names.

- Use JDBC for database access, and try to use generic SQL to make porting between databases easier.

- Considering that MiniJMS is only an example program, realize that enterprise applications are large and can take a lot of time to write and test. Of course, you probably knew that already! This bullet is for your boss, who disagrees with you and wants it tomorrow, bug-free.

- Rely on thread synchronization to protect shared resources, keeping in mind that you may not be able to protect something with only synchronized methods. For example, when we read messages, we both retrieve and remove them. If we relied on synchronized messages, another thread could perform an operation between the retrieve and remove. Synchronizing a block of code protects against this type of interference.

XML Data Backup Utility

YOU WILL NEED

✔ JDK 1.1 or 1.2

✔ Java programming experience

✔ An XML parser for Java (This project uses IBM's XML 4 Java library)

✔ Experience with SQL and XML is helpful

✔ MySQL database

✔ JDBC driver to connect to the database

Although this project is implemented using MySQL, you could port it to other databases available on Linux, including Postgres and mSQL.

Memo

To: Stephen
From: Novice Programmer

Stephen, I keep losing the data from the database when I rebuild it for my project. What can I do?

Also, what is XML? I keep reading about it. Is it like HTML? Do I need a new browser?

Novice Programmer

Memo

To: Novice Programmer
From: Stephen

Novice, I created the following project for converting databases to XML documents. I have been using it to back up and restore data during development. Let me know if it solves your problem.

Stephen

About This Project

I don't know about you, but I have learned more document formats than I care to think about—HTML, RTF, structured PostScript, and on and on. And then there are the formats I wrote for catalogs and online courses. All of these required custom parsers and special handling. If you are like me, then you want to know about XML. Now you have probably heard the marketing hype about what XML is. But often what you hear and read is wrong. What XML really does is make it easy to define data formats. By defining a common method for defining formats, XML makes it possible to build generic, well-defined libraries for handling XML documents. XML also makes it possible to build tools that work on multiple formats, such as a search utility or format validator.

This project creates a small Java program that takes data from a relational database and stores it in an XML file. The XML file then can be used to restore the database or transfer the data to another database. XML, the extensible markup language, is a language for defining file formats. The format you define in this project will support basic numerical and text data organized into tables, rows, and columns. Certainly, some databases will require a richer set of data formats and layouts. The intention of this project is not to create a fully functional, professional database backup utility because that would require too many lines of code. This project forms the beginning for that type of product, and it focuses on the basic data backup that is very useful during development. For example, this type of utility comes in handy when you are still designing and developing a database application and need to rebuild the database but don't want to lose data.

I chose Java for this project because it has become one of the most common and popular ways to build applications that work with XML. There are also a fair number of Java libraries for working with XML, making it an obvious choice.

Basic Concepts and Design

The basic design for this project is to create a backup utility that takes data from a database and stores it in an XML file. A restore utility reads this file and inserts the data into a database. XML is used to define the data format for the intermediary file. Today most programs save files in various formats. Some use binary, some use text. Often formats don't work across platforms. Until a couple years ago, Microsoft Word files for Mac differed from those for Windows. Framemaker even created an intermediate format called MIF to deal with platform and version differences. XML solves this problem by providing a standard way to define file formats. XML isn't a format itself, but a way to create formats.

The file that defines how the data will be formatted is called the *Data Type Definition (DTD)*. Developers use a DTD to undertstand the files that they want to create or read. The XML files themselves should look familiar to anyone who has seen an HTML file because data is organized using tags contained in the < and > characters.

This brings up one of the biggest misconceptions about XML. Many marketing documents imply that XML will replace HTML and allow all programs to communicate with each other. This is misleading, to say the least. XML is a way to define data *formats*; it is not a format itself. Given an XML file, a program doesn't know what to do with it unless it has some way to understand the data inside the format. For example, a program reading an address book XML file would need to know what the <person> tags represent. If the programmer did not build in an understanding of the format, a program can read the XML file but it can't do anything meaningful with it.

The only exception to this limitation is an emerging XML format called *XSL*, the extensible style language. XSL is used to create a map between any XML file and a page layout definition, such as HTML. For example, XSL might say that customer names are in bold and customer addresses are indented. For situations where you want to display the data from an XML file in a Web page, XSL will become a standard way to define the look of your data. This is still an ignorant mapping, however, and it does not tell the program reading the file what the data means.

On the other hand, the fact that all XML files use the same tag-based architecture means that programmers can use a standard parser for reading files, regardless of the data inside. In this project, you will use a parser from IBM to take an XML file and turn it into a tree of elements based on the tags. This tree is called the *Document Object Model (DOM)*. You can traverse the document's tree to access the data it contains. The same parser also supports an interface called *SAX* that uses callbacks to notify a program as tags are encountered while a file is being parsed. Because XML defines the meta-format, you can use this IBM parser that has been highly tuned and tested to create your custom program regardless of the XML format you decide to use. In the past, defining a format meant writing your own parser from scratch. Ultimately, standardizing the parsing technology can save you a lot of time and energy defining new file formats and reading existing ones.

The main difference between HTML and XML is that the developer defines the tags in XML. Also, at a fundamental level, XML has a more formal set of rules, while HTML was created over time and has several tags that don't fit the normal rules. XML's rules allow tags to be defined, whereas HTML specifies that all unknown tags are ignored, and there is no way to teach the language about a tag.

Because there isn't room here to introduce XML in its entirety, let's just look at the eight main differences between XML and HTML.

1. XML requires tags to form a well-defined hierarchy. For example,

   ```
   <B>this is bold <EM>emphasized</B></EM>
   ```

   is valid HTML but invalid XML because the <EM> tag straddles the <B> tag.

2. XML requires that all documents contain a root-level tag. This is like the <HTML> tag in an HTML file. So, for example, your database files will have the form:

   ```
   <DATABASE>

   . . .

   </DATABASE>
   ```

   The entire file is contained in these two tags.

3. XML handles empty tags differently from HTML. These are tags that don't have a closing tag, like <HR> in HTML. But in XML the tags must be marked empty with a / character. So the <HR> tag in HTML is invalid, and it would be replaced with <HR/> in an XML format.

4. XML is case sensitive. If the DTD defines the tag as all caps, then it is all caps. For example, in HTML <b> and <B> are the same tag. In XML they are not.

5. XML pays attention to white space between tags. In this project you will see how the restoring program has to ignore white space added by the backup program to enhance readability.

6. XML supports numerous character encodings including ASCII and UTF-8; while HTML has been augmented and updated to support internationalization, XML has been designed that way from the beginning.

7. All attributes in XML tags must be in quotes. HTML allows this but doesn't require it.

8. XML supports constants called entities.

The goal for the creators of XML was to leverage SGML and HTML, both standard formats, while creating an extensible language for creating new formats. One driving factor behind the differences between HTML and XML is the desire to have testable validity. It is possible for a parser to take a DTD and an XML file and test if the file is valid, without understanding the format. Again,

XML allows for the creation of some generic tools, while still requiring specific tools to deal with the meaning of the data.

Like HTML, XML has some special characters that have to be encoded. These include <, &, >, ' and ". You won't run into these in the project, but they are there.

NOTE

To learn more about XML, access www.xml.com, www.w3c.org, and www.software.ibm.com/xml. All of these sites have a lot of useful information for the XML novice and programmer. The IBM site, in particular, has a number of great tutorials. Also, pick up a copy of *Applied XML: A Toolkit for Programmers* by Alex Ceponkus and Faraz Hoodbhoy (Wiley, 1999). For a complete guide to the XML standard, get the *XML Specification Guide* by Ian S. Graham and Liam Quin (Wiley, 1999).

Step 1: Creating the DTD

The format for an XML file is defined by a DTD file. This file uses custom syntax to define the tags, attributes, and constants for an XML format. In the future, these DTDs may be written in XML themselves, making XML a self-defined format and allowing tools that work on XML files to work on the DTD as well.

The DTD for this project needs to define only five tags. The discussion that follows shows these tag definitions. The complete DTD is available on the CD-ROM in the file Project6/jdbc.dtd.

All of the data in the files will be inside the root <DATABASE> tag. This tag is defined as an element in the DTD. The database is made up of tables. Each table is organized into a pair of <TABLE> tags. The definition for the database tag says that a database element contains 0 or more table elements.

```
<!ELEMENT DATABASE (TABLE)*>
```

The tables contain 0 or more rows and a NAME attribute. Notice in the definition that follows that the attributes are defined separately from the tag itself. Also, the key word CDATA is used to indicate that the name attribute is character data. The #REQUIRED tells the XML parser that NAME is a required attribute and must be present for the document to be valid. Depending on the XML parser you use, a document containing an unnamed row could have the problem ignored or could throw an exception. Validating parsers will get mad at improperly formed documents and throw exceptions or fail to parse them. Nonvalidating parsers, the kind you will use in this example, will ignore mistakes, making it the developer's responsibility to handle errors in the XML.

```
<!ELEMENT TABLE (ROW)*>
<!ATTLIST TABLE
    NAME CDATA #REQUIRED>
```

Each row in the table is delimited by a pair of ROW tags defined next. Inside the row are tags to indicate numeric and text data. By using separate tags to indicate the data type, the parser easily can identify the type of data to insert into the database.

```
<!ELEMENT ROW (NUMERIC,TEXT)*>
```

The NUMERIC and TEXT tags are defined similarly, and both contain a required NAME attribute, as shown here.

```
<!ELEMENT NUMERIC (#PCDATA)>
<!ATTLIST NUMERIC
      NAME CDATA #REQUIRED>

<!ELEMENT TEXT (#PCDATA)>
<!ATTLIST TEXT
      NAME CDATA #REQUIRED>
```

These two tag definitions rely on the PCDATA key word. PCDATA indicates that the content of these tags is textual data.

Given this DTD, the backup utility will create files with the form:

```
<DATABASE>
<TABLE NAME="BUGS">
<ROW>
<NUMERIC NAME="id">1</NUMERIC>
<TEXT NAME="shortdesc">This+is+a+test.</TEXT>
<TEXT
NAME="description">This+test+has+several+lines%0D%0Aand+it+has+%27quoted%27
+values%0D%0Aas+well+as+%2Ccommas%2C+and%0D%0Aother+devices.</TEXT>
<TEXT NAME="workaround">working</TEXT>
<TEXT NAME="date_reported">1999-05-30</TEXT>
<TEXT NAME="category">minor</TEXT>
<TEXT NAME="environment">the+environment</TEXT>
</ROW>
</TABLE>
</DATABASE>
```

when used to back up the bugs database from Project 3. You may notice from this example that the strings in the database have been encoded using URL encoding that takes special characters and replaces them with a percent sign (%) followed by a hexadecimal number. For example, quotes (") are replaced with %27. Spaces are encoded with pluses (+). This ensures that the special XML characters, as well as non-ASCII characters, are not allowed in the file. In the next step, you'll look at the classes used to manage these encodings.

Step 2: Handling String Encodings

This project relies on two types of string encodings. First, you use URL encoding to store data in the XML file. Second, standard string escaping is required to create SQL insert statements in the restore utility. Both encodings require bidirectional code.

For URL encoding, there is a class in the java.net package called URLEncoder. On the CD-ROM I have included a class called URLDecoder that performs the decoding process. This class has a single static method called decode.

NOTE

In JDK 2.0 (Java2) there is a new library class called java.net.URLDecoder.

The database requires that certain characters be treated specially in SQL. These include the standard escape characters in C and Java, such as double quote becoming \" and new line becoming \n. To handle these characters, as well as encoding unicode characters, the CD-ROM contains a class called StringUtils. This class has static methods to escape and unescape a string. Both methods rely on four constants, defined here, to identify the characters to escape and their unescaped equivalent. Constants are also used for the octal and hex digits used to encode unicode characters.

```
final static String octalDigits = "01234567";
final static String hexDigits = "0123456789abcdefABCDEF";
final static String escChars = "\n\t\b\r\f\\\'\"";
final static String unescChars = "ntbrf\\\'\"";
```

The unescape method, shown here, takes a string and returns its unescaped equivalent. This process converts encodings such as \n into special characters, such as the new line character. A StringBuffer object is used during the encoding to build up the unescaped version.

```
public static String unescape(String cstring)
{
    if(cstring==null) return cstring;

    int len = cstring.length();
    StringBuffer sb = new StringBuffer(len);
    int val;
    int unesc;
```

Unescape loops over the string looking for the \ character to indicate a special encoding.

```
    for(int i=0; i<len; i++)
    {
```

```
char ch = cstring.charAt(i);

if(ch=='\\')
{
        i++;
        ch = cstring.charAt(i);
```

The backslash followed by an octal digit indicates an encoded character value. These are converted from a two-digit octal code into a character using the code that follows.

```
if(ch>='0' && ch<='7')
{
  val=0;

  for (int j=i
        ; j-i<3
        && octalDigits.indexOf(ch=cstring.charAt(j))!=-1
        ; j++)
  {
         val = val*8 + (((int)ch)-'0');
  }

  ch = (char)val;
  i+=3-1;
}
```

The backslash followed by a u indicates a Unicode character encoded as a four-digit hexadecimal number. Convert the Unicode string to a char using the code shown here.

```
else if(ch=='u')
{
  i++;
  val=0;

  for(int j=i; j-i<4; j++)
  {
        ch=cstring.charAt(j);

        if (hexDigits.indexOf(ch)==-1)
        {
            return null;
        }

        val *= 16;

        if (Character.isDigit(ch))
            val += (((int)ch)-'0');
        else if (Character.isLowerCase(ch))
            val += (((int)ch)-'a');
        else val += (((int)ch)-'A');
  }

  i+=4-1;
```

```
            ch = (char)val;
        }
```

If the character following the backslash is in the unescChars string, then the equivalent character is obtained from the escChars string and the encoding is replaced with the real character. Otherwise, this encoding is unknown, so the character is included after the backslash as is. The code for these last two steps looks like this:

```
        else if((unesc=unescChars.indexOf(ch))!=-1)
        {
            ch = escChars.charAt(unesc);
        }
        else
        {
            //leave it
        }
    }
```

Each character from the encoded string is converted if necessary and appended to the string buffer.

```
        sb.append(ch);
    }
```

Finally, the string buffer is converted to a string and returned to the caller.

```
        return sb.toString();
    }
```

The escape process goes the other direction, but it also uses a StringBuffer object to store up the return value.

```
    public static String escape(String raw)
    {
        if(raw==null) return raw;

        int max = raw.length();
        StringBuffer sb = new StringBuffer(max*2);
        int unesc;
        int len;
        String hex;
```

By looping over the input string, get the next character and convert it to an integer for testing.

```
        for (int i=0; i<max; i++)
        {
            char ch = raw.charAt(i);
            int ich = (int)ch;
```

If the character is in the escChars string, replace it with the \x equivalent from the unescChars string.

```
if ((unesc=escChars.indexOf(ch))!=-1)
{
    sb.append('\\');
    sb.append(unescChars.charAt(unesc));
}
```

If the character is a non-ASCII equivalent Unicode character, convert it to a hexidecimal code.

```
else if(ch<' ' || ich>=0x7f /*|| ich>0xff*/)
{     // not printable or Unicode
    sb.append("\\u");

    hex =   Integer.toHexString(ich);
    len = hex.length();

    for(int j=len;j<4;j++) sb.append('0');

    sb.append(hex);
}
```

Next, append the normal characters without change.

```
else
{
    sb.append(ch);
}
}
```

Finally, convert the string buffer to a string and return it.

```
    return sb.toString();
}
```

NOTE

The version of StringUtils on the CD-ROM also has methods to split strings into vectors and join vectors into strings, although this functionality is not used in this project.

Step 3: Creating the Backup Utility

You create the backup utility for this project in a single class called DBBackup. This class needs to define only a couple of methods. The solution, shown next, uses a main method to create a DBBackup object and tell it to perform the backup. The backup object uses its constructor for initialization, provides a method for performing the backup, and provides a second method to initiate cleanup. Configuration parameters for this utility can be passed in on the command line to make it usable in a shell script.

```
import java.io.*;
import java.util.*;
```

```
import java.net.*;
import java.sql.*;

public class DBBackup extends Object
{
```

Once configured, the DBBackup object will need to keep track of its connection to the database, the statement it will use to execute database commands, the name of the XML file in which to save data, and the name of the table to save. This last configuration parameter, the table name, is optional to the script but could be required by the JDBC driver that you use. If possible, this script uses metadata to save all of the tables in a database. Unfortunately, some databases and drivers won't provide this metadata accurately. In this case, the utility can be configured to save a specific table. This feature is also useful if you wanted to save only one table of the database. Define the variables you need to perform the backup, including the database connection, database statement, name of the XML file, and the name of the table to save.

```
Connection connection;
Statement statement;
String xmlFile;
String tableToSave;
```

When constructed, using the constructor included here, the solution DBBackup object takes parameters to indicate the database driver and connection information. This information is used to create a connection and statement for the database to back up. Parameters are also used to indicate the XML file to which to save the data and the table to save, if any. Exceptions during the configuration are handled by a single try-catch block that prints an error when an exception is thrown.

```
public DBBackup(String url, String driverName,
                String user, String passwd,
                String file, String table)
{
    try
    {
        //load the driver
        Class.forName(driverName);

        connection =
                DriverManager.getConnection(url, user, passwd);

        statement = connection.createStatement();

        xmlFile = file;
        tableToSave = table;
    }
    catch (Exception exp)
    {
```

```
                    System.out.println("Error connecting: "+exp);
        }
    }
```

Actually backing up the database requires a number of steps and loops. First, the backup utility creates a PrintWriter for the XML file. This writer is used to write XML throughout the method. Next, the utility has to make a list of the available tables in the database, or if a specific table was requested, add that single table to the list. Trying to back up all of the tables in a database that won't provide the correct metadata will result in an exception or an empty XML file.

Looping over the tables, the performBackup method selects all of the data from the table and writes out each row to the XML file. Each field in the row is written as either a NUMERIC or TEXT tag, so the backup utility checks the type of data in that column of the database and writes the data appropriately. The entire method is in a try-catch block to print errors to the console if they occur.

The discussion that follows pinpoints each of these steps in the performBackup method. To see the complete method, refer to the CD-ROM.

```
    public void performBackup()
    {
```

DatabaseMetaData is used to get a list of the tables in the database. The completeness of this object is one measure of your JDBC driver. Many drivers shortcut the implementation of this class. Others are limited by the database in the knowledge that they can get.

```
        DatabaseMetaData dbMetaData;
```

A ResultSet is used to return the table information from the DatabaseMetaData. Use a variable named tables to store these results.

```
        ResultSet tables=null;
```

The data from each table will also be returned in a ResultSet. Use a variable named resultSet to store this data. Keep in mind that this result set will have different columns for each table, so you will use its MetaData to get information about the current results. Store the metadata in a variable called metaData.

```
        ResultSet resultSet=null;
        ResultSetMetaData metaData;
```

To separate the getting tables process from the backing up tables process, use a vector as an intermediary. Create a vector called allTables to store the tables to backup. If only one table is requested, add it to the vector. Otherwise, add all of the tables in the database.

```
        Vector allTables = new Vector();
```

Next, define a PrintWriter called out for writing to the XML file.

```
PrintWriter out;
```

This method requires a number of temporary variables. These are defined here, named to indicate their use in the two loops that follow.

```
String tableName,colName;
int curType;
int i,max;
int k,maxTables;
String data;

try
{
```

Start by opening a writer for the XML file. This writer is used throughout the method to save data to file.

```
out = new PrintWriter(
                new BufferedWriter(
                new FileWriter(xmlFile)));
```

If a specific table is requested, add it to the allTables vector. Otherwise, get the database metadata and request a list of the available tables. Loop over this list and add the name of each table to the allTables vector. Upon completion, close the metadata result set to clean up any resources being used.

```
if(tableToSave == null)
{
    dbMetaData = connection.getMetaData();
    tables = dbMetaData.getTables("","","*",null);

    while(tables.next())
    {
        allTables.addElement(tables.getString("TABLE_NAME"));
    }

    tables.close();
}
else
{
    allTables.addElement(tableToSave);
}
```

Output the header for the XML file. The first two lines are used to identify the version of XML used to define the file and its DTD. Then the opening <DATA-BASE> tag is used to start the data.

```
out.println("<?xml version=\"1.0\"?>");
out.println("<!DOCTYPE jdbc SYSTEM \"jdbc.dtd\">");
out.println();
out.println("<DATABASE>");
```

Loop over all of the tables, possibly just the requested one, and output the data for each table.

```
maxTables = allTables.size();

for(k=0;k<maxTables;k++)
    {
```

The allTables vector stores the names of the tables to save. Use this name to output the <TABLE> tag and to select all of the data from that table from the database. This selection process returns a ResultSet.

```
tableName = (String) allTables.elementAt(k);

out.println("<TABLE NAME=\""+tableName+"\">");
resultSet = statement.executeQuery("select * from "
                +tableName);
```

Get the metaData from the ResultSet and use it to get the number of columns in the table.

```
metaData = resultSet.getMetaData();

max = metaData.getColumnCount();
```

The ResultSet is like an Enumeration. Use the next method to loop over the results. This moves the results from one row to the next, returning false when no more rows are available. If no rows were returned, the first call to next will return false.

```
while(resultSet.next())
    {
```

Start the data from each row with the <ROW> tag.

```
out.println("<ROW>");
```

Loop over the columns in each row.

```
for(i=1;i<=max;i++)
    {
```

For each column, get its name and type. This type is an integer associated with a static constant in the java.sql.Types class.

```
curType = metaData.getColumnType(i);
colName = metaData.getColumnLabel(i);
```

Use a switch statement to handle each type appropriately.

```
switch(curType)
    {
```

Character types should be treated as a string. For simplicity, binary types are also treated this way in the solution. One extension to the project is to add true support for binary data. To add this support, however, you need to encode the binary data into text before adding it to the XML file. One possible encoding would be Base64, a common binary to text encoding used for the Web and e-mail.

```
case Types.CHAR:
case Types.VARCHAR:
case Types.LONGVARCHAR:
case Types.BINARY:
case Types.VARBINARY:
case Types.LONGVARBINARY:
```

Take the string data from the resultSet and URL encode it before writing out a <TEXT> tag with the appropriate column name and contents. Don't add extra new lines to the data during output because these will be read in by the restore utility as part of the text data. The parser considers everything between the > of the first tag and < of the end tag to be part of the data, including white space like tabs and new line characters.

```
data = resultSet.getString(i);

if(data == null) data = "";
else data = URLEncoder.encode(data);

out.print("<TEXT NAME=\""
  +colName+"\">");
out.print(data);
out.println("</TEXT>");
break;
```

Numeric data should be written in <NUMERIC> tags. Write all integer types as longs and all floating point types as doubles. In the future, you might enhance the utility to handle these types more efficiently. For example, you might use a binary encoding to reduce the space a number uses. Currently, a number like 16 takes two characters (bytes) of space when it could take only one byte if stored in binary.

```
case Types.TINYINT:
case Types.SMALLINT:
case Types.INTEGER:
case Types.BIGINT:
    out.print("<NUMERIC NAME=\""
            +colName+"\">");
    out.print(resultSet.getLong(i));
    out.println("</NUMERIC>");
    break;

case Types.FLOAT:
case Types.DOUBLE:
    out.print("<NUMERIC NAME=\""
            +colName+"\">");
```

```
        out.print(resultSet.getDouble(i));
        out.println("</NUMERIC>");
        break;
```

Dates, times, and time stamps are handled differently by the result set so they need to be broken out in the switch statement. For simplicity, all can be written as strings in the XML file.

```
    case Types.DATE:
        out.print("<TEXT NAME=\""
            +colName+"\">");
        out.print(resultSet.getDate(i));
        out.println("</TEXT>");
        break;

    case Types.TIME:
        out.print("<TEXT NAME=\""
            +colName+"\">");
        out.print(resultSet.getTime(i));
        out.println("</TEXT>");
        break;

    case Types.TIMESTAMP:
        out.print("<TEXT NAME=\""
            +colName+"\">");
        out.print(resultSet.getTimestamp(i));
        out.println("</TEXT>");
        break;
```

All other column types are ignored by this version of the backup utility, so provide an empty default cause at the bottom of the switch statement.

```
    default:
        //do nothing
    }
}
```

Conclude the data for each row with the </ROW> tag.

```
    out.println("</ROW>");
}
```

Close the result set for this table after writing all of its data. This cleans up any connection information.

```
    resultSet.close();
```

Once each table is processed, write the </TABLE> tag.

```
    out.println("</TABLE>");
}
```

Once all of the tables are processed, write the </DATABASE> tag and close the XML file.

```
        out.println("</DATABASE>");
        out.close();
    }
    catch (Exception exp)
    {
        System.out.println("Error performing backup: "+exp);
        exp.printStackTrace();
    }
}
```

The main method tells the backup object to close its database connections after the backup is complete. The close method simply tells the statement and connection to close, handling any exceptions that occur.

```
public void close()
{
    try
    {
        statement.close();
        connection.close();
    }
    catch (Exception exp)
    {
        System.out.println("Error closing DB connection: "+exp);
        exp.printStackTrace();
    }
}
```

Users interact with the backup utility via the command-line arguments passed to the main method. Each argument is stored in a local variable, then used as a parameter to the constructor for a DBBackup object. Once the DBBackup is created, it is told to perform the backup and close.

```
public static void main(String args[])
{
    String url=null,driver=null,user=null;
    String password=null,file=null,table=null;
    DBBackup backup;
    int i,max;
```

DBBackup expects arguments; however, if none are provided then there is no need to process them.

```
    if ((args != null) && (args.length > 1))
    {
```

Processing the arguments relies on a for loop that iterates over the string array looking for arguments by name. When an argument is encountered, its value is captured in a local variable.

```
        max = args.length;

        for (i = 0;i < max;i++)
        {
            if (args[i].equals("-url"))
                url = args[++i];
            else if (args[i].equals("-driver"))
                driver = args[++i];
            else if (args[i].equals("-user"))
                user = args[++i];
            else if (args[i].equals("-password"))
                password = args[++i];
            else if (args[i].equals("-file"))
                file = args[++i];
            else if (args[i].equals("-table"))
                table = args[++i];
        }
    }
```

After processing the arguments, the main method checks that the required command-line arguments were provided using the if statement shown here. If the database URL, JDBC driver, and XML file were not provided, a usage message is printed to the console and the program exits.

```
    if((url == null)||(driver == null)||(file == null))
    {
        System.out.println("usage: DBBackup"
                        +" -url url"
                        +" -driver driverClassName"
                        +" [-user user]"
                        +" [-password pass]"
                        +" -file XMLFileName"
                        +" [-table tableName]");

        System.exit(0);
    }
```

Finally, the DBBackup object is created, used, and closed.

```
        backup = new DBBackup(url,driver,user,password,file,table);
        backup.performBackup();
        backup.close();
    }
}
```

Although this backup utility does not handle every data type or arbitrary databases, it is a generic tool that should work with few, if any, changes on most databases accessible via a JDBC driver. It also demonstrates how programs can create XML files for use by other programs.

Step 4: Creating the Restore Utility

The basic design for the restore utility created in this project is similar to that of the backup utility. A single class called DBRestore is used to implement the restoration process. The main method is used to process command-line arguments and a DBRestore object is used to perform the work.

Unlike the backup utility, the restore utility has to parse the XML file to get the data out. This task relies on an XML parsing library. For my solution I used XML4J from IBM, but other libraries are available, including one from Sun. If you want to use the IBM library, it is available at www.alphaworks.ibm.com. Once you download the library you need to install it. If you are using Java 2, install it in the JRE directory under lib/ext. If you are using JDK 1.1 you can install it anywhere, as long as you add the jar file to your CLASSPATH environmental variable.

The restore utility also uses the URLDecoder and StringUtils classes discussed in Step 2.

```
import java.io.*;
import java.util.*;
import java.sql.*;
import org.w3c.dom.*;
import URLDecoder;
import StringUtils;

public class DBRestore extends Object
{
```

Like the backup utility, a DBRestore object uses instance variables to store the database connection objects and the name of the XML file. Instead of keeping track of the table to restore, this class uses a flag to indicate if the database should be cleared before the restore is performed. The table names already exist in the XML file so the user doesn't need to pass that information into the script.

```
    Connection connection;
    Statement statement;
    String xmlFile;
    boolean deleteExisting;
```

The constructor for DBRestore takes configuration information as arguments, creates the database connection, and stores the XML file name and deletion flag. All of the constructor code is in a try-catch block to handle any exceptions thrown during the database connection process.

```
    public DBRestore(String url, String driverName,
                     String user, String passwd,
                     String file, boolean delete)
```

```
{
    try
    {
        //load the driver
        Class.forName(driverName);

        connection =
                DriverManager.getConnection(url, user, passwd);

        statement = connection.createStatement();

        xmlFile = file;
        deleteExisting = delete;
    }
    catch (Exception exp)
    {
        System.out.println("Error connecting: "+exp);
    }
}
```

The real restoration work is in the performRestore method. This method parses
the XML file, traverses the data from the file, and inserts it into the database.
Numerous local variables are defined in this method. These variables are described in the following paragraphs.

```
public void performRestore()
{
```

This version of the backup utility uses an XML parser provided by IBM called
xml4j. I chose to use the nonvalidating parser because the XML is created by the
backup utility and should be valid. In situations where you want to ensure that
XML is valid before using it, a validating parser can be used to check the file
against the DTD.

```
com.ibm.xml.parsers.NonValidatingDOMParser parser =
        new com.ibm.xml.parsers.NonValidatingDOMParser();
```

When the parser parses the file it generates a tree of objects that represent the
elements in the XML file. At the root of this tree is a Document object that represents the entire document. Store this root element in a variable called doc.

```
Document doc;
```

As you traverse the tree you need to store the objects for each node in the XML
tree. In particular, you need to track the root DATABASE element, the current
TABLE, the current ROW, and the current field. Each of these can be stored in
a generic Node object. Node is defined in the org.w3c.dom package that describes the standard Document Object Model for XML document.

```
Node dbElement;
Node curTable,curRow,curField;
```

Processing the XML file requires iterating over the tables, rows, and fields. Each Node can provide a list of its children in the form of a NodeList object. For example, the curTable node can be used to receive the list of rows, while the dbElement can return the list of tables. Use local variables to store these lists of nodes, as well as integers for iterating over the lists and storing the number of elements in each list.

```
NodeList tables;
int i,maxTables;
NodeList rows;
int j,maxRows;
NodeList fields;
int k,maxFields;
```

Use local variables to store temporary values like the name of a table or row.

```
String tableName;
String rowName;
String fieldName,fieldType;
String data;
```

The restore utility has to generate SQL for each insert statement that will put data into the database. Use a StringBuffer for this data to minimize memory allocation. Also, declare a Boolean to use as a flag when iterating over fields. This flag will be used to determine when the first comma is required in a list of SQL elements.

```
StringBuffer sql = new StringBuffer();
boolean gotOne;
```

Wrap the restoration code in a try-catch block that prints a message if an exception occurs.

```
try
{
```

The parser created above parses any XML file. Use the parse method and pass in a file name to perform the parse operation. This creates the DOM tree. By asking the parser for its document, you will get the Document object that represents this tree.

```
parser.parse(xmlFile);
doc = parser.getDocument();
```

Next, ask the document for the document element. This is the root XML element, or the DATABASE tags in this case. Everything else that you need to get to is considered a child of this root element.

```
//set dbElement to the root database element
dbElement = doc.getDocumentElement();
```

Specifically, the TABLE tags are converted to child nodes of the dbElement initialized previously. To get these nodes, ask the dbElement for its child nodes. Store the length of this node list for use in a for loop. In general, iterating the child list is easy. The one trick is that there can be children of the DATABASE element that aren't TABLES. In particular, the white space used to make the XML file human readable will be converted into text elements. Your loop will skip these nontable elements.

```
//get the table elements
tables = dbElement.getChildNodes();
maxTables = tables.getLength();
```

Loop over the tables list, storing the current table node in the curTable variable.

```
for(i=0;i<maxTables;i++)
{
    curTable = tables.item(i);
```

Double-check that curTable is really a table by getting its node name and comparing it to TABLE. If you encounter a nontable, skip it using continue to move to the beginning of the loop.

```
//skip any text elements surrounding tables
if(!"TABLE".equals(curTable.getNodeName())) continue;
```

Get the name from the table by getting its attributes and asking for the NAME attribute.

```
tableName =
    curTable.getAttributes()
      .getNamedItem("NAME").getNodeValue();
```

If the user passed in the –D command line argument, the deleteExisting flag will be true. In this case, try to delete all of the data from the tables as they are encountered.

```
if(deleteExisting)
{
    statement.executeUpdate("delete from "+tableName);
}
```

In the same way that the dbElement was used to get the tables, the curTable node can be used to get the rows. Again, there can be some nonrow nodes that you need to skip by comparing the name of each node with ROW.

```
rows = curTable.getChildNodes();
maxRows = rows.getLength();

for(j=0;j<maxRows;j++)
{
    curRow = rows.item(j);
    if(!"ROW".equals(curRow.getNodeName())) continue;
```

Given a row, you know that you need to insert some data in the database, so initialize the SQL buffer to include the table name.

```
sql.setLength(0);
sql.append("insert into ");
sql.append(tableName);
sql.append(" (");
```

Use the curRow node to get the column values as children nodes. Initialize the gotOne variable to false for use when creating comma-delimited lists of column names and values. The final SQL for each insert statement will look like:

```
insert into BUGS (name,date) values ("stephen","5/5/99");
```

where the names of the columns to insert appear in the first list and the values appear in the second. To create this SQL, loop over the list of fields twice, once to create the list of names, and then to add the values.

```
fields = curRow.getChildNodes();
maxFields = fields.getLength();

gotOne = false;
```

Loop over the fields performing two checks for each field, as shown in the code that follows. First, make sure that the field node is a NUMERIC or TEXT node. Otherwise, skip it. Next, make sure that the node has a child. This child will be the data in the node. For example:

```
<B>this is the child</B>
```

has a child, while:

```
<B></B>
```

does not.

```
//Build the column names for the insert statement
for(k=0;k<maxFields;k++)
{
    curField = fields.item(k);

    fieldType =
        curField.getNodeName();

    if(!"NUMERIC".equals(fieldType)
            &&!"TEXT".equals(fieldType)) continue;

    if(curField.getFirstChild()==null) continue;
```

All but the first field requires a comma in front of them. Add a comma if got-One is true, and set gotOne to true for the next pass through the loop.

```
if(gotOne) sql.append(",");

gotOne = true;
```

Next, get the field's name by accessing the NAME attribute, and add it to the SQL buffer.

```
fieldName =
    curField.getAttributes()
            .getNamedItem("NAME").getNodeValue();

sql.append(fieldName);
}
```

At this point, the SQL is half built. Insert the connector, and get ready to add the values for each field.

```
sql.append(") values (");
```

Loop over the field, as you did previously.

```
gotOne = false;

//Build the column values for the insert statement
for(k=0;k<maxFields;k++)
{
    curField = fields.item(k);

    fieldType =
        curField.getNodeName();

    if(!"NUMERIC".equals(fieldType)
            &&!"TEXT".equals(fieldType)) continue;

    //Skip blank tags
    if(curField.getFirstChild()==null) continue;

    if(gotOne) sql.append(",");

    gotOne = true;
    data = null;
```

For TEXT elements, get the data from their first child. Decode the URL encoding, and escape the string for insertion into the database. Finally, add the data to the SQL statement, surrounding it with quotes.

```
if("TEXT".equals(fieldType))
{
    data =
     curField.getFirstChild().getNodeValue();

    if(data == null) data = "";
    else
    {
        data = URLDecoder.decode(data);

        data = StringUtils.escape(data);
    }

    sql.append("\"");
```

```
                                sql.append(data);
                                sql.append("\"");
                        }
```

Numeric values can be included in the SQL as they appear in the XML file, without quotes.

```
                        else if("NUMERIC".equals(fieldType))
                        {
                            sql.append(
                                curField.getFirstChild().getNodeValue());
                        }
                    }
```

Conclude the SQL statement and execute it. You may want to print the SQL to the console for debugging, but this is an optional step.

```
                    sql.append(")");

                    //System.out.println(sql.toString());
                    statement.executeUpdate(sql.toString());
                }
            }
        }
        catch (Exception exp)
        {
            System.out.println("Error performing backup: "+exp);
            exp.printStackTrace();
        }
    }
```

Like the backup utility, the restore object has a close method for cleaning up the database connection or printing a message if an error occurs.

```
    public void close()
    {
        try
        {
            statement.close();
            connection.close();
        }
        catch (Exception exp)
        {
            System.out.println("Error closing DB connection: "+exp);
            exp.printStackTrace();
        }
    }
```

The main method for the DBRestore class is almost identical to the DBBackup class. The only real difference is the use of a unary flag "-D" to indicate if the utility should delete existing data during the restoration process.

```java
public static void main(String args[])
{
    String url=null,driver=null,user=null;
    String password=null,file=null;
    boolean doDelete=false;
    DBRestore restore;
    int i,max;

    if ((args != null) && (args.length > 1))
    {
        max = args.length;

        for (i = 0;i < max;i++)
        {
            if (args[i].equals("-url"))
                url = args[++i];
            else if (args[i].equals("-driver"))
                driver = args[++i];
            else if (args[i].equals("-user"))
                user = args[++i];
            else if (args[i].equals("-password"))
                password = args[++i];
            else if (args[i].equals("-file"))
                file = args[++i];
            else if (args[i].equals("-D"))
                doDelete = true;
        }
    }

    if((url == null)||(driver == null)||(file == null))
    {
        System.out.println("usage: DBBackup"
                        +" -url url"
                        +" -driver driverClassName"
                        +" [-user user]"
                        +" [-password pass]"
                        +" -file XMLFileName"
                        +" [-D]");

        System.exit(0);
    }

    restore = new DBRestore(url,driver,user,password,file,doDelete);
    restore.performRestore();
    restore.close();
}
}
```

Again, this utility provides a useful basic tool for restoring data to a database from your XML files. Enhancements might include creating tables before restoring them, so that an empty database could be restored to the backed up version.

Wrap Up

This project gives you both a useful pair of database utilities and a reasonable understanding of what XML is and how it can be used. As you need to create new file formats for applications, consider using XML to define the format. Also, research existing XML formats, as new standards are being proposed and agreed on regularly. Ultimately, the XML community may make it possible to transfer data in a standard format for many applications.

A Performance Toolkit

YOU WILL NEED

✔ **JDK 1.2 (You can use 1.1, but you need to install Swing and update the JDBC example)**

✔ **Java programming experience; Swing experience is helpful**

✔ **MySQL database**

✔ **A JDBC driver to connect to the database**

Although this project is implemented using MySQL, you could port it to other databases available on Linux, including Postgres and mSQL.

Memo

To: Stephen
From: The Project Manager

Stephen, we are having some performance issues with our applications. In particular, our servlets are spending a lot of time connecting to the database compared to the amount of time they spend handling user requests. Could you develop something to fix this problem? Also, the client application takes a long time to process queries, and we would like to be able to process more than one at a time. Can you create a library for managing multiple background processes?

Thanks,

The Project Manager

Memo

To: The Project Manager
From: Stephen

ProjMan, attached please find a toolkit for fixing these two problems. I have also included a couple of other tools that may help with general performance issues.

Stephen

About This Project

Programmers always need to increase the performance of their applications. In this project, you create a number of classes and frameworks that help you improve the performance of your Java applications on Linux. Along with this toolkit, you may want to research books on algorithms and the documentation for your servers such as mysql and Apache. Also look into the new interpreters, like Sun's HotSpot, and compilers, IBM's jikes and TowerJ, that can improve the performance of running programs regardless (well, almost regardless) of the code they contain. The techniques discussed here are more global in nature and should be applicable to many of your application development projects.

This project creates four toolkits—one each for managing simultaneously executing tasks, managing database connections, pooling threads, and keeping a process alive. Put together, these four subprojects create a nice toolkit for improving the performance, and possibly the development time, of your applications on Linux and other Java-enabled platforms.

Basic Concept and Design

Performance is a loaded term for many programmers. First, it is important to realize that improving performance is not the first step in application development. Often, applications perform admirably without any performance tuning. When the time comes to improve performance, however, there are numerous approaches ranging from updating algorithms to buying hardware. This project focuses on a middle ground including four key concepts.

First, you will create a framework for managing background operations. This framework provides feedback to users so that they perceive that work is occurring even if the task takes a long time to finish. Ultimately, this type of solution improves the user experience while possibly reducing real performance. Each background task created with the framework will have a progress indicator so that the user can see what is happening, and even cancel a task that he or she does not want to continue.

The second step in this project discusses a set of classes for controlling the number of threads that an application uses. This solution minimizes resource usage and, as a result, improves the performance of the working threads, although possibly making the user wait for his or her work to be queued.

Similar to thread pooling is the concept of connection pooling. Often the time it takes to connect to a database can be a significant part of the data access process. You will create a small framework for managing connections, allowing them to be reused when possible. This database connection manager can be a very valuable part of your applications. A number of expensive application server solutions provide this functionality, but with this toolkit, you can build pooling into all of your applications directly.

Finally, you will create a class for managing processes that need to be reliable. This is really a last-ditch performance tuning that ensures that if the application fails, it will be restarted, thus improving the reliability of your applications.

Step 1: A Framework to Improve Perceived Performance

The first element of your performance toolkit is a small framework for managing parts of a program that can happen in a background thread. For example, I use this toolkit in a program that downloads multiple files from the network simultaneously. This framework extends the Swing classes, provided by Sun to build user interfaces, by defining a window for monitoring the progress of a background task or canceling it. A picture of this panel in action can be seen in Figure 9.1. Notice that tasks can display either a progress or an animation indicating that an unknown amount of work is to be done.

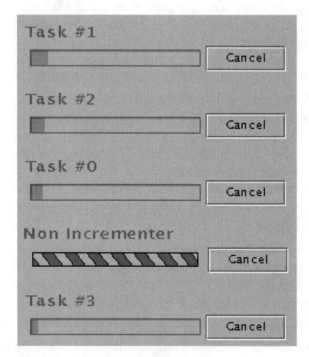

Figure 9.1 Background action monitor.

Swing uses the concept of an Action to describe an object that implements a specific function in a program. For example, the Open Action could implement the open file menu. These Action objects are also ActionListeners, so they can be used to listen for notification from Menu Items, Buttons, Toolbars, and other GUI elements. Because the ActionListener interface is so minimal, it forms a great generic interface to your background task management framework.

BackgroundAction

At the heart of this framework is the BackgroundAction class. This class, described here, extends the AbstractAction class provided in javax.swing. By extending AbstractAction, a BackgroundAction automatically implements a number of Action methods via a hashtable that the AbstractAction class manages. BackgroundAction is defined as an abstract class with a single Abstract method called doWork. To implement a background action, programmers subclass BackgroundAction and implement doWork. The framework then manages the entire monitoring process for the background task, as well as spawning the background thread.

Subclasses also could want to update their status, which will be reflected in the task monitor, and can use the isCancelled method to test if they have been cancelled. Note that in JDK 1.1 it is possible to stop threads, but as of 1.2 it is considered inappropriate to kill a thread externally, thus the need for a polling mechanism. This process will be demonstrated in two example actions discussed here.

```
package bgaction;

import javax.swing.*;
import javax.swing.event.*;
import java.awt.event.*;
import java.awt.*;

abstract public class BackgroundAction extends AbstractAction
implements ActionListener, Runnable
{
```

The BackgroundAction class defines three instance variables. The t variable stores the actions thread, cancelled tells the action if it has been cancelled by the user, and progressBar provides a reference to an object that displays the task's current progress. This object, a ProgressIndicator, displays either a progress bar or an animation, depending on whether the task has a fixed progress or an unknown duration.

```
    protected Thread t;
    protected boolean cancelled;
    protected ProgressIndicator progressBar;
```

Provide accessors for the instance variables.

```
public synchronized ProgressIndicator getIndicator()
{
    return progressBar;
}

public Thread getThread()
{
    return t;
}

public synchronized boolean isCancelled()
{
    return cancelled;
}
```

Subclasses of BackgroundAction can override the methods getMin and getMax to indicate the extent of their work. By default, the amount of work is unknown so the progress indicator animates without indicating a current status. In cases where you know a numeric indication of the amount of work to do, however, use these methods. For example, if the action is copying a file, the min could be 0 and the max the number of bytes in the file. As bytes are copied, the progress would be updated to indicate the current number of bytes copied.

```
public int getMin()
{
    return 0;
}

public int getMax()
{
    return 0;
}
```

As you can see in Figure 9.1, each indicator displays the name of the task. By default this is the actual Name as defined by the Action interface. You can change this value or just use the putValue method to set the name in your subclasses constructor.

```
public String getNote()
{
    return (String)getValue(Action.NAME);
}
```

Some background tasks can require preparation before they begin processing. For example, a File operation could want to check that the file exists. The prepareForTask method is provided to allow subclasses of BackgroundAction to indicate that they are ready to go by returning a Boolean flag. By default, true is returned. A subclass could perform some work before determining what value is appropriate for the task. PrepareForTask normally will be called from the main event-handling thread so it is a safe place to show FileDialogs or OptionPanes to get information from the user about the task to perform.

```
protected synchronized boolean prepareForTask()
{
    return true;
}
```

A single method starts the task executing. This method, startTask, begins by stopping itself. At first this seems weird, but this step is required for background actions that are initiated from the user interface. In a moment, I discuss another class in this framework that can be used when you want to allow multiple copies of the same background task simultaneously. By default, each task will perform its task only in a single background thread. If you start it before it finishes it will restart.

That explains the stopTask call, but then there is a loop checking if the indicator is null. The indicator is used as a flag to tell you when the task has really stopped. Remember that the stop command can't just kill the background thread. Instead it updates the cancel flag. Then the getIndicator method is used to wait for the task to really stop before proceeding.

Finally, the task prepares itself, notifies a central object called the TaskManager that it is ready to go, and starts a background thread. The TaskManager is discussed here; it manages the monitor pictured in Figure 9. 1.

```
public synchronized void startTask()
{
    stopTask();

    while(getIndicator() != null)
    {
        try
        {
            wait();
        }
        catch(Exception exp)
        {
        }
    }

    cancelled = false;

    if(!prepareForTask()) return;

    TaskManager tasker = TaskManager.getTaskManager();
    progressBar = tasker.addTask(this);
    t = new Thread(this);
    t.setPriority(t.getPriority() -1);
    t.start();
}
```

```
public synchronized void stopTask()
{
    cancelled=true;
}
```

When a task completes its work it notifies the TaskManager and resets its thread and progressBar instance variables. Notice the call to notifyAll. This ensures that the startTask command will be notified if it is waiting in another thread for the task to complete.

```
private synchronized void finish()
{
    if(t != null)
    {
        TaskManager tasker = TaskManager.getTaskManager();
        tasker.removeTask(this);
        t = null;
        progressBar = null;
        notifyAll();
    }
}
```

When attached to a GUI element, notifications should result in a call to startTask. Thus the actionPerformed command is implemented to just call the startTask method.

```
public void actionPerformed(ActionEvent evt)
{
    startTask();
}
```

Finally, the run method for your abstract class calls the abstract doWork method and when that completes, calls the finish method to perform any cleanup.

```
public void run()
{
    doWork();
    finish();
}

//Method for subclasses to override and implement the work
abstract protected void doWork();
}
```

SpawningBackgroundAction

For situations in which you want to have an action associated with a GUI element, such as a menu item, but you want to be able to have multiple tasks working simultaneously, you need to create a new BackgroundAction object for each task. To simplify this process, create a class called SpawningBackgroundAction that takes a BackgroundAction subclass and performs the spawning process automatically. The example at the end of this section demonstrates how this action can be used.

```
package bgaction;

import javax.swing.*;
import javax.swing.event.*;
import java.awt.event.*;
import java.awt.*;

public class SpawningBackgroundAction extends AbstractAction
implements ActionListener
{
```

Each spawning action keeps track of a class we'll call the worker class. An instance of this class is created each time the spawning action receives actionPerformed. A constructor argument is used to tell the spawning action its name. This name should correspond to the task performed by the worker class.

```
    private Class workerClass;

    public SpawningBackgroundAction(String name)
    {
        putValue(Action.NAME, name);
    }

    public void setWorkerClass(Class wrkr)
    {
        workerClass = wrkr;
    }
```

When a new worker object is needed, the getNewWorker method is called. This method can be overridden by subclasses of SpawningBackgroundAction so that a nondefault constructor can be used to create the worker object.

```
    protected BackgroundAction getNewWorker()
    {
        BackgroundAction retVal = null;

        try
        {
            if(workerClass != null)
                retVal = (BackgroundAction)workerClass.newInstance();
        }
        catch(Exception exp)
        {
            retVal = null;
        }
        return retVal;
    }
```

```
    public void actionPerformed(ActionEvent evt)
    {
        BackgroundAction newW;

        newW = getNewWorker();

        if(newW != null) newW.actionPerformed(evt);
    }
}
```

ProgressIndicator

The progress for each background action is displayed by a ProgressIndicator object. This object displays either a JProgressBar or a ProcessingView for the task. ProcessingView is included on the CD-ROM but is not discussed here because it is mainly drawing code and not part of our performance theme. The ProgressIndicator also displays a cancel button and a text message or note. The constructor for an indicator instantiates all of the necessary objects and builds the appropriate user interface. In order to determine if a progress bar or processing view should be used, the indicator asks its background action for the max and min values. If these are equal, a processing view is used; otherwise, the progress bar is used.

```
package bgaction;

import java.awt.*;
import java.awt.event.*;
import javax.swing.*;
import javax.swing.border.*;
import javax.swing.event.*;

public class ProgressIndicator extends JPanel implements ActionListener
{
    transient private JProgressBar bar;
    transient private ProcessingView procV;
    transient private JButton cancelButton;
    transient private Jlabel note;
    transient private BackgroundAction action;

    public ProgressIndicator(BackgroundAction action)
    {
        TitledBorder b;
        JPanel spacer;

        setOpaque(true);

        this.action = action;

        // set the border of the component

        JPanel p = new JPanel(new GridLayout(2,1,0,0));
        JPanel top = new JPanel(new BorderLayout(4,0));
```

```
        note = new JLabel("");

        setNote(action.getNote());

        spacer = new JPanel(new FlowLayout(FlowLayout.LEFT,4,0));

        if(action.getMax()==action.getMin())
        {
            procV = new ProcessingView();
            spacer.add(procV);
            procV.start();
        }
        else
        {
            bar = new JProgressBar();
            bar.setMaximum(action.getMax());
            bar.setMinimum(action.getMin());
            spacer.add(bar);
        }

        cancelButton = new JButton("Cancel");
        cancelButton.addActionListener(this);
        cancelButton.setFont(new Font("Dialog", Font.PLAIN, 10));
        spacer.add(cancelButton);

        top.add(note,"Center");

        p.add(top);
        p.add(spacer);

        add(p);
    }


    public BackgroundAction getBackgroundAction(){ return action; }
```

Other objects can test the current progress using the getValue method. This returns 0 if a processing view is being used. Setting the indicator's value will update the progress bar or be ignored. Subclasses of background action that want to display their progress should call this method when they want to update their progress for the user.

```
    public int getValue()
    {
        int retVal = 0;

        if(bar != null) retVal = bar.getValue();

        return retVal;
    }

    public void setValue(int val)
    {
        if(bar != null)
        {
```

```
        bar.setValue(val);
    }
}
```

Provide accessors for the note, minimum, and maximum values associated with the indicator's background action.

```
public int getMaximum() { return action.getMax(); }
public int getMinimum() { return action.getMin(); }
public String getNote() { return action.getNote(); }
```

Setting the current note for the indicator will either display a new string message or stop the message at 36 characters to save space.

```
public void setNote(String message)
{
    String newMsg = message;

    if((message!=null)&&(message.length() > 36))
    {

        newMsg = message.substring(0,36) + "...";
    }

    note.setText(newMsg);
}
```

Each indicator is attached to its cancel button as an ActionListener. When the cancel button is pressed, the indicator receives actionPerformed and should stop the task. The task then notifies the indicator that it is done by calling finish. Finish updates the user interface appropriately.

```
public void actionPerformed(ActionEvent evt)
{
    action.stopTask();
}

public void finish()
{
    setValue(getMinimum());
    if(procV != null) procV.stop();
}
```

Background actions also can use two increment messages to update the progress. One simply adds one to the progress, calling finish when the value exceeds the maximum. The other sets a note as well. The code for these two increment methods is shown here.

```
public void increment(String message)
{
    setNote(message);
    increment();
}
```

```
public void increment()
{
    int value;

    value = getValue();

    setValue(++value);

    if(value >= getMaximum())
    {
        finish();
    }
}
}
```

Perhaps the core of the background action framework is the TaskManager class. This class defines a custom Frame component that displays the progress indicators for each task. One feature of the manager is that it displays itself only after a specified delay. This allows a task that performs quickly to avoid displaying its status. Remember that we are trying to improve perceived performance. When the user performs a copy operation that takes half a second, he or she won't notice the delay. But if the same operation takes five seconds, the progress indicator should be made visible. This implementation of the TaskManager is also limited to eight indicators at a time. If more tasks are registered, they will wait in the queue until others finish before being displayed. You could expand this class by providing tabs to hold tasks beyond the eighth, or you could expand the window further as new tasks are added.

TaskManager

TaskManager is designed to be a Singleton object, meaning that there is only one per program. To implement this pattern, the constructor is marked private and a static method is used to access the one instance. This method, getTaskManager, creates a new object the first time and returns this object on subsequent calls.

```
package bgaction;

import javax.swing.*;
import java.util.*;
import java.awt.*;
import java.awt.event.*;

public class TaskManager extends JFrame
implements ActionListener
{
    private static TaskManager frame;
    private JPanel panel;
    private Vector progs;
    private Timer watcher;
```

```
public static final int DELAY = 400;
public static final int MAX_ROWS = 8;

private TaskManager()
{
    super("Task Panel");
    watcher = new Timer(DELAY,this);
    panel = new JPanel();
    panel.setDoubleBuffered(true);
    getContentPane().add(panel,"Center");

    progs = new Vector();
}

public static TaskManager getTaskManager()
{
    if(frame == null)
    {
        frame = new TaskManager();
    }
    return frame;
}
```

Each time the number of background tasks changes the TaskManager updates its UI by creating a new grid layout with up to eight rows. Then the frame recalculates its size to match the new number of tasks.

```
protected void updateLayout()
{
    int i,max;

    panel.removeAll();

    max = Math.min(progs.size(),MAX_ROWS);

    panel.setLayout(new GridLayout(max,1,4,4));

    for(i=0;i<max;i++)
    {
        panel.add((JComponent)progs.elementAt(i));
    }

    panel.revalidate();

    if(isVisible()) pack();
}
```

When a task is started, it notifies the process manager. The manager returns a new ProgressIndicator to the background action and updates its user interface. Also, a Timer is used to notify the manager when it is time to display. Of course, if the manager is already visible, it doesn't need to display again so the timer is ignored.

```
public synchronized
  ProgressIndicator addTask(BackgroundAction action)
{
    ProgressIndicator p = new ProgressIndicator(action);

    progs.add(p);

    updateLayout();

    if(!isVisible())
    {
        watcher.start();
    }

    return p;
}
```

When a task stops it removes itself from the TaskManager. This results in re-moving the indicator, and if this is the last registered background action, the window is removed from the screen.

```
public synchronized void removeTask(BackgroundAction task)
{
    Component[] children;
    ProgressIndicator indicator = task.getIndicator();

    indicator.finish();
    progs.remove(indicator);

    if(progs.size() == 0)
    {
        setVisible(false);
        watcher.stop();
    }
    else
    {
        updateLayout();
    }
}
```

For style, the TaskManager displays itself in the upper right corner of the screen. You could alter this code to center the window on the screen or place it somewhere else.

```
public void setVisible(boolean tf)
{
    if(tf)
    {
        Dimension screenSize =
            getToolkit().getScreenSize();
        Dimension curSize;
```

```
            int x,y;

            this.pack();

            curSize = getSize();

            x = (screenSize.width-curSize.width);
            y = 0;

            setBounds(x,y,curSize.width,curSize.height);
        }

        super.setVisible(tf);
    }

    public void actionPerformed(ActionEvent evt)
    {
        //timer fired
        setVisible(true);
        watcher.stop();
    }
}
```

Test Program

The following two classes define sample Background actions. The first, Test-Action, implements an action that counts from 0 to a maximum that defaults to 5000. After each iteration, the action sleeps to allow the task to take some time. Notice the code in bold that shows how the task checks if it is cancelled and updates its progress for each iteration of work.

```
package bgaction;

import javax.swing.event.*;
import javax.swing.*;
import java.awt.event.*;

public class TestAction extends BackgroundAction
{
    private static int counter = 0;
    private static int max = 5000;

    public TestAction()
    {
        String name = "Task #" + Integer.toString(counter);
        putValue(Action.NAME, name);
        counter++;
    }

    public int getMax()
    {
        return max;
    }
```

```
public void doWork()
{
    int i=0;

    while((i<=max)&&(!isCancelled()))
    {
        try
        {
            Thread.sleep(5);
                getIndicator().setValue(++i);
        }
        catch(Exception exp)
        {
        }
    }
}
}
```

The second test action is like the first one but doesn't have a maximum value. As a result, it uses the processing view instead of the progress bar to indicate status.

```
package bgaction;

import javax.swing.event.*;
import javax.swing.*;
import java.awt.event.*;

public class NoIncTestAction extends BackgroundAction
{
    public NoIncTestAction()
    {
        putValue(Action.NAME, "Non Incrementer");
    }

    public void doWork()
    {
        int max = 200;
        int i=0;

        while((i<=max)&&(!isCancelled()))
        {
            try
            {
                Thread.sleep(100);
                i++;
            }
            catch(Exception exp)
            {
                i++;
            }
        }
    }
}
```

I have included a small test program on the CD-ROM called BackgroundTest, shown here, that uses these two test actions. This test program displays a menu item that can be used to initiate actions.

```
package bgaction;

import javax.swing.event.*;
import javax.swing.*;
import java.awt.event.*;

public class BackgroundTest
{
    public static void main(String[] args)
    {
        JFrame f = new JFrame("Test");
        JMenuBar mb = new JMenuBar();
        f.setJMenuBar(mb);
        JMenuItem mi;
        Class actCls;
        SpawningBackgroundAction action;

        System.setErr(System.out);

        JMenu filem = new JMenu("Tests");

        mb.add(filem);
```

The first action added to the menu is a spawning background action that uses the TestAction class as its worker. Each time this menu is selected, a TestAction is created and started.

```
        actCls = TestAction.class;
        action = new SpawningBackgroundAction("Start new thread");
        action.setWorkerClass(actCls);
        mi = filem.add(action);
        mi.setMnemonic('s');
```

The second two menu items create a single TestAction and a NoIncTestAction. Selecting these menus either starts or restarts the action.

```
        mi = filem.add(new TestAction());
        mi = filem.add(new NoIncTestAction());

        f.pack();
        f.show();
    }

}
```

Try running the test program to see the behavior of each action. In particular, notice how the spawning action creates a new task while the nonspawning actions restart the existing task. You should see something like the window pictured in Figure 9.2.

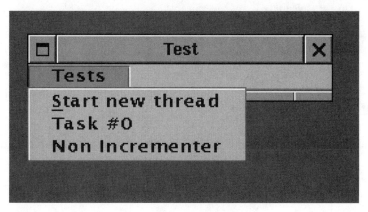

Figure 9.2 Background action test program.

Step 2: A Technique for Managing Thread Usage

The second part of the performance toolkit is a pair of classes that can be used to manage a pool of threads. This thread pool is a set of threads that are created already and waiting to execute the run method of a Runnable object. To keep things simple, the threads can be started only, not joined or interrupted. For most situations, though, this is exactly the type of library you need to keep a limited number of threads active for performing specific tasks. The library is designed to hold any requests beyond a limiting number until one of the threads is available.

The main class for this library is called ThreadPool. Programs use ThreadPool to acquire and initialize threads. The ThreadPool class maintains a shared pool, but programs can also create their own pools. For example, a program could assign three threads to perform input and three different threads for output. Or you might use six threads shared between both.

```
package threadpool;

import java.util.*;

public class ThreadPool
{
```

The threads themselves are stored in two vectors. Actually, a subclass of Thread called PoolThread is used to allow the reuse of a system-level thread for multiple Runnables. Each pool also maintains the maximum number of threads it can hold.

```
public static ThreadPool sharedPool;
private int maxThreads;
private Vector availThreads;
private Vector workingThreads;

static
{
    sharedPool = new ThreadPool();
}
```

Programmers can either take the default number of threads, 10, or assign a new maximum during construction.

```
public ThreadPool()
{
    this(10);
}

public ThreadPool(int maxT)
{
    maxThreads = maxT;
    availThreads = new Vector();
    workingThreads = new Vector();
}
```

Once created, the pool's size can be adjusted. In the current implementation, the maximum cannot be reduced to a number below the number of running threads.

```
public synchronized void setMaxThreads(int i)
{
    if(i>0) maxThreads = i;
}
```

When created, the pool has not actually created any system threads. The initialize method can be used to create the maximum number of available threads. If initialize is called after a few threads are created, only the remaining available threads are created. Available threads are stored in the availThreads vector.

```
public synchronized void initialize()
{
    int i,max;
    int curSize;

    max = Math.min(maxThreads
        ,maxThreads-workingThreads.size()-availThreads.size());

    for(i=0;i<max;i++)
    {
        availThreads.addElement(new PoolThread(this));
    }
```

```
            notifyAll();
    }
```

To use the ThreadPool, a program calls getThreadFor passes a Runnable as the argument. This method tries to get a thread from the availThreads vector. If that fails, and if there are still less than maxThreads running, a new thread is created. Otherwise, the program waits for a thread to become available.

```
    public synchronized Thread getThreadFor(Runnable runner)
    {
        PoolThread retVal = null;
        int curThreads = availThreads.size()
                        + workingThreads.size();

        if(availThreads.size() > 0)
        {
            retVal = (PoolThread) availThreads.elementAt(0);
            availThreads.removeElementAt(0);
            workingThreads.addElement(retVal);
        }
        else if(curThreads < maxThreads)
        {
            retVal = new PoolThread(this);
            workingThreads.addElement(retVal);
        }
        else
        {
            while(availThreads.size() < 1)
            {
                try
                {
                    wait();
                }
                catch(Exception exp)
                {
                }
            }

            retVal = (PoolThread) availThreads.elementAt(0);
            availThreads.removeElementAt(0);
            workingThreads.addElement(retVal);
        }

        retVal.setRunnable(runner);

        return retVal;
    }
```

Threads are made available when they are released. The release method is called by the PoolThread object when it completes executing its current Runnable's run method.

```
    synchronized void release(PoolThread t)
    {
        workingThreads.remove(t);
        availThreads.addElement(t);
        notifyAll();
    }
}
```

That's the entire code for the pool. The PoolThread class defines the Thread
subclass that is placed into the pool. These objects take a Runnable in their
setRunnable method and execute inside their own run method. When no
Runnable is available, the PoolThread waits for one. Telling a PoolThread to
start actually sets a flag that initiates the run method. This way the syntax for
running a pool thread is similar to that of running a regular thread. First, you
get it from the pool, then you start it. If you don't start it, it won't run.

```
package threadpool;

public class PoolThread extends Thread
{
    private Runnable runner;
    private boolean running;
    private ThreadPool pool;

    public PoolThread(ThreadPool p)
    {
        pool = p;
        running = false;
        super.start();
    }

    public synchronized void setRunnable(Runnable r)
    {
        runner = r;
    }

    public void start()
    {
        synchronized(this)
        {
            running = true;
            notifyAll();
        }
    }

    public void run()
    {
        while(true)
        {
            synchronized(this)
            {
                while(!running || (runner == null))
```

```
                    {
                        try
                        {
                            wait();
                        }
                        catch(Exception exp)
                        {
                        }
                    }

                    runner.run();
                    runner = null;
                    running = false;
                    pool.release(this);
                }
            }
        }
    }
```

Test Program

To test this ThreadPool library, I created two classes. The first has a short main method that creates 30 Runnable objects and tries to execute them. The second class implements Runnable. The code for these two classes is shown here.

```
package threadpool;

public class ThreadPoolTest
{
    public static void main(String args[])
    {
        int i;
        Tester tester;
        Thread thread;

        for(i=0;i<30;i++)
        {
            tester = new Tester(i);

            thread = ThreadPool.sharedPool.getThreadFor(tester);
            thread.start();
        }
    }
}

class Tester implements Runnable
{
    int num;

    public Tester(int i)
    {
        num = i;
```

```
        }
        public void run()
        {
            for(int i=0;i<5;i++)
            {
                try
                {
                    Thread.sleep(1000);
                }
                catch(Exception exp)
                {
                }
            }

            System.out.println(""+num+" done " + Thread.currentThread());
        }
    }
}
```

When run, this test program outputs a screen like the one in Figure 9.3.

```
[stephen@brisco Project10]$ java threadpool.ThreadPoolTest
0 done Thread[Thread-0,5,main]
1 done Thread[Thread-1,5,main]
2 done Thread[Thread-2,5,main]
3 done Thread[Thread-3,5,main]
4 done Thread[Thread-4,5,main]
5 done Thread[Thread-5,5,main]
6 done Thread[Thread-6,5,main]
8 done Thread[Thread-8,5,main]
7 done Thread[Thread-7,5,main]
9 done Thread[Thread-9,5,main]
10 done Thread[Thread-0,5,main]
11 done Thread[Thread-1,5,main]
12 done Thread[Thread-2,5,main]
13 done Thread[Thread-3,5,main]
14 done Thread[Thread-4,5,main]
15 done Thread[Thread-5,5,main]
16 done Thread[Thread-6,5,main]
18 done Thread[Thread-7,5,main]
17 done Thread[Thread-8,5,main]
19 done Thread[Thread-9,5,main]

[stephen@brisco Project10]$ []
```

Figure 9.3   ThreadPoolTest output.

Notice that the pool reuses threads with a maximum thread count of 10, which is the default.

Step 3: Minimizing Database Connection Times

The third part of the performance toolkit is a database connection pool. In general, the connection time for a database can be a performance block when many connections are used to perform small operations. As you will see from the test program created at the end of this discussion, if you are creating only a few connections, or if they are used for a long time, this pool will not add a great deal of performance improvement.

 **NOTE**

This driver pool is roughly based on the GNU toolkit.

PoolDriver

The first class in the database pool library is the PoolDriver. This class defines the driver object as defined in JDBC. A class called the PoolDriverManager is used to manage the actual pool of connections, and the PoolConnection class represents each connection.

Like all drivers, the PoolDriver registers itself with the JDBC driver manager when its class is loaded.

```
package     dbpool;

import      java.sql.*;
import      java.util.Properties;

public class PoolDriver implements Driver
{
    // Register driver with JDBC
    static
    {
        try
        {
            PoolDriver d = new PoolDriver();
            java.sql.DriverManager.registerDriver(d);
        }
        catch(SQLException e)
        {
        }
    }

    public PoolDriver() throws SQLException
```

```
    {
        // Driver has already been registered by static initializer
    }
```

To access the pool driver, you use a URL that starts with the string jdbc:pool:. The remaining portion of the URL should be a valid JDBC URL, like jdbc:mysql://127.0.0.1:3306/bugs.

```
public boolean acceptsURL(String url) throws SQLException
{
    return url.startsWith("jdbc:pool:");
}
```

Whenever a program uses the JDBC driver manager to get a URL of this type, the PoolDriver is notified and told to connect to the database using the connect method. In this case, the PoolDriver checks that the URL is valid and then tries to get the connection from the PoolDriverManager class. This class returns an existing connection, if one is available, or creates a new one based on the URL that is passed in. Notice that the URL has been chopped to remove the jdbc:pool: string at the front.

```
public Connection connect(String url, Properties info) throws
SQLException
    {
        String realURL;

        // check whether we accept this URL
        if(!acceptsURL(url)) return null;

        // get connection from pool
        return PoolDriverManager.getConnection(url.substring(10), info);
    }
```

The remaining implementation for PoolDriver simply implements the Driver interface with minimal effort.

```
public DriverPropertyInfo[] getPropertyInfo(String url, Properties
info) throws SQLException
    {
        return new DriverPropertyInfo[0];
    }

public int getMajorVersion()
    {
        return 1;
    }

public int getMinorVersion()
    {
        return 0;
    }

public boolean jdbcCompliant()
```

```
     {
         return false;
     }
 }
```

PoolDriverManager

Perhaps the main class in this pooling package is the PoolDriverManager. The implementation on the CD-ROM uses another package called ptimer. This package implements a timer framework that is similar to the Personal Java specification. In this implementation a timer is used to kill connections if they remain unused for a specified amount of time. The default for this expiration is three minutes, although it could be extended as appropriate.

```
package    dbpool;

import java.sql.*;
import java.util.Enumeration;
import java.util.Properties;
import java.util.Vector;
import ptimer.*;

public class PoolDriverManager implements PTimerWentOffListener
{
    private static int POOLCLEANER_MILLIS = 30000,      // 30 seconds
                       TIMEOUT_MILLIS = 3 * 60000;       // 3 minutes
```

The PoolDriverManager uses static variables to track the timer and connections. A private instance is used to act as the pool cleaner; otherwise, it has no value.

```
    private static Vector poolConnections;
    private static PoolDriverManager cleaner;
    private static PTimerSpec spec;
```

When created the PoolDriverManager initializes the cleaner and prepares a Vector to hold the connections that are created. The connections themselves are created on demand.

```
    static
    {
        spec = new PTimerSpec();

        poolConnections = new Vector();

        cleaner = new PoolDriverManager();
        spec.setTime(POOLCLEANER_MILLIS);
        spec.setRepeat(true);
        spec.addPTimerWentOffListener(cleaner);
        PTimer.getTimer().schedule(spec);
    }
```

```
private PoolDriverManager()
{
}
```

When a connection is requested, the driver manager tries to find a Pool-Connection object that has the same URL and info as the one being requested. If this connection is found, it is returned. Otherwise, a new connection is created and returned. In some applications you could augment this code to implement a maximum like the ThreadPool class discussed previously.

```
public static Connection getConnection(String url, Properties info)
 throws SQLException
{
    Enumeration connections;
    PoolConnection pc=null;
    int curPoolSize;

    synchronized(poolConnections)
    {
        curPoolSize = poolConnections.size();

        connections = poolConnections.elements();

        while(connections.hasMoreElements())
        {
            pc = (PoolConnection) connections.nextElement();

            if(!pc.initFor(url, info))
            {
                pc = null;
            }
        }

        if(pc == null)
        {
            pc = new PoolConnection(url, info);

            poolConnections.addElement(pc);
        }
    }

    return pc;
}
```

Several connection methods are provided for convenience. All of these ultimately use the method defined previously.

```
public static Connection getConnection(String url, String user, String
password)
    throws SQLException
{
    Properties info = new Properties();
```

```
        info.put("user", user);
        info.put("password", password);
        return getConnection(url, info);
    }

    public static Connection getConnection(String url) throws SQLException
    {
        return getConnection(url, new Properties());
    }
```

When the expiration timer goes off, the pool is enumerated and each connection is asked if it should be destroyed using the destroyIf method. This method returns true if the connection should go away and false otherwise. The decision to destroy a connection is based on the current time.

```
    public void timerWentOff(PTimerWentOffEvent e)
    {
        long inactiveSince;
        PoolConnection pc;
        int i,max;

        synchronized(poolConnections)
        {
            max = poolConnections.size();

            // check for inactive connections
            inactiveSince = System.currentTimeMillis() - TIMEOUT_MILLIS;

            for(i=(max-1);i>=0;i--)
            {
                pc = (PoolConnection) poolConnections.elementAt(i);

                if(pc.destroyIf(inactiveSince))
                {
                    poolConnections.removeElementAt(i);
                }
            }
        }
    }
```

Each connection in the pool is an instance of PoolConnection. A pool connection maintains a real connection and provides the methods used by the PoolDriverManager to initialize and destroy it. In order to implement all of the Connection methods, the PoolConnection forwards requests to the real connection, maintaining a record of key changes. The connection also keeps track of its lastUse in order to calculate if it should be destroyed.

```
package     dbpool;

import      java.sql.*;
import      java.util.Enumeration;
```

```java
import    java.util.Properties;

class PoolConnection implements Connection
{
    private Connection realConn;
    private String realURL;
    private Properties realInfo;
    private long lastUse;
    private boolean shouldRestoreAutoCommit = false,
                    shouldRestoreCatalog = false,
                    shouldRestoreReadOnly = false,
                    shouldRestoreTransactionIsolation = false;
    private boolean savedAutoCommit;
    private String savedCatalog;
    private boolean savedReadOnly;
    private int savedTransactionIsolation;

    PoolConnection(String url, Properties info) throws SQLException
    {
        realInfo = (Properties) info.clone();
        realConn = DriverManager.getConnection(url, info);
        realURL = url;
        lastUse = 0;
    }

    public String toString()
    {
        return "Pool connection to: "+realURL;
    }

    public void close() throws SQLException
    {
        try
        {
            if(!realConn.getAutoCommit())
                realConn.rollback();
        }
        catch(Exception exp)
        {
        }
        try
        {
            if(shouldRestoreAutoCommit)
            {
                shouldRestoreAutoCommit = false;
                realConn.setAutoCommit(savedAutoCommit);
            }

            if(shouldRestoreCatalog)
            {
                shouldRestoreCatalog = false;
                realConn.setCatalog(savedCatalog);
```

```
            }

            if(shouldRestoreReadOnly)
            {
                shouldRestoreReadOnly = false;
                realConn.setReadOnly(savedReadOnly);
            }

            if(shouldRestoreTransactionIsolation)
            {
                shouldRestoreTransactionIsolation = false;

realConn.setTransactionIsolation(savedTransactionIsolation);
            }
        }
        catch(Exception exp)
        {
        }

        try
        {
            realConn.clearWarnings();
        }
        catch(Exception exp)
        {
        }

        lastUse = System.currentTimeMillis();
    }

    boolean initFor(String url, Properties info) throws SQLException
    {
        Enumeration pnames;
        String pname, pval;

        if((lastUse == 0) || !url.equals(realURL) || isClosed())
          return false;

        pnames = realInfo.propertyNames();

        while(pnames.hasMoreElements())
        {
            pname = (String) pnames.nextElement();
            pval = realInfo.getProperty(pname);

            if((pval == null) || !pval.equals(info.getProperty(pname)))
            {
                return false;
            }
        }

        pnames = info.propertyNames();

        if(realInfo.size() != info.size()) return false;

        while(pnames.hasMoreElements())
```

```
            {
                pname = (String) pnames.nextElement();
                pval = info.getProperty(pname);

                if(pval == null || !pval.equals(realInfo.getProperty(pname)))
                {
                    return false;
                }
            }

            synchronized(this)
            {
                if(lastUse == 0)
                {
                    return false;
                }

                lastUse = 0;
            }

            return true;
        }

        boolean destroyIf(long inactiveSince)
        {
            if((lastUse != 0) && (lastUse < inactiveSince))
            {
                synchronized(this)
                {
                    if((lastUse != 0) && (lastUse < inactiveSince))
                    {
                        try
                        {
                            realConn.close();
                        }
                        catch(SQLException ignore)
                        {
                        }

                        realConn = null;

                        return true;
                    }
                }
            }

            return false;
        }

        protected void finalize()
        {
            try
            {
```

```java
            realConn.close();
        }
        catch(SQLException ignore)
        {
        }
    }

    public void clearWarnings() throws SQLException
    {
        realConn.clearWarnings();
    }

    public void commit() throws SQLException
    {
        realConn.commit();
    }

    public Statement createStatement() throws SQLException
    {
        return realConn.createStatement();
    }

    public Statement createStatement(int i,int j) throws SQLException
    {
        return realConn.createStatement(i,j);
    }

    public boolean getAutoCommit() throws SQLException
    {
        return realConn.getAutoCommit();
    }

    public String getCatalog() throws SQLException
    {
        return realConn.getCatalog();
    }

    public DatabaseMetaData getMetaData() throws SQLException
    {
        return realConn.getMetaData();
    }

    public int getTransactionIsolation() throws SQLException
    {
        return realConn.getTransactionIsolation();
    }

    public SQLWarning getWarnings() throws SQLException
    {
        return realConn.getWarnings();
    }

    public boolean isClosed() throws SQLException
    {
```

```java
        return ((realConn == null) || realConn.isClosed());
    }

    public boolean isReadOnly() throws SQLException
    {
        return realConn.isReadOnly();
    }

    public String nativeSQL(String sql) throws SQLException
    {
        return realConn.nativeSQL(sql);
    }


    public CallableStatement prepareCall(String sql) throws SQLException
    {
        return realConn.prepareCall(sql);
    }

    public PreparedStatement prepareStatement(String sql)
      throws SQLException
    {
        return realConn.prepareStatement(sql);
    }

    public CallableStatement prepareCall(String sql,int i,int j)
      throws SQLException
    {
        return realConn.prepareCall(sql,i,j);
    }

    public PreparedStatement prepareStatement(String sql,int i, int j)
     throws SQLException
    {
        return realConn.prepareStatement(sql,i,j);
    }

    public void setTypeMap(java.util.Map m) throws SQLException
    {
    realConn.setTypeMap(m);
    }

    public java.util.Map getTypeMap() throws SQLException
    {
    return realConn.getTypeMap();
    }

    public void rollback() throws SQLException
    {
        realConn.rollback();
    }

    public void setAutoCommit(boolean autoCommit) throws SQLException
    {
```

```
        synchronized(this)
        {
            if(!shouldRestoreAutoCommit)
            {
                shouldRestoreAutoCommit = true;
                savedAutoCommit = realConn.getAutoCommit();
            }
        }

        realConn.setAutoCommit(autoCommit);
    }

    public void setCatalog(String catalog) throws SQLException
    {
        synchronized(this)
        {
            if(!shouldRestoreCatalog)
            {
                shouldRestoreCatalog = true;
                savedCatalog = realConn.getCatalog();
            }
        }

        realConn.setCatalog(catalog);
    }

    public void setReadOnly(boolean readOnly) throws SQLException
    {
        synchronized(this)
        {
            if(!shouldRestoreReadOnly)
            {
                shouldRestoreReadOnly = true;
                savedReadOnly = realConn.isReadOnly();
            }
        }

        realConn.setReadOnly(readOnly);
    }

    public void setTransactionIsolation(int level) throws SQLException
    {
        synchronized(this)
        {
            if(!shouldRestoreTransactionIsolation)
            {
                shouldRestoreTransactionIsolation = true;
                savedTransactionIsolation
                    = realConn.getTransactionIsolation();
            }
        }
```

```
        realConn.setTransactionIsolation(level);
    }
}
```

I have included a small test program on the CD-ROM to test this connection pooling. The program takes two URLs as argument. One should be a pool URL and the other a regular URL; the Pool and mysql drivers are assumed, although you can update the test to use any driver. The connection times are compared for a specified number of tests. The results of several of these tests are shown in Figure 9.4.

Notice that the value of the pool is seen only at larger connection rates. For example, a servlet or another server process that needs a connection for each client might benefit from this type of package:

```
import java.sql.*;

public class DBPoolTest
{
```

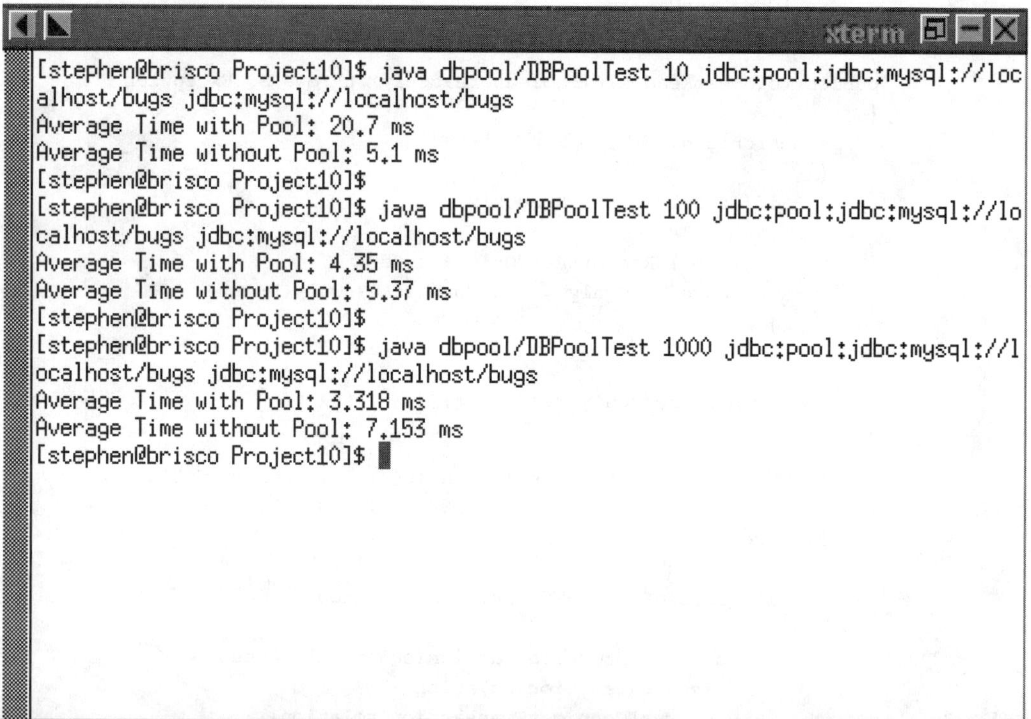

```
[stephen@brisco Project10]$ java dbpool/DBPoolTest 10 jdbc:pool:jdbc:mysql://loc
alhost/bugs jdbc:mysql://localhost/bugs
Average Time with Pool: 20.7 ms
Average Time without Pool: 5.1 ms
[stephen@brisco Project10]$
[stephen@brisco Project10]$ java dbpool/DBPoolTest 100 jdbc:pool:jdbc:mysql://lo
calhost/bugs jdbc:mysql://localhost/bugs
Average Time with Pool: 4.35 ms
Average Time without Pool: 5.37 ms
[stephen@brisco Project10]$
[stephen@brisco Project10]$ java dbpool/DBPoolTest 1000 jdbc:pool:jdbc:mysql://l
ocalhost/bugs jdbc:mysql://localhost/bugs
Average Time with Pool: 3.318 ms
Average Time without Pool: 7.153 ms
[stephen@brisco Project10]$
```

Figure 9.4 DBPoolTest results.

```java
public static void main(String args[])
 throws Exception
{
    int i,max;
    long start,end;
    long total=0;
    double averageWPool,averageWOPool;
    Connection conn;
    Statement s;

    if(args.length<3)
        {
        System.out.println("usage: DBPoolTest tests "
                            +"poolurl plainurl");
        System.exit(0);
        }

    max = Integer.parseInt(args[0]);

    Class.forName("dbpool.PoolDriver");
    Class.forName("org.gjt.mm.mysql.Driver");

    total = 0;

    for(i=0;i<max;i++)
    {
        start = System.currentTimeMillis();

        conn = DriverManager.getConnection(args[1]);
        s = conn.createStatement();
        s.close();
        conn.close();

        end = System.currentTimeMillis();

        total += end-start;
    }

    averageWPool = ((double)total)/max;

    total = 0;

    for(i=0;i<max;i++)
    {
        start = System.currentTimeMillis();

        conn = DriverManager.getConnection(args[2]);
        s = conn.createStatement();
        s.close();
        conn.close();

        end = System.currentTimeMillis();

        total += end-start;
    }
```

```
                        averageWOPool = ((double)total)/max;

                        System.out.println("Average Time with Pool: "+averageWPool+" ms");
                        System.out.println("Average Time without Pool: "+averageWOPool+"
            ms");

                        System.exit(0);
                }
        }
```

Step 4: Improving Reliability

The last part of your toolkit is a single Java program whose job is to watch another Java program and restart it if it fails. This monitor program is implemented in two classes. The first, ProcessMonitor, performs the task of starting
the child process and restarting it if it doesn't exit with a code of 0. The second
class, called StreamForwarder, is used to pass input to the child process and
read output from the child process.

The arguments passed to the ProcessMonitor class's main method are used to
create the command line for the child process. Currently, the first argument is
assumed to be the name of a Java class. You could alter this code to support
other types of arguments, including arbitrary programs.

```
package procmon;

import java.io.*;

public class ProcessMonitor
{
    public static void main(String args[])
    {
        StringBuffer command = new StringBuffer();
        String cmd;
        int i,max;
        Process child;
        Thread t;
        boolean hasSpace;

        max = args.length;

        if(max == 0)
        {
            System.out.println("usage: ProcessMonitor Class [args]");
            System.exit(0);
        }

        command.append("java");

        for(i=0;i<max;i++)
        {
```

```
        command.append(" ");

        if(args[i].indexOf(" ") >= 0) hasSpace = true;
        else hasSpace = false;

        if(hasSpace) command.append("\"");
        command.append(args[i]);
        if(hasSpace) command.append("\"");
    }

    cmd = command.toString();
```

Once the command is recreated, the child process is created and StreamForwarders are used to forward bytes for the in, out, and err streams. If the child fails with an exit code that is not 0, the monitor creates it again and starts up a new set of forwarders. You might want to update this code to reuse the existing stream forwarding objects so that bytes cannot be lost from the input streams. If the child process exits with a code of 0 the monitor considers its job done and exits.

```
    try
    {
        child = Runtime.getRuntime().exec(cmd);

        do
        {
            try
            {
                t = new Thread(new StreamForwarder(
                        System.in
                        ,child.getOutputStream()));
                t.start();

                t = new Thread(new StreamForwarder(
                            child.getInputStream()
                            ,System.out));
                t.start();

                t = new Thread(new StreamForwarder(
                            child.getErrorStream()
                            ,System.err));
                t.start();

                child.waitFor();
            }
            catch(Exception exp)
            {
            }

            if(child.exitValue()==0) break;

            child = Runtime.getRuntime().exec(cmd);
        }
```

```
            while(true);

            System.exit(0);
        }
        catch(Exception exp)
        {
            System.out.println("Error creating child process.");
            System.out.println(exp);
        }
    }
}
```

As implemented in the code that follows, a StreamForwarder is a very simple-minded object that copies bytes from one stream to another, exiting if an error occurs.

```java
class StreamForwarder implements Runnable
{
    InputStream in;
    OutputStream out;

    public StreamForwarder(InputStream i,OutputStream o)
    {
        in = i;
        out = o;
    }

    public void run()
    {
        int cur;

        try
        {
            while((cur = in.read())!=-1) out.write(cur);
        }
        catch(Exception exp)
        {
        }
    }
}
```

To test the ProcessMonitor class I created another Java class that implements a main method and can be run as a Java program. This class uses a random number to exit with a code of 0, exit with a code of –1, or exit by throwing an exception.

```java
package procmon;

public class ProcessMonitorTest
{
    public static void main(String args[])
```

```
        throws Exception
{

        double rand=Math.random();
        int i,max;

        System.out.println("Starting...");

        max = args.length;

        if(max > 0) System.out.print("\tGot "+max+" args ");

        for(i=0;i<max;i++)
        {
            System.out.print(args[i]);
            System.out.print(" ");
        }

        if(max > 0) System.out.println();

        try{Thread.sleep(1000);}catch(Exception exp){}

        if(rand>0.6)
        {
            try
            {
                int x;

                x = 2-1;
                x--;

                x = 1/x;
            }
            catch(Exception exp)
            {
                System.out.println("Throwing... "+exp);
                throw exp;
            }
        }
        else if(rand>0.1)
        {
            System.out.println("Failing...");
            System.exit(-1);
        }

        System.out.println("Exiting...");
        System.exit(0);
    }
}
```

The output of running this test program is shown in Figure 9.5.

Because a random number is used to determine behavior, the output of this test will change each time. As a result, it shows how the various exit codes are handled, and the test restarts when necessary and exits when appropriate.

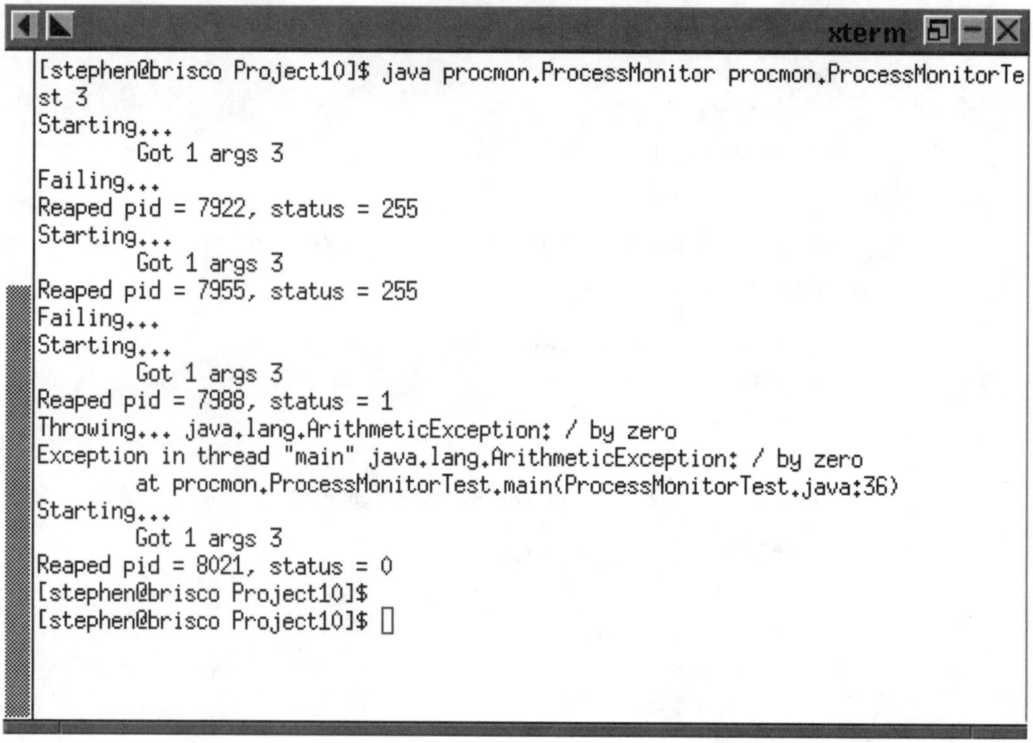

```
[stephen@brisco Project10]$ java procmon.ProcessMonitor procmon.ProcessMonitorTe
st 3
Starting...
        Got 1 args 3
Failing...
Reaped pid = 7922, status = 255
Starting...
        Got 1 args 3
Reaped pid = 7955, status = 255
Failing...
Starting...
        Got 1 args 3
Reaped pid = 7988, status = 1
Throwing... java.lang.ArithmeticException: / by zero
Exception in thread "main" java.lang.ArithmeticException: / by zero
        at procmon.ProcessMonitorTest.main(ProcessMonitorTest.java:36)
Starting...
        Got 1 args 3
Reaped pid = 8021, status = 0
[stephen@brisco Project10]$
[stephen@brisco Project10]$ []
```

Figure 9.5 ProcessMonitor test.

Wrap Up

This set of four packages provides you with useful tools for your Java applications. Keep in mind that performance is a complex topic and that the main philosophy when tuning a program is to test it first before applying any effort tuning. A great example of this is the connection pool that shows a performance gain only in the long run and would actually be overkill in a situation where only a few connections are used.

In addition to these four tools, keep in mind that there are other ways to improve performance. Look into books on algorithms. Get the best compiler and interpreter for your computer; try www.javaworld.com for frequent reviews of compilers and interpreters on various platforms including Linux. Work on minimizing the code run for each component of your application and, most importantly, keep the user happy so that even those slow tasks don't seem to take that long.

A Parallel Program

Project Objectives

To complete this project, you will learn how to:

- Create a parallel job server
- Create a parallel job client

 YOU WILL NEED

- ✔ PVM, a parallel virtual machine
- ✔ C programming experience

Memo

To: Stephen
From: Programmer

Stephen, I am supposed to write a program that looks at our company database and identifies trends. I know the algorithms for performing this operation, but the program is too slow for the computer I am running it on. My boss says we can't buy another computer, but I do have access to several other Linux workstations. Can you point me in the right direction for breaking my program up so that it can run on several machines at once?

Programmer

Memo

To: Programmer
From: Stephen

Programmer, you might want to try PVM. It makes it easy to write programs that run on multiple machines. I have included a small program below to help with the basics of creating a PVM program.

Good luck,

Stephen

About This Project

Parallel programming has gained momentum in the scientific community for at least the last decade. Until recently, few companies considered programs that ran on numerous processors to be a useful tool because of all the issues with parallel programming. The primary issue with parallel programming has been that you needed, or wanted, to use a computer that contained a number of processors. This could be a customized piece of hardware that cost millions of dollars. The other choice for parallel programming was to use multiple computers on a network, but managing multiple computers introduced communication and administration issues. With the advent of multiterabyte databases, ERP systems, the Web, and the general glut of information that has taken over, our enterprise landscape companies and other institutions have become more interested in moving to parallel programs. Luckily, the technology for grouping computers together, often called clustering, has become more approachable and, with Linux, inexpensive. For problems that can be split into independent tasks, such as data mining and numerical simulations, this means that companies will soon be competing for the most Linux nodes in their corporate network instead of the biggest computers in their mainframe-housing, super-cooled IS office.

In this project, you will create a simple parallel program that computes prime numbers. Although parallel programming in general is beyond the scope of this book, this project should give you an idea of how a program can be split into pieces and distributed onto a cluster of computers.

Basic Concepts and Design

For the purposes of this project, you are going to use a package called the *Parallel Virtual Machine* (PVM) to create a distributed application. This application will calculate prime numbers starting from 0 and increasing to a user-defined maximum. By adding computers to the task, the calculations can happen more quickly. Although I picked a very simple algorithm for this project, in order to focus on the parallel issues, you can easily use this project as a model for a more complex application.

There are two basic ways to take a program and break it into parallel components: *functional parallelism* and *data parallelism*. In functional parallelism, different machines do different tasks based on their specific capabilities while sharing the same data. For example, a fast processor could be used to perform calculations, and a high-end graphics workstation could be used to view the data. This type of parallelism was used to create the dinosaurs in Jurassic Park, where racks of Sun computers performed the actual generation but SGI graphics workstations controlled and checked the rendering process.

In data parallelism, the data is distributed to all of the tasks in the virtual machine. Operations are performed on each set of data, and information is passed between processes until the problem is solved. PVM programs also can use a mixture of both models to fully exploit the strengths of different machines.

PVM is a message-passing system that enables a network of computers, possibly of various makes and models, to be used as a single distributed memory parallel computer. This network is referred to as the virtual machine. PVM can be used at several levels:

Transparent mode. Tasks are automatically executed on the most appropriate computer.

Architecture-dependent mode. The user specifies which type of computer is to run a particular task.

Low-level mode. The user may specify a particular computer to execute a task.

In all of these cases, the PVM libraries and daemon take care of any data conversions from computer to computer as well as low-level communication issues.

PVM supports C and Fortran. There are even some folks working on libraries for Perl and Java. For the purposes of this exercise, you will focus on the C API. Other languages can be deduced from this basic discussion. A few techniques or steps are common to all PVM programs written in C.

1. Programs must include the PVM header file. For version 3 this means including the line

   ```
   #include "pvm3.h"
   ```

2. Next, the program must notify the PVM daemon of its existence. The easiest way to do this is to call the function pvm_mytid(). This notifies the daemon and returns an integer that uniquely identifies the client. If an error occurs a negative number is returned.

3. Finally, a PVM program should conclude with a call to pvm_exit(). This cleans up the connection with the server, and notifies it that this program is no longer part of the virtual machine.

PVM is a pretty low-level API for creating a parallel program. Although there are higher-level APIs built on top of PVM, it is important to first understand the low-level concepts. Perhaps the most important of these is the management of computing tasks on multiple processors. PVM provides both a library and a daemon. The daemon's job is to track all of the tasks in the virtual machine. The rsh command is used to launch tasks on other computers, including the PVM daemon. This will require that the system administrator configure the computers to except rsh commands from each other. It is up to your program to request that tasks are run, and to request which processors they run on.

To create new tasks you use the pvm_spawn() function.

```
slavesStarted = pvm_spawn("prime_slave",(char**)0, 0,"",numtasks,tids);
```

This spawns numtasks copies of the program "prime_slave" on the computers that PVM chooses. The actual number of tasks started is returned to slavesStarted. The task ID of each task that is spawned is returned in the integer array tids. These task IDs are assigned when the subtasks call pvm_mytid().

After creating the master task and subtasks, the next step is to get all of the tasks working on the same problem. This is accomplished through message passing. A message can consist of an arbitrary collection of data that compartmentalizes your problem. In this project, you send a number that the subtask will test for primeness. A data-mining program could send the query and a filter indicating the subset of the database for that process to search.

To send a message, you first call pvm_initsend(). This clears the default send buffer and specifies the message encoding. In this project you will use the default data encoding. After initialization, the sending task packs all of the data it wishes to send into the buffer. Various functions are provided to pack data by type. Once packed, the message is sent using the pvm_send() function. This function takes two arguments, the task ID for the destination and a message tag. The tag is an integer that programs can use to identify a message. It has no meaning to the PVM system but could be used to control what or how the child task works.

To receive a message you call pvm_recv():

```
bufid=pvm_recv(tid, msgtag)
```

pvm_recv waits for a message from task tid with tag msgtag to arrive. Use a -1 for either the tid or msgtag to match anything. Other functions are provided to perform a receive with timeout and a nonblocking receive. After receiving the message you unpack it in the same order. Then the child task performs its work and uses another message to send the results back to the master, or manager, task.

On top of this model, you can also use groups that the PVM daemon will manage to organize tasks that perform similar tasks. Functions are provided to keep the group together and to make queries about the group. You also can build higher-level APIs on top of this model. A number of people have added load-balancing algorithms that parcel out work to various tasks, assigning new work as old work is completed. In this project you will use a simple type of load balancing to keep all of the subtasks busy until the job completes.

As you take the techniques from this project and extend them to larger enterprise applications, keep some basic performance issues in mind. First, you want to maximize the ratio of work to messages. Messaging will be the slowest part of the application so the more work that a program can do between messages the better. Of course, the more work each task does on its own, the more autonomous it is, so this is an important design consideration.

Along the same lines, try using a few large messages rather than a lot of small messages. Depending on your application you may want to go one way or the other, and you will need to test your design in order to optimize it. For example, an application that runs on a set of computers networked by modems could find it more efficient to send a few big messages, then process for a long time. A fast ethernet cluster of computers can send more frequent, smaller messages.

Finally, the computers and network themselves are a key part of the parallel programs' performance. Load balancing should ensure that the most work is happening, but you also want to optimize the network. The Beowulf project at NASA, www.beowulf.org/, has done a lot of work on improving Linux network performance and managing clusters of computers.

With these basic concepts under our belt, let's look at our parallel job server.

Step 1: Creating a Parallel Job Server

For this project, you can perform all of the work in a single main function. You are going to calculate primes up to a specified maximum, so define a small default maximum for testing.

```
#include <stdio.h>
#include "pvm3.h"

#define MAX 10

int main(int argc,char **argv)
{
```

This program uses a number of local variables. Although I defined these variables at the top of the main function, they are described where they are used in the code that follows. Note that the array called tids that you are going to use to store available child tasks is statically allocated. In a larger application you will want to assign this array dynamically.

```
    int numhost, numarch;
    int slavesStarted;
    int mytid;
    int tids[32];
    struct pvmhostinfo *hostp;
    int i,nextVal,max;
    int returntid,returnflag,returnnum;
```

Connect to the PVM daemon and get your task id. Store it in a variable called mytid.

```
mytid = pvm_mytid();
```

Use pvm_config to access the number of available hosts and architectures. Store the number of hosts in a variable called numhost.

```
pvm_config( &numhost, &numarch, &hostp);
```

Now pretend that there are three times as many hosts, but not more than 32. This ensures that your static tids array will hold all of the task ids you create. You could also dynamically allocate the array at this point.

```
numhost = 3*numhost;

if(numhost > 32) numhost = 32;
```

The manage task for this project will be called prime. A separate program called prime_slave performs the actual calculations. Spawn numhost of these processes, and capture their task IDs in the tids array. The return value of pvm_spawn will be the number of successfully started processes.

```
slavesStarted = pvm_spawn("prime_slave",(char**)0, 0,"",numhost,tids);
```

If the number of slaves started is incorrect, then print failure messages and kill the child tasks that did start and exit.

```
if((slavesStarted==0) || (slavesStarted < numhost))
{
    printf("\n Trouble spawning slaves:\n");

    for(i=slavesStarted; i<numhost; i++)
    {
        printf("\tTID %d %d\n",i,tids[i]);
    }

    for(i=0 ; i<slavesStarted; i++)
    {
        pvm_kill( tids[i] );
    }

    pvm_exit();
    exit(1);
}
else
{
    printf("Started %d Slaves...\n",numhost);
}
```

Next, send out initial work requests to each slave. The request contains an integer indicating the number of tasks at work and the integer that the child should check for primeness. Use 0 for the message tag when sending a request.

```
for(i=0;i<numhost;i++)
{
    pvm_initsend(PvmDataDefault);
    pvm_pkint(&numhost, 1, 1);
    pvm_pkint(&i,1,1);

    /* send msg type 0*/
    pvm_send(tids[i], 0);
}
```

There are three ways to tell the program how many numbers to test for primeness. First, provide a number on the command line. The program will test that many numbers for primeness. Second, use the default. Finally, if the default is too small a test have each host test at least four numbers.

```
if(argc >= 2) max = atoi(argv[1]);
else if(MAX<numhost) max = numhost*4;
else max = MAX;
```

You already started numhost tasks working, so now you need to get the first set of results. Then as a result arrives, you send out another request. This simple load balancing reuses the child tasks.

```
for(i=0;i<max;i++)
{
```

The children will send back a message with an ID of 2 containing their task ID, the number they tested, and a flag indicating if the number is prime.

```
    pvm_recv( -1, 2);
    pvm_upkint( &returntid, 1, 1 );
    pvm_upkint( &returnnum, 1, 1 );
    pvm_upkint( &returnflag, 1, 1 );
```

Next, print a message with this information.

```
    printf("%d %s from %d\n",returnnum
        ,((returnflag==0)?"is prime":"is not prime")
        ,returntid);
```

Figure out the next prime to test, remembering that you started numhost going before you got in this loop.

```
    nextVal = i+numhost;
```

If you still have numbers to test, send them to the task that just finished. Otherwise send the task a value of –1 to tell it to exit.

```
    if(nextVal <  max)
    {
        pvm_initsend(PvmDataDefault);
        pvm_pkint(&numhost, 1, 1);
        pvm_pkint(&nextVal,1,1);
```

```
            pvm_send(returntid,0);
        }
        else
        {
            nextVal = -1;
            pvm_initsend(PvmDataDefault);
            pvm_pkint(&numhost, 1, 1);
            pvm_pkint(&nextVal,1,1);
            pvm_send(returntid,0);
        }
    }
}
```

When the loop completes, exit the program.

```
  pvm_exit();
}
```

In order to run your programs, you must compile them. On my machine,

```
gcc -L~/packages/pvm3/lib/LINUX prime.c -lpvm3 -o prime
```

will compile a program called foo.c. You will have to change the name LINUX to the architecture name of your computer. After compiling, you must put the executable file in the directory ~/packages/pvm3/bin/LINUX. Also, you need to compile the program separately for every architecture in your virtual machine. If you use dynamic groups, you must also add -lgpvm3 to the compile command.

Next, make sure that the PVM deamon, pvmd, is running. This daemon is in the bin directory under the appropriate architecture subdirectory. You can provide a configuration file to the daemon to indicate the other computers that it should use to perform tasks. By default, only your computer will be used. Complete Step 2 and install the client before testing the parent.

Step 2: Creating a Parallel Job Client

The child task for this project demonstrates how a single task can be used several times in the same program. This task uses a loop to receive instructions, execute work, return the results, and wait for more instructions.

```c
#include <stdio.h>
#include "pvm3.h"

int main(int argc,char **argv)
{
  int parentid;
  int mytid;
  int numhost,prime;
  int i,flag;
```

As with all PVM programs, start off by connecting to the system and getting your task ID. Also, because this is a child process, get the parent's task ID as well. This allows the child to message the parent. You can send task IDs in messages so it is possible to create more complex structures than the star used in this project.

```
mytid = pvm_mytid();
parentid = pvm_parent();
```

Loop, waiting for input from the server.

```
while(1)
{
    flag = 0;

    pvm_recv( -1,0);
    pvm_upkint(&numhost, 1, 1);
    pvm_upkint(&prime, 1, 1);
```

If the server sends a negative number to test, exit the loop and program. Otherwise, use a very simple algorithm to test the number for primeness.

```
    if(prime<0) break;

    for(i=2;i<prime;i++)
    {
        if(prime%i == 0)
        {
            flag = 1;
            break;
        }
    }
```

Have the program take a quick nap so that you can really see the effect of parallel programming.

```
    sleep(2);
```

Return the results to the server, then go back to the top of the loop and wait for another message.

```
    pvm_initsend(PvmDataDefault);
    pvm_pkint(&mytid, 1, 1);
    pvm_pkint(&prime,1,1);
    pvm_pkint(&flag,1,1);
    pvm_send(parentid,2);
}
```

When the loop completes, exit the PVM and the program.

```
pvm_exit();
}
```

Compile the child as you did the parent.

Wrap Up

With a library like PVM it is very easy to convert your applications from serial to parallel. At least the code is easy to write. The real work comes in designing the program and compartmentalizing the work. Once you complete the project, you should read through the PVM manual pages to learn more about each function and all of the available techniques. This will give you a basis for starting design work. You also should research parallel programs in general, keeping in mind that all problems will need some optimization work specific to their needs.

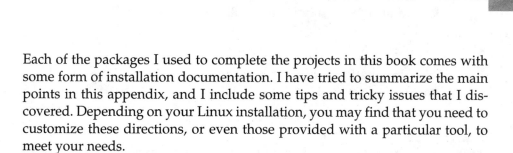

Installation Tips

Each of the packages I used to complete the projects in this book comes with some form of installation documentation. I have tried to summarize the main points in this appendix, and I include some tips and tricky issues that I discovered. Depending on your Linux installation, you may find that you need to customize these directions, or even those provided with a particular tool, to meet your needs.

Linux itself has gotten much easier to install over the last couple of years. For example, Caldera's OpenLinux 2.2, through its graphical installer called Lizard (short for Linux Wizard), can be launched from inside Windows and almost installs itself, as long as all hardware is on its supported list. Caldera also has a Linux version for Macintosh systems, LinuxPPC, which is also easy to install. Linux-Mandrake, unlike OpenLinux, forces you to learn a little about hard drive partitioning, but once you get past that barrier, you end up with a Windows-like interface on the desktop, full of utilities, ready to use. RedHat 6.0 is easier and faster to install than any of its predecessors. Debian 2.1 is less of a job to get going than previous versions. S.u.S.E., Pacific Hi-Tech, and plenty of others are also jumping onto the easy-to-install bandwagon.

Because most Linux distributions already include some tools, I have assumed that your computer already has the following:

- The Apache Web server
- Netscape Navigator, or another Web browser
- The GNU C and C++ tools, gcc and make
- Perl 5.0

NOTE
All of these installations should be performed as root.

JDK 1.2

To install the JDK:

1. Download the JDK from http://www.blackdown.org/.
2. Unpack the distribution, and place it somewhere that you want to access it from.

```
> tar xzf jdk1.2pre_v1.tar.gz
```

This will create a directory called JDK1.2 or equivalent.

3. Add the JDK1.2 subdirectory called bin to your PATH environment variable.

```
> export PATH=$PATH:~/jdk1.2/bin
```

Other installation instructions are available at http://www.blackdown.org/java-linux/docs.html.

JSDK 2.1

The JSDK requires the JDK. To install the JSDK:

1. Download the JSDK from http://java.sun.com/products/servlet/index.html. Get the Unix distribution so that it is in tar.gz format.
2. Unpack the distribution.

```
> tar xzf jsdk2_1-solsparc.tar.Z
```

3. Copy the jsdk.jar file from the JSDK distribution to your Java extensions directory.

```
> cp JSDK2.1/lib/jsdk.jar jdk1.2/jre/lib/ext
```

This will make it available to the compiler.

JServ

Apache supports two models for adding functionality, and either can be used to install JServ. If you have the Apache source code, you can compile modules into the server executable. Otherwise, you can use dynamic loading to add modules without recompiling the server. Your server must be set up to support dynamic shared objects (DSO) when it is compiled, however, or you cannot use this option. The RedHat 5.2 and SUSE 6.2 distributions used to write this book included Apache with DSO support.

JServ requires that the JSDK and JDK be installed before it. To install JServ:

1. Download JServ from http://java.apache.org.

2. Unpack the distribution.

   ```
   > tar xzf Apache-JServ-1_0.tar.gz
   ```

3. Rename the newly created JServ directory.

   ```
   > mv ApacheJServ1.0 jserv
   ```

4. Change directory to the jserv file.

   ```
   > cd jserv
   ```

5. Run the configure program, being sure to pass in the appropriate flags:

   ```
   > ./configure —with-apache-install=/usr —prefix=/root/jserv —with-jdk-
   home=/root/jdk1.2 —with-jsdk=/root/jsdk2.1
   ```

 NOTE

You may have to install the optional Apache development package to get all of the tools necessary to install JServ. The apache-install directory that you pass to the configure command should have the apxs command in its bin or sbin directory.

If the JServ configuration program, configure, can't find the Apache installation in the default location it may not notify you.

6. Run make and make install.

   ```
   > make
   > make install
   ```

If running make install does not conclude with a message indicating how to complete the installation, then the configuration failed.

This final screen also tells you that you need to add a line to the Web server's httpd.conf file. The line you add includes another configuration file in the httpd.conf without requiring you to copy it. This makes it easier to edit the configuration, as needed. By default a directory called example contains the configuration files for JServ. For now, use the files in this directory. In a real deployment you should rename this directory and its contents to a more accurate value.

7. Open the Apache httpd.conf file for editing. Mine was at /etc/httpd/conf/httpd.conf.

Insert the line:

```
Include /root/jserv/example/jserv.conf.
```

corrected for your JServ installation path.

8. Open the JServ configuration file under example.
   /root/jserv/example/jserv.conf on my installation.

Update the load module line to represent the correct path. In my case:

```
/usr/lib/apache/mod_jserv.so
```

9. Restart the Apache server. I use:

```
ps aux | grep httpd
```

to find the running processes. Then kill the process running as root. This should kill all of the others.

Restart the server with /usr/sbin/httpd, or appropriate.

JHTML Engine from Project 2

To install the JHTML engine:

1. Copy the jhtml.jar file from the CD-ROM to your jserv directory and your JDK extensions.

```
> cp jhtml.jar /root/jserv
> cp jhtml.jar /root/jdk1.2/jre/lib/ext
```

2. Edit the JServ example.properties file located in the example directory. Add the lines:

```
servlet.jhtml.code=com.pri.servlets.jhtml.JHTMLServlet
servlet.com.pri.servlets.jhtml.JHTMLServlet.initArgs=workingDir=/root/j
serv/pageCompile,compileCommand=/root/jdk1.2/bin/javac
```

3. Update these paths as you want for your installation.

4. Edit the jserv.conf file, located in the example directory. Insert the line:

```
ApJServAction .jhtml /example/com.pri.servlets.jhtml.JHTMLServlet
```

5. Edit the jserv.properties file. Insert the lines:

```
wrapper.classpath=/root/jserv/pageCompile
wrapper.classpath=/root/jserv/jhtml.jar
```

6. I used the directory /root/jserv/pageCompile as the working directory in this configuration. You may use a different directory, but you need to create the directory and make it writable by everyone, especially the Web server.

```
mkdir /root/jserv/pageCompile
chmod a+w /root/jserv/pageCompile
```

7. Restart the Web server.

JNDI

To install the JNDI:

1. Download the JNDI libraries from http://java.sun.com/products/jndi/index.html. Be sure to get the JNDI file and the LDAP provider file.

2. Make a directory for the files.

   ```
   > mkdir jndi
   ```

3. Copy the distribution to the new directory.

   ```
   > cp jndi1_2.zip jndi
   ```

4. Unpack the distribution.

   ```
   > unzip jndi1_2.zip
   ```

5. Copy the jndi.jar file to your JDK extensions directory.

   ```
   > cp lib/jndi.jar /root/jdk1.2/jre/lib/ext
   ```

6. Unpack the LDAP provider and copy all of the JAR files to the extensions directory as well.

MySQL

To install MySQL, you'll need to download the necessary files from http://www.tcx.se/download.html. You should be able to get an rpm package. If so, use rpm or your Linux distributions package manager to install MySQL.

While you are at the MySQL site, go to the Perl downloads section at http://www.tcx.se/download_perl.html. Get these files:

- Data-Dumper (for perl 5.004.X)
- Data-ShowTable (for perl 5.004.X)
- DBI 1.11
- Msql-Mysql-modules 1.2200

Unpack these tar.gz files, and follow the enclosed directions to install them. Many of these packages use a file called Makefile.pl to configure them for your system. Run this file by typing:

```
> perl Makefile.PL
```

MySQL JDBC Driver (mmmysql)

To install the MySQL JDBC driver:

1. Download the JDBC driver from http://www.worldserver.com/mm.mysql.
2. Unpack the distribution.
3. Copy the mysql.jar file to your JDK extensions folder.

```
> cp mysql.jar /root/jdk1.2/jre/lib/ext
```

XML4J

To install XML4J:

1. Download the XML Parser for Java, from http://www2.software.ibm.com/developer/tools.nsf/xml-parsing-byname.
2. Unpack the distribution.
3. Copy the xml4j.jar file to your JDK extensions folder.

```
> cp xml4j.jar /root/jdk1.2/jre/lib/ext
```

Check out http://www.ibm.com/developer/xml/ for lots of useful XML information.

OpenLDAP

Depending on your Linux distribution, you may have access to open LDAP on your CD-ROM. If not, do the following:

1. Download the distribution from http://www.openldap.org/software/download.
2. Unpack the distribution.

```
> tar xzf openldap-release.tar.gz
```

3. Change directory to the newly created ldap directory.
4. Run configure and make.

```
> ./configure
> make depend
> make
```

5. Go to the tests directory and run them to test your installation.

```
> cd test
> make all
```

I found that I had trouble with some tests, but the server would still run with the test database if I was in the tests directory and typed:

```
> ../servers/slapd/slapd —f data/slapd-master-conf
```

Perl LDAP

To install Perl LDAP:

1. Download the BER, lib-www, and LDAP modules from http://www.cpan .org/modules/00modlist.long.html. Search for ::BER, LWP::, and ::LDAP.
2. Unpack the distributions.
3. In each distribution, first BER, then LWP, then LDAP:

```
>perl Makefile.PL
> make
> make install
```

MICO

To install MICO:

1. Download the source for MICO from http://www.mico.org/.
2. Unpack the distribution.
3. CD to the distribution directory and build MICO.

```
> cd mico
> ./configure
> make
> make install
> /sbin/ldconfig -v
```

JacOrb

To install JacOrb:

1. Download JacORB from http://www.inf.fu-berlin.de/~brose/jacorb/.
2. Unpack the distribution.
3. Follow the installation directions provided; because JacORB is Java there really isn't much to do to get it working.

PVM

To install PVM:

1. Download PVM from http://www.epm.ornl.gov/pvm/.
2. Unpack the distribution and follow the directions in the provided Readme file. This worked great for me with no problems.

Additional References

As I was writing this book I thought it could be useful to provide additional references. Some of the books listed here are great introductions to the technologies used in these projects. Others will help you continue your study of the concepts and technologies discussed in this book. Of course, there are hundreds of great books available. These are just a few that I have used over the years and thought you could also find useful.

Asbury, Stephen, et al. *CGI How-To*. Corte Madera, CA: Waite Group Press, 1996.

Asbury, Stephen, et al. *Perl 5 How-To*, 2d ed. Corte Madera, CA: Waite Group Press, 1997.

Asbury, Stephen, and Weiner, Scott R. *Developing Enterprise Java Applications*. New York: John Wiley & Sons, 1999.

Binstock, Andrew, and Rex, John. *Practical Algorithms for Programmers*. Reading, MA: Addison-Wesley, 1995.

Flanagan, David, and Loukides, Mike. *Java in a Nutshell: A Desktop Quick Reference*, 2d ed. Sebastopol CA: O'Reilly and Associates, 1997.

Howes, Timothy A., and Smith, Mark C. *LDAP Programming Directory-enabled Applications with Lightweight Directory Access Protocol*. Indianapolis, IN: Macmillan Technical Publishing, 1997.

Kernighan, Brian, and Ritchie, David. *The C Programming Language.* Englewood Cliffs, NJ: Prentice Hall, 1988.

Lea, Doug. *Concurrent Programming in Java.* Reading, MA: Addison-Wesley, 1997.

Perry, Greg M. *Absolute Beginner's Guide to C.* Indianapolis, IN: Sams, 1994.

Ricart, Alberto. *The Complete Idiot's Guide to Linux.* Indianapolis, IN: Que, 1998.

Schwartz, Randal L., et al. *Learning Perl,* 2d ed. Sebastopol, CA: O'Reilly and Associates, 1997.

Seigal, Jon. *CORBA Fundamentals and Programming.* New York: John Wiley & Sons, 1996.

Wall, Larry, et al. *Programming Perl,* 2d ed. Sebastopol, CA: O'Reilly and Associates, 1996.

You should also check out the Web sites referred to within the various projects.

Index

Page references in *italic* type indicate illustrations.

**CUSTOMER NOTE: IF THIS BOOK IS ACCOMPANIED BY SOFTWARE,
PLEASE READ THE FOLLOWING BEFORE OPENING THE PACKAGE.**

This software contains files to help you utilize the models described in the accompanying book. By opening the package, you are agreeing to be bound by the following agreement:

To use this CD-ROM, your system must meet the following requirements:

Platform/Processor/Operating System. Pentium or better running Redhat Linux 5.2 or equivalent

RAM. 32MB or better

Hard Drive Space. 60 MB after Linux installation

Peripherals. CD-ROM drive, Web browser to navigate CD-ROM